THE SPANISH CIVIL WAR AS A RELIGIOUS TRAGEDY

The Spanish Civil War as a Religious Tragedy

José M. Sánchez

UNIVERSITY OF NOTRE DAME PRESS
NOTRE DAME, INDIANA

Library of Congress Cataloging-in-Publication Data

Sánchez, José M. (José Mariano), 1932–
    The Spanish Civil War as a religious tragedy.

    Bibliography: p.
    Includes index.
    1. Spain—History—Civil War, 1936–1939—Religious
aspects. 2. Catholic Church—Relations (diplomatic)—
Spain. 3. Spain—Foreign relations—Catholic Church.
4. Catholic Church—Spain—History—20th century.
I. Title.
DP269.8.R4S26 1987   946.081   86-40581
ISBN 0-268-01726-3

The University of Notre Dame Press
gratefully acknowledges the generous support of the
Program for Cultural Cooperation
between Spain's Ministry of Culture
and North American Universities
in the publication of this book.

Contents

Foreword

The Spanish Civil War was the dominant European event of the 1930s prior to the crisis that led to the outbreak of World War II in 1938–39. It polarized the political consciousness of a generation, in some respects more so than did the opening round of the World War itself, for the Spanish contest was held to be a true contest of principles, an international ideological civil war to a much greater degree than anything represented by the standard clash of rival national egotism. Even after World War II the Spanish struggle was still being fought by the partisans of both sides, and later, in the 1950s and 60s, when veterans of the Allied and Axis forces were able to look back on their own conflict with some detachment, the Spanish war remained a matter of intense passion.

The modern era has seen many civil wars, but the Spanish struggle was unique in being the only one to take place in a west European country during the twentieth century. Variously labeled by partisans as a contest between "fascism and democracy" or "Christianity and communism," it was essentially a revolutionary/counterrevolutionary civil war between left and right, and to that extent similar to the revolutionary/counterrevolutionary civil wars that had occurred some years earlier in eastern Europe and would take place subsequently in the Balkans and east Asia.

Three earlier civil wars had been fought in Spain between liberals and traditionalists in the nineteenth century (1821–23, 1833–40, 1869–76). Each of these had also had a significant religious dimension, but those struggles had been in large measure contests between progressivist Catholics (frequently anticlerical) and religious traditionalists (mainly in northeastern Spain). In no other Catholic country did the introduction of liberal government and market capitalist economics produce such a prolonged conflict, but the result was eventually to develop a new compromise—though never a real synthesis—in which Spanish Catholicism seemed increasingly aligned with the

new capitalist status quo. By the beginning of the twentieth century
a new scenario had emerged, in which the major new challenges would
stem from the revolutionary left, and in which the new anticlericalism would aim so much not at the reform of Catholicism as at its
destruction.

Religious factors, pro and con, have been of some importance
in all the revolutionary/counterrevolutionary civil wars, though the
degree of that significance has varied considerably. Prior to the rise
of liberation theology in the 1970s revolutionary movements tended
to be both anticlerical and anti-Christian, but in most revolutionary
civil wars religious factors did not play so large a role as in the case
of Russia (1918–21) and Spain (1936–39). In neither of these cases was
religion truly a major factor in the coming of the civil war, but in Russia and Spain the revolutionary assault on the national church unleashed the two most bloody and extensive persecutions in the modern history of Christendom. Since the antireligious forces won a
complete victory in Russia, it has not been possible to document
precisely the extent of the persecution there, while that in Spain has
been carefully measured. Conversely, in both Russia and Spain the
national church became fully identified with the counterrevolutionary forces and scandalously compromised with their own violence
and excess.

The counterrevolutionary Nationalists who won the Spanish
Civil War were an eclectic coalition representing a diversity of interests, but the single most prominent value that they came to espouse
was traditional Catholicism. The result was a restoration of religious
traditionalism in Spain on a formal scale that has had no analogy in
any other Western country of the twentieth century and has been ri-
valed or exceeded in recent times only in the Middle East. The main
consequence of the Nationalist victory was thus not so much to secure the triumph of "fascism" as to inaugurate the final stage in the
baroque and Tridentine culture of Spanish tradition.

The anticlerical fury of the revolutionary onslaught and the ruthless religious restorationism of the counterrevolutionaries reached
such extremes in the Civil War that commentators have often been
at a loss to account fully for them. Yet they had origins in concrete
developments of recent generations in Spain and can be analyzed by
professional scholars about as effectively as they have studied other
major aspects of the conflict. Nonetheless historians have heretofore
concentrated on major political and international issues, reflecting
the priorities of their standard agenda.

The present work by Professor José Sánchez is thus the first full investigation of the religious dimensions of the conflict in Spain. The author of an earlier study of the role of Catholicism and anticlericalism in the political turmoils of the prewar Republic, Sánchez is uniquely qualified to tread the minefield which such a theme comprises, and to elucidate the motivations and deeds of both sides in what may with only a little exaggeration be called the last of the religious civil wars.

Such a project requires both a great deal of careful investigation of ambience and facts, and also an unusual degree of detachment and objectivity to treat both sides fairly. Sensitivity to the nuances and feelings of anticlerical and of Catholic forces presents much more of a challenge than does the preliminary labor of research per se. It is a measure of Sánchez's achievement that he has succeeded in presenting the values and activities of both sides accurately and fairly, and thus for the first time explaining the exact character of the religious struggle within the greater Spanish conflict. As the years of the fiftieth centenary of the Civil War pass, scores of books are being published to coincide with the commemoration, but few will make a more important or original contribution to understanding the minds and motivations of the Spanish participants.

Stanley G. Payne
University of Wisconsin-Madison

Preface

I t is commonplace to call the Spanish Civil War a turning point in
history. It has been seen as the last great ideological armed conflict between liberalism and conservatism, the first between fascism
and communism, and in Spain itself as the last hope for progress or
the last attempt to preserve tradition. The Spanish dichotomy is a
false one, as the last two decades have proved, and as for the others
the point is arguable: so much has happened since World War I that
we are daily surrounded by turning points.

But one dimension of the war was an authentic turning point.
The Spanish war was the greatest and the last struggle between traditional triumphalist Catholicism and liberal-proletarian secularism.
It burst upon the religious world like a bombshell, an armed conflict
that drove men and ideologies to extremes. Priests were killed, in larger
numbers than ever before in history; churches were burned, statues
smashed, and the symbolism of Catholic Christianity was destroyed
in a fury that knew few limits. Militant Catholics, in turn, killed non-
Catholics and anticlericals in the name of the Prince of Peace, and
they supported an oppressive regime that restored the power of clerical Catholicism. Religion became the most clearly divisive issue of
the war, the single aspect that distinguished one faction from another.

The anticlerical fury was part of the revolutionary terror that
consumed Spanish leftist passions for over five months after the war
broke out in July 1936. By the time the fury had run its course in
early 1937 the religious issue became focused on the Basque problem
—the existence of a Catholic Basque autonomous movement actively
supporting the Republican government that in the eyes of the Nationalists was responsible for the attack on the Church. This open
breach in Catholic unity inflamed religious passions and was not ended
until the Nationalist armies conquered Vizcaya in the summer of 1937.
Shortly thereafter the Spanish bishops issued a collective letter explaining their views on the fury and calling upon Catholics through-

xiii

out the world to support the Nationalist regime. Attempts by Republican Catholics to obtain Vatican recognition of a twofold division of the Spanish religious organization foundered first on the problem of determining authority and ultimately upon the Nationalist victory in the spring of 1939.

Support abroad for the warring factions in Spain was frequently determined by religious sympathies. Working-class Catholics in France, Britain, and the United States, whose perceived class interests lay with the Republicans, pressured their governments toward tacit support of Franco's forces solely because the Spanish general and his followers took on the guise of defenders of the Church, while upperclass Protestants and anti-Catholics supported violent anticlericals who would have murdered them had they been Spaniards.

The war had a powerful impact upon religious thought as well. The theological and philosophical implications of the theory of a just war were publicly debated for the first time in centuries, and it is not just coincidence that some of the leading Catholic critics of Franco and the Nationalists became the ideological fathers of the Second Vatican Council.

The religious events of the war have not been fully explored, perhaps because they are an embarrassment for both factions. Republican supporters and historians have had a difficult time explaining the anticlerical fury. Frequently they choose not to mention it or to downplay it; it is difficult to speak of the Republic as a force for human progress, decency, and enlightenment and then to try to explain the blood lust that led to the death of nearly seven thousand clerics. Similarly, while Nationalist supporters and historians emphasize the fury, few have addressed the appalling scandal of silence and implied moral approval the clergy gave the Nationalists' retributions and reprisals, even to the dreadful crimes committed in the name of Christ.

The anticlerical fury and the scandal of silence are intimately connected. Neither happened in a vacuum. To understand the scandal one must relate it to the fury. And the fury must be linked to the earlier scandal of clerical support of establishment oppressors. That scandal, in turn, can be understood only in connection with anticlerical violence in the nineteenth and early twentieth centuries. To ignore these relationships is to lapse into the mythology of the war that views the anticlerical incendiaries and killers as downtrodden workers rising up in just wrath against their clerical oppressors who conspired with the military to deprive them of their freedom; or conversely to see them as agents of a communist or satanic conspiracy against God and God's representatives on earth.

The Spanish Church of 1936, despite its weaknesses, was a militant and aggressive institution with a dynamic impulse that derived from the belief that the institutional church represented a perfect society, one whose ethical and cultural values should be imposed on all humanity. It clashed with the equally aggressive and tenaciously held beliefs of working-class and intellectual secularists who held dearly to the idea that a new and more perfect human society should be based on principles having nothing to do with religious institutions.

The triumphalist Church clashed with the forces of secularism in a physical and ideological battle that had repercussions throughout the world, and while the triumphalist vision was immediately victorious, it came out much the worse for wear in the long run and is today an anachronism. The circumstances of the Spanish Civil War made the struggle a decisive event in the religious history of the Western world.

It need hardly be stated that this work is only an introduction to the religious aspects of the Spanish war. The topic is much too large, the literature too vast, and the sources too scattered for the sort of detailed treatment that would make it a definitive study. I have therefore relied on printed sources and secondary works for what is mainly a work of preliminary interpretation.

The work is intended to correct the mythology that has grown up around the topic; even in the past decade histories of the war have repeated the hoary myths of 1936, as if the war were still being fought. The confusion and misinformation about the religious issues and personalities is astounding, and in a sense they point to the continuing impact of the war. I also want to explore the effect of the war on Catholics and Catholic issues abroad, a subject that has been scarcely investigated, and which, I believe, offers insights into the religious and national histories of the countries involved.

I wish to express my thanks to Professor Stanley G. Payne for his foreword and to the Beaumont Foundation of Saint Louis University for a research grant that made this work possible.

A Note Concerning the Use of Terms

While there is general agreement about the meaning of such words as priest, brother, nun, bishop, and pope, some confusion exists over the terms clergy, laity, church, and Catholic. In this work

I have used clergy as a catchall term to describe anyone ordained or who was studying for ordination or for anyone, male or female, who took the three canonical vows of obedience, chastity, and poverty, or who was a novice with the intention of taking those vows. Thus, the term includes pope, bishops, priests, brothers, nuns, seminarians and novices, members of religious orders and congregations as well as secular (diocesan) priests.

Defining the Church is more difficult. The Second Vatican Council defined the Church as the people of God, the community of the faithful; this is a happy definition but unfortunately not useful for description or analysis. On the other hand, the commonly and popularly used definition of the Church as the clergy and those who supported the clergy is much too narrow. I shall avoid the term as much as possible, using it only when it would be stylistically awkward to do otherwise, and instead attempt more accurate descriptions of specific groups within the Church. Among these was the organized body of bishops known as the hierarchy or the episcopate; these ecclesiastics, along with Vatican officials, constituted the official Church, especially when their pronouncements were endorsed by the pope. I have used the term laity to refer to those persons who were practicing Catholics and usually obeyed the instructions of the official Church; it includes those who were organized into specific Catholic-oriented partisan political or social movements. I have not used the term laity to refer to those believers who did not practice the outward signs of their faith (often in protest against the actions of the official Church); I would note that dissension from the position of the official Church does not make anyone less a Catholic, nor is anticlericalism a barrier to membership in the community of the faithful, as numerous saints' lives will attest. As for the term Catholic, despite baptism, it seems most accurate to say that those who claimed to be Catholic, whatever their actions, were Catholic, while those who claimed otherwise were not.

As for the political and military factions, for the sake of simplicity and with no intention of prejudice, I have used the term Nationalist to apply to all those who fought for and supported the victors in the war. This includes those known otherwise as fascists, Falangists, Carlists, monarchists, Francoists, rebels, insurgents, and others. Similarly, for the defeated I have used the term Republican to apply to all, including anarchists, Communists, Loyalists, Socialists, liberals, Government forces, and others. I have, of course, used specific definitions when necessary.

CHAPTER 1

The Anticlerical Fury

There is a famous photograph taken a few days after the outbreak of the Spanish Civil War in July 1936 that shows a group of Republican militiamen aiming rifles at the statue of the Sacred Heart of Jesus atop the Cerro de los Angeles, the geographical center of Spain, a few miles outside of Madrid. The bullets, of course, did little harm to the massive stone structure that the exiled King Alfonso XIII had dedicated some seventeen years earlier, but the photo was published widely abroad as proof of the godlessness of the embattled Spanish Republic.[1]

The act of firing and the statue itself were both symbolic, and it is instructive to examine the symbolism. The militiamen were aiming, not at a statue of the Virgin Mary, surely the supreme patroness of Spanish Catholicism and the dearest symbol of the Christian religion in all centuries, but rather at the Sacred Heart, the symbol of nineteenth-century pious Jesuitism, of the union of church and state and throne and altar, of clerical power, of Catholic triumphalism, the symbol, in fact, of an entire cultural ethic.

In all probability few of the militiamen were aware of the high symbolism of their action. Perhaps some were firing because they believed that the clergy were supporting the military-fascist-monarchist uprising with both cash and armed force, and destroying the clergy's statue was one way to show their anger and determination; perhaps they were shooting at a statue because they could find no more churches to burn in the anticlerical fury that was raging throughout Republican Spain, and iconoclasm of one sort was as good as iconoclasm of another; or maybe they were conscious of being part of a

---

1. See the photo, among other places, in the *Espasa-Calpe Encyclopedia* (known more formally as *Enciclopedia universal ilustrada Europeo-Americano*), *suplemento anual, 1936–1939 (segunda parte)* (Bilbao, 1944), p. 1566. The monument was within the month dynamited to bits.

1

revolutionary surge that would sweep away the past, and with it all churchly and priestly things.

But all of these motivations shared one common target: the Catholic cultural ethic that had dominated the nation for nearly a century. That ethic was more than a religion. It was a way of life, a framework of reality that was intimately bound up with Spain's history; it was at root an attempt to recapture the role that Catholicism had once played in what was perceived as the Church's historic mission to the Spanish people.

The Spanish Church, like churches everywhere, had aspired to universality. At one time in the early modern era it had achieved that status. In a country of intense localism Catholicism had become the one belief that all Spaniards had in common, and the Church had become the only institution common to the entire peninsula. It was a force for the unity necessary for the remarkable expansion of Spain and Spanish culture throughout the world in the sixteenth century. And when Spain went into decline, foreign Protestants and some Spaniards blamed Catholicism. Throughout the rise and decline the people remained devoutly Catholic, and during the Bourbon renascence of the eighteenth century the enlightened monarchs were also pious adherents of the faith, despite their sometimes anticlerical policies. When nineteenth-century pressures turned Spaniards against one another and two Spains came into being—a progressive, urban, commercial Spain along side a rural, conservative, pastoral Spain—there was hope that Catholicism could bridge the two and continue to provide unity. But nineteenth-century clerics, from pope to curate, defined Catholicism too narrowly to appeal to all Spaniards, and the two Spains became clerical and anticlerical as well.

From the universality of 1500 the Spanish Church had become by 1900 a cult, a religion of a particular time and place and group. But the clergy continued to believe in the Church's universality, to the point that they considered those who rejected their interpretation of Catholicism to be less than complete Spaniards, and they imposed their cultural ethic on everyone. Little toleration and often civil disabilities existed for non-Catholics. Most Spaniards responded not by turning anti-Catholic but by becoming anticlerical. Church attendance dropped, in some areas to less than one in ten. But the cultural ethic prevailed because the clergy controlled education. The Catholic catechism was taught in all public elementary schools, and the religious orders—Dominicans, Jesuits, Christian Brothers, Augustinians, and others—ran practically all the secondary schools. Tridentine Catholicism was the theology and culture of the country; the Catholic catechism, the ethical standard of the nation. Spain's greatest philosopher, Miguel de Unamuno, defined the ethic cogently: "Here in Spain," he once commented acidly, "we are all Catholics, even the atheists."[2]

The Spanish Catholic cultural ethic emphasized religion as the center of man's being; and while it strove to develop an inner spiritual life, it was emphatic in its stress on formalism, on the outward manifestation of faith. This manifestation had become bound up with pious practices—novenas, rosaries, processions, devotions—all of them harmless in themselves, according to anticlericals, but dangerous because they cultivated clerical attitudes. The ethic, they argued, encouraged mindless formalism, emphasized ignorant humility, and preached a worldview that stressed the transitory nature of this life, one that held a contemplative monk or nun as more valuable to society than a trained scientist or merchant. It stressed obedience to the clergy in all aspects of life. Clerical virginity was deemed more pleasing to God than the most devoted parenthood; pious devotional tracts were prized more highly than works of learning and scholarship; the pope, whoever he might be, was portrayed as a paragon of virtue, and even taste. Furthermore, the ethic was intolerant of all other faiths and all other views. Error, the clergy stated, had no rights; and all that was not clerically approved was erroneous. Worst of all, the ethic identified the clergy—and therefore the Church—with the possessing classes in what had become a cold class war.[3]

The Spanish Catholic ethic was born out of the experiences of the nineteenth century. It was a defensive reaction to a series of attacks upon the clergy that politicians and statesmen had made in an attempt to solve national problems. Even before the devastating 1808 war against Napoleon, these policymakers had eyed clerical lands (about one-fifth of the national territory) as a solution to Spain's economic instability. Confiscation began on a small scale in the eighteenth century; the major attack came between 1836 and 1876, when clerical institutions lost most of their land. The effect upon the Church was profound. The clergy lost their land rents; as recompense the government made them salaried civil servants. This did not provide

---

2. Quoted in Margaret Thomas Rudd, *The Lone Heretic* (Austin, 1963), p. 153.
3. For insights into and further elaborations of the ethic, see William J. Callahan, *Church, Politics, and Society in Spain, 1750–1874* (Cambridge, Mass., 1984), pp. 232ff.; Stanley G. Payne, *Spanish Catholicism: An Historical Overview* (Madison, 1984), pp. 97–122; Frances Lannon, "Modern Spain: The Project of a National Catholicism," *Religion and National Identity*, ed. Stuart Mews (Oxford, 1982), pp. 567–69; and the portrayal of the ethic in fiction in Soledad Miranda, *Religión y clero en la gran novela española del siglo XIX* (Madrid, 1982).

enough income to meet their needs, so they turned to the emerging middle class for subsidies. In doing so they were compromised into accepting economic liberalism, and they came to sanctify capitalism and defend private property with sermons and pastoral letters.[4] In their own minds the clergy saw themselves engaged in an apocalyptic struggle against the forces of materialistic secularism; at the same time they defended their alliance with the possessing classes, the most materialistic group in modern history. The paradox was only dimly perceived by those involved.[5]

The clergy also lost their centuries-old role as the nation's dispensers of charity. They could no longer afford the outlay to remain the chief agents of public welfare. Gradually the Church was transformed from an urban to a rural institution. In the process it lost the support of the urban working classes, and the clergy became further identified with the middle class.

Another sign of the clergy's loss of prestige was the incidence of anticlerical violence: priests were killed and churches burned in 1822 and 1834. This violence was partly of the clergy's own making, for they had actively engaged in armed warfare in the various liberal-conservative conflicts of the first half of the nineteenth century. Anticlerical violence was a reaction to clerical violence. After 1834 the violence moderated somewhat for the rest of the century, but the clergy were constantly aware of the threat.[6]

By the time the restoration settlement was achieved in 1876 the clergy had accepted the loss of their lands, but they remained defensive, for it appeared as if Spain's problems were being solved at their expense. This defensiveness took the form of an aggressive elaboration of their role in Spain's history and an attempted revival of their past glories. These became essential elements of the Catholic cultural ethic.

Greater problems loomed. As the secular working-class movements of socialism and anarchism grew, the clergy found themselves even more on the defensive. Having accepted the implicit individual-

---

4. See Richard Herr, "El significado de la desamortización en España," *Moneda y Crédito* 131 (1974), pp. 55–94; and also the sociological analysis of the middle-class connection in Juan González-Anleo, "Vida religiosa," *Informe sociológico sobre la situación social de España, 1970* (Madrid, 1970), p. 441.

5. But not by the Socialists. Rafael García Ormaechea pointed out the irony in an article in *La Nueva Era* in 1902: see Victor Manuel Arbeloa, *Socialismo y anticlericalismo* (Madrid, 1973), p. 157.

6. See the analysis of the clerical ethic and modern anticlericalism in José María Díaz Mozaz, *Apuntes para una sociología del anticlericalismo* (Barcelona, 1976).

ism of middle-class values, they were ill-prepared to minister to workers with collectivist aims.[7] And as Spain's problems intensified, the clergy became less able to face the demands of modernization. Not that other institutions could cope either: Spanish life was rocked with a series of disasters that accompanied attempts at national regeneration. In 1898 Spain lost the last of her overseas colonies, and the prestige of empire went with them. Attempts to found a new empire in Morocco led to a destructive week of rioting in Barcelona in 1909 in which the Church became the most visible target of the destroyers. Continued economic problems produced more upheavals in 1917. Dissidents offered their solutions: Basques and Catalans proposed regional autonomy as a means of cutting themselves off from the diseased body politic; socialists and anarchists agitated for their collectivist visions. Politics degenerated into violence, martial law, and assassination. Finally the army stepped in. In 1923 General Miguel Primo de Rivera overthrew the constitutional government and established a military dictatorship.

Through all of this turmoil the clergy reacted defensively, condemning modern secular life. Unable to cope with problems that few of them understood, they cultivated their Catholic ethic as a defense against the modern world. They concentrated upon the nourishing of a devotional, pious religiosity with romantic overtones that found its outlet in the externalia of religious life, and they developed a secondary school system to train students in the practice of the ethic. In both these instances the religious orders became the specialists of the religious revival, proving their expertise in preaching, teaching, and publication.[8]

The numbers of regular clergy increased dramatically after 1870. Since the middle of the eighteenth century they had been the targets of anticlerical hostility, and they had suffered legislative attempts to limit their numbers and possessions along with anticlerical violence against their persons and churches. Now they provided the Church with some of the manpower needed to meet not only the growth of secularism but also the changes caused by the urban population shift. The regulars came to bear the brunt of anticlerical hostility as well.[9]

---

7. Callahan, *Church, Politics, and Society*, pp. 235ff., treats this growing individualism as it affected all aspects of Spanish Catholicism.

8. Hugh McLeod, *Religion and the People of Western Europe, 1789–1970* (Oxford, 1981), p. 49, places this development in the context of the entire Catholic world.

9. See the comments on the regulars in Joan Connelly Ullman, "The Warp and Woof of Parliamentary Politics in Spain, 1808–1939: Anticlericalism versus 'Neo-Catholicism,'" *European Studies Review* 13 (1983), p. 149. José Manuel Castells, *Las*

The Catholic revival was international. It was perhaps more pronounced in Spain (and there were some peculiarly Spanish aspects to it), but the Church was hostile to the secular world everywhere. Pope Pius IX (1846–78) emphasized defensive values as he took a stand against the modern world in his *Syllabus of Errors* (1864) and discouraged any opposition to his stance when he defined papal infallibility at the First Vatican Council in 1870. Pious values and devotionalism became common Catholic characteristics, and the emotional experiences of such visionaries as the French girl Bernadette Soubirous at Lourdes set the tone for an age. Clergy everywhere became more ultramontane, more papal, more Roman.

In Spain the Catholic revival awakened an interest and renewed the faith of many Catholics, but at the same time the limited success of the revival encouraged the growth of a more aggressive anticlericalism. By this time anticlericals had a clear idea of the cultural ethic they wanted to destroy, and they also had some notion of what they wanted to put in its place. Working-class leaders talked about a classless society, one without priests, with neither moral nor religious coercion; the middle classes had visions of a secularized Western nation, an English Spain. Anticlericals from the professional classes argued that even if most Spaniards passively accepted the Catholic cultural ethic's values, these should not be imposed on everyone. Nor should the future be mortgaged to it, they said, arguing that it fettered the nation's youth to superstitious beliefs, focused the nation's energy on tasks of a narrow cultish nature, and perverted the national character to parochial ends. Manuel Azaña, the prototypal anticlerical intellectual and president of the Spanish Republic, the symbol of all that was right and wrong with that republic (and a fine coiner of phrases), said in 1931 that prohibiting the clergy from teaching the nation's youth was a matter of "public mental health."[10]

Azaña was the spokesman for a generation of liberals who believed that Spain would be left behind in the modern world unless

asociaciones religiosas en la España contemporánea (1767–1965): un estudio jurídico-administrativo (Madrid, 1973), catalogues the legislation against the regulars.

10. To accusations that he was anti-Catholic, Azaña answered that "to call me an enemy of the Church is like calling me an enemy of the Pyrenees or the Andes. What I could never accept was that my country should be governed by bishops, priors, abbots, or priests. I have never opposed the clergy in their mission of teaching Christian doctrine to whoever wants to hear them. I do oppose their teaching philosophy, law, history, and science to laymen and women." Manuel Azaña, *Obras completas,* vol. II: *Una política* (México, 1966), p. 57; vol. IV: *Memorias de política y de guerra* (México, 1968), p. 765. For examples of clerical pressures in education in the 1920s see Schlomo Ben-Ami, *Fascism from Above: The Dictatorship of Primo de Rivera in Spain, 1923–1930* (Oxford, 1983), pp. 104–6.

the cultural ethic could be changed. And, in fact, change was in the air. While Spain's economic and social crisis intensified, the nation underwent a remarkable cultural renascence in the half-century before the Civil War. Unamuno and José Ortega y Gasset were giants among the world's philosophers. Antonio Machado was a poet worthy of any nation in the West. Pablo Picasso came to dominate painting. The writers of the Generation of '98 made literary history. In medicine Santiago Ramón y Cajal founded modern neurology. But none of these great minds defended the Catholic cultural ethic, even though (or perhaps because) most of them were products of Church schools.

The advent of a new government gave liberal anticlericals hope: in 1931 the monarchy was overthrown and the Second Republic was proclaimed. A liberal-socialist coalition took power in an optimistic attempt to solve Spain's problems (which now included the fiscal effects of the worldwide depression of 1929). Reforms aimed at satisfying rural and urban working-class needs, regionalist aspirations, and antimilitarist demands were legislated, but they were only partially implemented because of disagreement within the government and opposition without. But on one matter within the governing coalition there was little disagreement: the liberal and socialist reformers were all anticlerical. They passed laws prohibiting the regular clergy from teaching in any schools; the Jesuits were dissolved and their property confiscated; clerical salaries were abolished; processions were banned; and other legislation further diminished the Church's public role. Only the anti-Jesuit laws were fully implemented, however, and after the anticlerical coalition fell in the autumn of 1933 and was replaced by a center-right government dependent on Catholic support, the other laws were not enforced at all. Moreover, the legislative attack upon the clergy had nourished clerical political fears and ambitions, so that the clergy came to play a most active political role, campaigning and supporting Catholic political parties.[11]

The overthrow of the monarchy had also signalled widespread anticlerical violence for the first time in a quarter of a century. A month after the proclamation of the Republic, in May 1931, churches were burned in Madrid and throughout much of Andalusia. The government stood by helpless, unwilling to use its police force to stop the destruction, fearful that it would lose popular support.[12] Worse,

---

11. See my earlier work *Reform and Reaction: The Politico-Religious Background of the Spanish Civil War* (Chapel Hill, 1964) on the Republic and the Church.

12. Manuel Azaña, then minister of war, responded to an urgent plea to stop the incendiaries with the comment that "all of the *conventos* in Spain are not worth

in 1934 when the Catholic political party, the CEDA, demanded representation in the ministry and leftist groups responded with an abortive rebellion, 34 priests, brothers, and seminarians were killed by violent anticlericals in the Asturias mining region; it was the first time in a century that so many clergy had been slain, an ominous portent of the fury to come. By the time the center-right government fell in early 1936, the religious issue had caused complete polarization. Anticlerical violence had created violent clericals. The clergy were rapidly becoming confirmed in their apocalyptic beliefs.

The elections of February 1936 returned a Popular Front government to power. This coalition of liberals, socialists, and communists, with anarchist support, once again began the process of implementing agrarian, industrial, regionalist, and anticlerical reform. Like its predecessor of 1931 the government was unable or unwilling to stop anticlerical violence as churches were put to the torch again. Tensions grew. In July 1936 elements of the military and the right rose against the Popular Front government. The government armed the working-class organizations in response, and the uprising turned into a civil war.

One of the first targets of the simultaneously harried and exultant defenders of the Republic was the Catholic cultural ethic. Hence the militiamen posed atop the Cerro de los Angeles, firing at a symbol. But the action went beyond symbolism: there were other targets for whom there were no photographers, thousands of flesh and blood targets, symbols and souls alike, the targets of an anticlerical attack unsurpassed in all of history.

The anticlerical fury of 1936 has a special meaning and significance. It was the greatest clerical bloodletting in the entire history of the Christian Church. No other fury in modern times approaches the Spanish conflict in the total number of clerics killed, or the percentage of victims of the total, or in the short time span involved: not the French Revolution of 1789, the Mexican conflict of the 1920s, certainly none of the church-state struggles in Latin America, and not even the Russian Soviet terror.[13] Antonio Montero Moreno, the most meticulous recorder of the Spanish fury, argues that it even sur-

---

the life of a single Republican." Reported by Miguel Maura, the home minister, in *Así cayó Alfonso XIII* (Barcelona, 1966), p. 251.

13. John McManners, *The French Revolution and the Church* (New York, 1969), p. 106, says that "perhaps two thousand were executed, perhaps as many as five thousand," this out of a clerical establishment twice the size of Spain's. John S. Curtiss, *The Russian Church and the Soviet State 1917–1950* (Boston, 1953), pp. 87, 89, says that the Soviet authorities "executed a relatively small number of clergy"; by 1920 about 1,200 Orthodox clerics had been killed.

passed the persecution of the early Christians by the Roman emperors, a contention difficult to prove, but difficult to disprove as well.[14] The stark facts, and they are the best recorded among the many deaths in the Spanish war and its associated terrors, are that nearly seven thousand clerics were killed, most of them within the six-month period from July to December 1936. These were not priests killed while serving as chaplains in the Nationalist army, nor those who died natural deaths while in hiding, but those who were killed purposely because they were clerics in Republican Spain.

Montero Moreno has broken down the statistics in his monumental study of the fury: of those clerics killed, 4,184 were secular (diocesan) clergy, 2,365 were male regular clergy (those belonging to a religious order or congregation), and 283 were nuns, all together for a total of 6,832.[15]

Depending upon the estimates for noncombatants killed in the terror and during the war, the clerical figure is a significant proportion of the total. Ramón Salas Larrázabal's thorough study indicates that 72,500 persons were killed by the Republicans; if so, then clerical deaths would constitute nearly 10 percent of this number.[16]

These figures must be seen in proportion to the total clerical establishment. There were nearly 30,000 secular priests and about 3,500 seminarians, for a total of 33,500; of these about 12 percent were killed.[17] The number of clergy killed in each diocese depended on the success or failure in each city and town of the military uprising that began the war, and also on the movement of military lines in the first six months of the war. For example, the diocese of Pamplona, where the uprising was a complete success, lost no clergy. In Barbastro, in Aragon, where the uprising failed and the area became the site of transit of the violently anticlerical anarchist Durruti column, the diocese suffered the loss of 123 of its 140 priests (88 percent). Most of the arch-

---

14. Antonio Montero Moreno, *Historia de la persecución religiosa en España, 1936–1939* (Madrid, 1961), pp. xiii–xiv.

15. Ibid., pp. 758–68. See also the critical review by Arturo Alonso Lobo, OP, "¿Se puede escribir así la historia?" *La Ciencia Tomista* 88 (1961), pp. 301–76, which does not, however, disagree with the statistics.

16. Ramón Salas Larrázabal, *Pérdidas de la guerra* (Barcelona, 1977), pp. 428–29. Gabriel Jackson, *Entre la reforma y la revolución 1931–1939* (Barcelona, 1980), p. 392, argues that only 20,000 persons were killed by the Republicans; if true, this would raise the clerical deaths to 34 percent.

17. There is some confusion about the actual number of clerics in Spain in 1936. Ricardo de la Cierva, *Historia de la guerra civil española*, vol. I: (1898–1936) (Madrid, 1969), p. 463, carefully weighs all of the figures from the different sources; his figures are used here.

diocese of Seville was captured for the Nationalists in the first days of the rising, and only 24 of 657 priests (4 percent) were killed. Between these extremes, of the three large dioceses which remained in Republican hands throughout most of the war, Barcelona lost 279 of 1,251 (22 percent), Valencia lost 327 of 1,200 (27 percent), and Madrid-Alcalá lost 334 of 1,118 (30 percent).

Thirteen bishops were killed: those of Siguenza, Lérida, Cuenca, Barbastro, Segorbe, Jaén, Tarragona (auxiliary), Ciudad Real, Almería, Guadix, Barcelona, Teruel, and the apostolic administrator of Orihuela.

Of the regular clergy, of which there were some 11,000 professed (including both ordained and nonordained) and another 9,000 novices and assorted unprofessed for a total of 20,000, 11 percent were killed.[18] Of those orders that lost over a hundred of their members, the Claretians lost 259, the Franciscans 226, the Piarists 204, the Brothers of Mary 176, the Christian Brothers 165, the Augustinians 155, the Dominicans 132, and 114 Jesuits were killed.

Of the orders of nuns, the largest losses were those of the Daughters of Charity of Saint Vincent de Paul with 30, the Carmelites of Charity with 26, the Adoratrices also with 26, and the Capuchins with 20. These were out of a total female religious establishment of 60,000 professed and novices.[19]

In all of these cases the proportions and comparisons take on more significant meanings when it is considered that probably half of Spain's clerical establishment was safely behind Nationalist lines within a week after the uprising; thus, the percentage of clergy killed should be doubled to reflect the loss. Taking these facts into consideration, it can be concluded that about a quarter of the male clergy behind Republican lines was killed.

In addition to these deaths an incalculable number of lay persons were killed because of their religious associations, either as well-known churchgoers, members of fraternal and charitable religious organizations, or as the fathers, mothers, brothers, sisters, and friends of clerics. Some were killed because they professed their faith by wearing some outward symbol of belief, perhaps a religious medal or scapular. Some were killed for acts of charity, for granting refuge to clerics

---

18. Manuel Ramírez Jiménez, *Los grupos de presión en la segunda república española* (Madrid, 1969), pp. 198–201, has the best statistics on the regulars.

19. As there are no figures available for the numbers of male and female religious in each order in Republican Spain, it is difficult to draw any conclusion as to which order suffered the most deaths per capita or the reasons thereof.

attempting to escape the fury. It is impossible to determine the number of these lay persons who were slain for their faith.

Nor was the anticlericalism limited to killing. Thousands of churches were burned, religious objects were profaned, nuns' tombs were opened and the petrified mummies displayed to ridicule, and religious ceremonies were burlesqued. Indeed, practically any imaginable anticlerical act was not only possible but likely.

The reality of the fury was bad enough, but popular belief abroad exaggerated it to be a constant persecution during the entire three years of the war. This was not so. The fury lasted some six months, through the remainder of 1936. An analysis of clerical assassinations shows this to be the case. About 80 percent of the clergy were killed in the first two and a half months of the war, from the beginning of the uprising in mid-July to October 1. Another 15 percent occurred in the following three months, up to the end of the year on December 31, 1936. Thus, 95 percent of the killings took place within the first six months of the war. Assassinations were sporadic after that, with the remaining 5 percent killed almost entirely in the first quarter of 1937 and only an occasional killing in 1938 and 1939.

For example, of some 976 clerics killed throughout the war in the diocese of Barcelona, 23 (2 percent) were killed within the first four days following the uprising, and by the end of July the number had risen to 214 (22 percent). In the following months the numbers are: August, 233 (23 percent); September, 151 (15 percent); October, 123 (13 percent); November, 99 (10 percent); December, 56 (6 percent); for the year 1937, from January through May, 59 (6 percent); after that the killings ended except for the assassination of the bishop of Teruel and his aides within the geographical confines of the diocese of Barcelona in February 1939.[20]

Most of the anticlerical violence occurred, then, during the revolutionary terror which resulted from the Popular Front government's arming of the labor unions and left-wing political organizations as a response to the military-rightist uprising. The government lost effective control of internal security as power was dispersed to the lowest level. Nearly anyone who had arms could act with impunity. Not until the beginning of the following year, after six months of terror, did

---

20. These figures have been extracted from José Sanabre Sanromá, *Martirologio de la iglesia en la diócesis de Barcelona durante la persecución religiosa* (Barcelona, 1943). The Barcelona fury has been perhaps the best studied, although in many ways it was atypical because of the strength of the anarchists, the large numbers of regular clergy, and the confusing political situation.

the government regain power (although there were some revolutionary elements that preserved their independence until the end of the
war). Surveying the damage in January 1937, as the government re-
established control, Manuel de Irujo, the only practicing Catholic in
the ministry, presented an accurate portrait of the fury in a memorandum to his colleagues in which he outlined what had happened to
the Church in Republican Spain since the previous July: all statues,
altars, and objects of worship had been destroyed; all churches had
been closed to worship; most churches in Catalonia had been burned;
official organizations had taken metallic objects of worship (bells,
crucifixes, etc.) and melted them down for military use; church
buildings had been turned into garages, offices, factories, and shops;
all *conventos*[21] had been emptied; police had been searching private
homes for religious objects and destroying them; clergy had been arrested, imprisoned, and killed by the thousands; and there were hundreds of clerics still in prison who were there only because they were
clerics.[22]

Irujo's memorandum dealt in generalizations. Already other accounts, more descriptive of the fury, had appeared, and many more
would be written in the next few years. Most were eyewitness accounts,
and dealing with individual attacks, they lend a greater feeling of in-
timacy, understanding, and insight into the events.[23] From these it
is possible to develop two general scenarios of the fury. In the first,
the clergy were killed in the days immediately following the uprising, either when the churches were stormed or after a day or two of
imprisonment. In most of these cases the clergy were pictured as conspirators with the military, and it was believed that they had arms
hidden in their churches and rectories or else had actually fired at
the enemies of the uprising. For example, Manuel González-Serna y
Rodríguez, pastor of the church of Constantino in Seville province,
was arrested on the day following the uprising and was accused of keep-

---

21. A convento is a residence of the regular clergy, male or female, and is usually attached to a church or chapel, and for teaching orders, to a school.

22. Quoted in A. de Lizarra, *Los vascos y la república española: contribución
a la historia de la guerra civil, 1936–1939* (Buenos Aires, 1944), pp. 200–2.

23. Many of the accounts have been filed in Rome on behalf of causes for canonization. A large number appeared during the war and were published abroad to create
sympathy and support for the Nationalists. Some were written by foreign journalists,
and these appear to be more disinterested and therefore more reliable, although there
have been some distortions. One of the best accounts is fictional, but utterly true to
reality: José María Gironella's description of the fury in Gerona in *The Cypresses Believe in God*, trans. Harriet de Onís (New York, 1955), pp. 927–39; 994–97, captures
the mood and tone of the fury better than most reminiscences.

ing arms; he was interrogated by a popular tribunal for three days. During his imprisonment the church was vandalized. Four days after his arrest he was taken to view his looted church and was killed with a bullet shot in his face.[24]

The Barcelona Jesuit José Murall survived an attempt and related the incident. He was at the Jesuit retreat house in the Bonanova district with two other priests and a Jesuit brother on July 21, 1936, three days after the uprising began. A short time after 9:00 A.M.

an officer and six men armed with rifles came to the door. The terrified housekeeper told me that I was wanted. When I presented myself they asked me if we had any weapons in the house. I replied that we had none and thereupon they searched the house.

The man in charge of the soldiers made the search. I accompanied him when we went up to my room but he scowled at me and said, "Get behind me or I'll kill you on the spot." All of us went outside and while we were being marched off I pleaded for Father Cots, saying that they should spare him because he did not belong to that house, but that he had come there merely to pay a visit. The officer, however, paid no attention.

In the street there were two cars bearing the letters FAI and CNT [anarchist organizations]. We three priests got into the first car and Brother Iriondo followed in the second. The orders were: "To the Union headquarters. . . ." The chauffeur intimated that he was forced to act against his will and told us that if we wished he would speed up in order to free us. But we refused because we believed that it would be worse for him as well as for ourselves. During the ride Father Cots remarked: "They are going to shoot us!" I added that we ought to prepare ourselves for death and we did so by confessing to one another.

Having arrived at the Union headquarters, we waited in the autos for about seven minutes. During that time several members of the crowd insulted us in a most horrible manner saying, among other things, "We are going to kill you because you are priests; not one of you will be left!"

Then we left the Union headquarters. After driving along the highway for about ten minutes they made us leave the car. I was the first out. Behind me followed Fathers Cots and Romá.

24. Aniceto de Castro Albarrán, *Este es el cortejo: héroes y mártires de la cruzada española* (Salamanca, 1938), pp. 277–85.

We were ordered to climb a nearby hill. Before leaving the road I said, "I die for Jesus Christ and I have no regrets whatever. I forgive all of you." The other priests expressed similar sentiments. Just then the other auto arrived with Brother Iriondo who called to us, "Give me absolution!" In a loud voice Father Romá absolved him, at the same time making the sign of the cross. Then Brother Iriondo joined us. We marched along together, I on the left, Brother Iriondo on the right, and between us were Fathers Cots and Romá. When we had gone some ten or fifteen feet they poured a shower of bullets upon us. I instinctively raised my right arm. A bullet grazed my head and struck me in the arm which I had raised. I did not, however, lose consciousness. It felt as though I had been stunned by an electric shock and I fell in a heap supporting my head on my wounded arm. Then I heard these words: "Bandit, assassin, he's trying to escape!" It seemed to me that it was Brother Iriondo who was moving along in the grass. Then they shot him.

I remember the thoughts that flashed through my mind: "Am I not dead? Shall I not have the happiness of being a martyr?" I could not but breathe heavily. Then one of the men said, "This fellow is still breathing." But the other replied, "Still breathing? Nonsense! Why, his brains are blown out!" The reason he thought so was because I had been bleeding freely from the wound in my head. From then on I heard nothing more.

Two or three minutes later, rising slightly, I saw my companions. Fathers Cots and Romá were crumpled over, heads nearly touching. What a consolation it was to behold those martyrs! I tried to raise myself but I fell back again. My wounded arm was like a piece of lead. Later I climbed back on the road but again I fell exhausted. Little by little I moved ahead. . . .

An auto belonging to the FAI drove up. . . . The driver of the car asked me where I wished to go. I told him that I would like to be taken to a hospital. After hesitating for a moment he consented, and muttered, "Bah, it's always a piece of humanity to take care of a wounded man!" On arriving there, he told the Superioress that he was bringing a priest. At the hospital they put a few stitches in the wound in my head and put my arm in a sling. Since the anarchists knew where I was they tried on several occasions to come and take me. But about all this the Doctor and the Sisters kept me blissfully ignorant.

At the hospital I called the Superioress and told her who I was and asked her to get me in touch with some of our Jesuit fathers. The following day Father Soler de Morell and Brother Massip arrived, and I told them everything that had happened. . . .

I stayed in the hospital almost a month—until the 16th of August. On that day I was taken to a private home and there I remained another month, til divine Providence saw fit to bring me to Italy.[25]

In the second scenario, more typical, most clerics survived the first few days of the war. Most were arrested in their rectories or conventos. Some were on the streets, dressed in secular clothing, and were recognized and denounced. They were taken to the local jail, or if the prison was full, to a convento or school requisitioned for use as a prison, and the clergy were put in with others arrested by the proletarian committees (which were spontaneously-organized groups whose aim was to carry out the terror by arresting, sometimes trying, and frequently executing enemies of the revolution—usually conservative politicians, employers, landlords, priests, and laymen). Then, each night for a week or two, or sometimes for a month, a number of prisoners would be taken out and shot, usually in or near a cemetery or else in a remote spot outside of town. Occasionally kangaroo courts would be held, but in the first weeks militiamen simply read off lists of names of those to be executed. Sometimes priests would be given an opportunity to save themselves by apostasizing, by denying their faith, but there is no record of any of them having done so. The foreign journalist and Nationalist sympathizer H. Edward Knoblaugh says that he was told by a militiaman about a priest arrested on suspicion of saying a clandestine mass in a private home who was taken out seven successive nights before he was killed: "That *fraile* died seven deaths before we shot him."[26]

The French writer Simone Weil, who went to Spain as a volunteer for the Republicans, was told by two anarchists of the capture of two priests. She says, "they killed one of them on the spot with a revolver, in front of the other, and then told the survivor that he could go. When he was twenty yards away they shot him down. The man who told me this story was much surprised when I didn't laugh."[27]

In the smaller villages and towns the cleric might be taken to

25. As quoted in Antonio Pérez de Olaguer, *El terror rojo en Cataluña* (Burgos, 1937), pp. 26–32. There is an English translation by P. Burns in *The Jesuit Bulletin* 16 (January 1938), pp. 4–5. See also the various accounts in Montero Moreno, pp. 589–626.

26. H. Edward Knoblaugh, *Correspondent in Spain* (London, 1939), p. 74.

27. From a letter to Georges Bernanos, in Murray Sperber, ed., *And I Remember Spain* (London, 1974), p. 261.

a larger city for jailing and later killed or, if he survived until 1937 or 1938, released when the fury was over. After August 1936 many clerics were killed when they were found hiding during searches in the larger cities.

Most clerics had this sort of experience. Included with them were known Catholic laymen. Sometimes students in the religious schools were taken along and killed with their teachers. Many of the slain clergy were young men; there are numerous instances of collective assassinations in which all of the slain were under thirty years of age. Of the 20 priests and novices of the Missionaries of the Immaculate Heart of Mary in the diocese of Barbastro who were killed, the oldest was twenty-four. Any and all kinds of experiences were possible, and for every generalization that can be made there is an exception. Some priests were saved from death by committee members who vouched for them, sometimes for remembered acts of charity or degrees of kinship, sometimes simply for their physical skill at evading their pursuers or for their courage. Some were released out of pity. Some individual conventos were not molested, and the clergy continued to live a communal life throughout the war.[28]

Nor were all clerics killed by their own parishioners. In both Aragon and Valencia much of the killing was done by outsiders, by anarchist members of the military units moving toward the front. In Aragon the Durruti column and in Valencia the Iron column both attacked local churches and priests who had been spared by the local populace, or agitated among rural folk with tales of conspiracy in the larger cities, or else urged them to kill the priests as enemies of the Republic and the revolution.[29]

Many assassinations defy analysis. Some are simply inexplicable, certainly in terms of hot-blooded motivation. The murders of dozens of Brothers of Mary illustrate this point. Their story is instructive. One hundred fifty-two Marists (not including novices) operated 15 schools with some 6,000 students in the diocese of Barcelona. When the uprising began, some were arrested, but most sought refuge in the homes of friends and relatives. Many of the novices simply stayed in their seminary dormitories. Some of those arrested were killed, the earliest on July 23, four days after the uprising. Throughout the rest

---

28. Montero Moreno, pp. 82–83, identifies one Gabrielist and two Salesian houses in Catalonia, a Dominican one in Santander, and a Hospitalers convento in Madrid.

29. See Montero Moreno, pp. 211ff. for Aragon and pp. 248ff. for Valencia. On the Durruti column see Abel Paz, *Durruti: The People Armed*, trans. N. MacDonald (New York, 1977), pp. 224ff.

of July and August additional Marists were killed, to a total of 15 by September 20. The number of assassinated increased to 36 by October 6.

By this time the provincials and superiors of the order, themselves in mortal danger, prepared a plan to secure the emigration of the remaining Marists. A meeting was set up with anarchist committeemen who were offered 200,000 francs (to be collected from the Marists' French province) to allow the remaining Marists security of passage to France. After half this sum was paid, 117 novices were allowed to proceed to the frontier at Puigcerdá on October 4, but only those aged twenty or under were permitted to leave. The remainder (there were only a few) were returned to Barcelona, where they were promised that they would be allowed to leave by sea passage.

The success of this exodus prompted the superiors of the order to make further arrangements, and a new agreement was made for the payment of 100,000 francs to allow the passage of all the remaining Marists aboard a steamship to France.

The word was spread, and dozens of Marists came out of hiding; 107 gathered at the Port of Barcelona, where they boarded the steamship *San Agustín* on October 7. After waiting a few hours, they were ordered off the boat and taken to the convento of San Elías, which had been commandeered as a prison. They remained there throughout the next day. The following night 45 of the imprisoned Marists were taken to the Moncada cemetery where a machine gun had been set up. Without explanation their captors began to fire at them. All 45 were killed. The remaining 62 Marists were saved when the natural brother of one of the imprisoned informed the government authorities, who then transferred the survivors to the safety of the Model Prison in Barcelona.[30]

Some clerics were beaten and tortured before they were killed. The pastor of the church in El Hornillo (Ávila) was jabbed with sharp axes and picks like a bull in the ring before he was shot to death.[31]

Among the better-researched assassinations are those of the thirteen bishops. Ten were killed within six weeks of the uprising, most after having spent two or three weeks in prison. Only one, the bishop of Ciudad Real, was shot on the same day he was arrested, August 22, 1936. None was shot in the vicinity of the prisons; they were taken to highway stops outside of towns or to local cemeteries. The bishop

---

30. Sanabre, pp. 150–52, and Montero Moreno, pp. 230–32.

31. See Teodoro Toni Ruíz, *Iconoclastas y mártires (por Ávila y Toledo)* (Bilbao, 1937), pp. 31–32.

of Jaén was taken by train to Madrid but was shot before he reached the capitol. The bishops of Guadix and Almería were taken aboard sea vessels off the coast of Almería, where they were forced to clean the decks and serve meals to the sailors before being taken ashore and shot. Other bishops were subjected to abuse and beatings before being killed. The bishop of Barcelona hid with friends until he was found on a routine search on December 1, 1936, and was shot two days later. The bishop of Teruel was arrested in January 1938 and was killed in February 1939 in the last days of the war.[32]

The Catholic world, both in Spain and abroad, was shocked by the fury. Before the war ended and an accurate count could be made, estimates of clerical deaths ranged as high as 20,000, nearly three times the actual number. All of the dead were claimed by their orders or their bishops to be martyrs to the faith. Rome was petitioned. But before this claim could be admitted, the question of the motivation of their assassins had to be clarified. And so the terrible questions were asked. Why? Were the murdered priests immolated on the altars of an outmoded cultural ethic? Were they the victims of a diabolical plot arranged in Moscow and carried out in Spain? Were the clerics armed conspirators with the military? How was it that a Catholic people could rise up against their clergy and allow them to be killed with impunity? Why?

---

32. All of the bishops' assassinations are recounted in Montero Moreno, pp. 364–430.

CHAPTER 2

The Fury and the Uprising

There are two conventional pictures of the anticlerical violence that gripped Spain in the summer and fall of 1936. One is the liberal-left version familiar to American and British readers (but not to Spaniards) of an enraged citizenry rising up against a parasitical clergy, of oppressed peasants storming baroque churches and comfortable rectories inhabited by smug, fat, and tyrannical priests, of downtrodden workers torching churches in moments of driven passion and killing conspiring Jesuits in hot-blooded bursts of anger. The aroused masses are depicted as true Christians, purging God's Church of the unworthy servants.

The other portrait of anticlerical violence is that painted by the conservative-right, one more familiar to Spanish readers. It views the anticlerical fury as the work of a small group of cold-blooded, willful, and God-hating men following the orders of Soviet communism, international freemasonry, or, in the most reactionary view, zionistic Judaism; and sometimes all three.[1] These conspirators entered into the chambers of government, or else had the ear of those who governed, and they kept the government from preventing or stopping the fury, which in turn was being directed by the conspirators' more criminal elements, greasy rabble paid off in foreign currency.[2]

Enough truth exists in both views to have kept them alive for

---

1. Manuel de Castro Alonso, the archbishop of Burgos, said in his pastoral letter of February 14, 1937: "The Popular Front was nothing more than a conglomeration of atheists, masons, Jews, and enemies of God and Spain." Cited in Victor Manuel Arbeloa, "Anticlericalismo y guerra civil," *Lumen* 24 (1975), p. 171.

2. Indeed, sketches by Carlos Sáenz de Tejada for the Nationalist official history of the uprising, Joaquín Arrarás, ed., *Historia de la cruzada española* (Madrid, 1940–43), depict the incendiaries and murderers with Slavic and typically un-Iberian features; and the first attempt at a book-length analysis of the fury, Juan Estelrich, *La persecución religiosa en España* (Buenos Aires, 1937), claimed a Marxist plot. See also Luis Carreras, *The Glory of Martyred Spain* (London, 1939), pp. 19ff.

half a century. Given the variety of circumstances possible in the killing of over six thousand clerics and the assault on over ten thousand churches, it is not surprising that anything could and probably did happen. There *were* oppressed peasants, just as there were God-hating communists and freemasons, criminals, and tyrannical priests. There were killings done both in the heat of passion and in cold-blooded calculation. There were churches burned as an exultation to freedom from oppressive obscurantism just as there were churches burned by criminal pyromaniacs. All of these facets of the violence are true.

But they are not the whole truth. There are discernible patterns in the violence and the motivation behind it that disprove the simplistic views of the conventional theorists. In many ways the conservative-right conspiracy theory is more difficult to disprove if only because the liberal-left view is so idealistic and romantic as to be patently unreal.

The proof of the conspiracy usually cited by clerical authors consists of cryptic masonic lodge instructions, statements of a most general nature from the ideological founders of socialism, occasional obscure newspaper articles or confessions by equally obscure communists turned repentent. Marx, Lenin, and Trotsky are hauled out, and their views on religion aired to explain the motivation for the fury. Masonic lodge minutes and letters are cited as proof of masonic intervention.

The documents and citations are probably valid—there is usually a bit of truth in all conspiracy theories—but they are only a small part of the reality of the anticlerical fury. There is no question that the Spanish Communist party (and that of the Soviet Union) wanted to put an end to Catholicism. That it was the directing spirit behind the fury is another matter. The fact is, of course, that anticlericalism predated Marxism in Spain by decades. Before Marx began to write, churches were being burned and priests were being killed in Spain. It is of course possible (and even probable) that local working-class leaders took advantage of circumstances to direct their followers' ire against the clergy and channeled their deep anticlerical instincts into violent activity, but they were not following orders from abroad. The most authoritative studies on the role of the Communist party reject the notion that it was the motivating force behind the anticlerical fury.[3]

---

3. In fact, the Communists wanted to end the fury and terror so as to attract moderate Western democratic support for the Republic. See Burnett Bolloten, *The Spanish Revolution: The Left and the Struggle for Power During the Civil War* (Chapel Hill, 1979), and David Cattell, *Communism and the Spanish Civil War* (Berkeley, 1955).

As for the masonic conspiracy theory, there were lodges promoting anticlerical ideas in the nineteenth century, but they had become a bulwark of middle-class anticlericalism by the twentieth century, and however much they may have promoted restrictions on clerical privilege, they were opposed to violence which might easily be turned against the middle class and engulf it.[4]

No, the dominant fact is that violent anticlericalism runs deeply throughout modern Spanish history, and this anticlericalism was caused by clericalism, or by perceptions of clericalism, and by very specific circumstances. It may very well be that these perceptions of clericalism did not conform to reality—a point that will be examined — and that Marxist and masonic conspirators exaggerated clericalism beyond what it actually was. But they did not manufacture clericalism nor did they make the religious problem. These conspirators may have provided the spark for the anticlerical fury, but to carry the analogy through, the spark had to ignite vast amounts of fuel.[5] The Spanish urban working classes in general perceived the clergy to be their enemies, and the absence of governmental restraint and the atmosphere of war gave them the opportunity to display their anticlericalism in violent ways.

The conservative-right conspiracy theorists do not face the fact that anticlericalism has been an intensely Spanish phenomenon with deep historical roots. How else can the ferocity of some of the attacks, the complacency of many of the people observing the acts of destruction, or the unwillingness of the government to intervene be explained? And this, of course, is why they resort to the facile explanation of a conspiracy theory. If, after centuries of christianization, of clerical domination and selection of cultural determinants, the people turned against the clergy of their own accord, this would be a striking confession of failure, an indictment of the clergy's efforts. It is infinitely easier to blame a foreign ideology, outside agitators, or diabolical international forces in a scenario that smacks of an apocalyptic cosmology. But motivation is seldom that simple.

---

4. But the influence of the lodges—however slight—cannot be dismissed out of hand. They did provide a meeting place for anticlericals, and during the course of the Republic a number of left-wing politicians and even socialists joined. See Juan Ordóñez Márquez, *La apostasia de las masas y la persecución religiosa en la provincia de Huesca, 1931–1936* (Madrid, 1968), pp. 255–415, for information on the lodges and an obsession with freemasonry that mars an otherwise fine work.

5. The anarchist press, especially *Solidaridad Obrera* (Barcelona), urged its readers on to anticlerical violence, as did that of the POUM (the Trotskyist party); see Montero Moreno, pp. 55–56.

The liberal-left has its own mythology. This is that all of the killings were done as acts of passion in a blind rage of fury at years of oppression. Probably some of the first assassinations and burnings were done so, but a careful analysis of the record indicates that the vast majority of clerics were killed after the first month of the uprising. For example, over three-fourths of the assassinations in the diocese of Barcelona occurred over two weeks and more after the uprising began.[6] It is difficult to see how these killings can be considered as having been committed in anything but cold blood.

A variation of the liberal-left explanation, especially among foreigners, argues a conspiracy of expectation. They say that Spaniards killed their clergy because it was expected of them; violence was a way of life in Spain. If Spaniards burned churches, it was because churchmen once burned Spaniards. Cathedral blazes were simply the other side of the coin of the fires of the Inquisition.

These differing explanations raise the question of who exactly the arsonists and assassins were. The question has implications beyond the fury. Liberal Republicans either pointed to criminal elements in order to dissociate themselves from the violence or else elevated the workers as justifiable purifiers: condemn as criminals or extol as masses. Nationalists, on the other hand, saw the arsonists and assassins as representative Republicans leavened with anti-Spanish bolsheviks.

There does seem to be a general agreement that most of them were young men.[7] Many were probably common criminals, turned loose as the prisons were opened to free political prisoners when the uprising began.[8] In rural areas many were outsiders, alien to the vil-

---

6. Sanabre Sanromá, pp. 227ff.; 332–69. Consider the killings in the month of September 1936, when it can be assumed that most of the passions aroused by the uprising were abated. Of the 151 clergy killed that month in Barcelona, 73 were assassinated within one day after arrest; 44 were killed after a longer period of detention, but most of them within three days. Of the remaining 34 there is no record of the period between arrest and execution. Some of those killed had been arrested in July right after the uprising and then had been released, only to be arrested again in September and killed. Some were arrested and killed at the frontier while they were trying to flee the country.

7. Hugh Thomas, *The Spanish Civil War*, rev. and enl. ed. (New York, 1977), p. 280, claims that men under twenty-four on both sides carried out most of the terrorist (both red and white) activities. Franz Borkenau, *The Spanish Cockpit: An Eyewitness Account of the Political and Social Conflicts of the Spanish Civil War* (London, 1937), p. 94, interviewed a sixteen-year-old militiaman as ecstatic over the destruction of the clergy and churches.

8. See Bolloten, p. 56.

lages whose churches they burned and whose priests they killed. Sometimes local folk joined in the acts of destruction.[9] These arsonists and assassins are usually referred to as "uncontrollables."

But many were not common criminals. There were idealists also, and there were those who had been goaded by years of poverty, misery, and frustration at the hands of the possessing classes and the clergy who counseled humble acceptance; there were also those powerful enough to intimidate others, those at the bottom of the economic scale who had everything to gain and nothing to lose, and those who had either visions of a glorious future or else simply scores to settle with those who had wronged them in the past. Many were the same ones who would and did support rightist organizations and fascists in those areas where the Nationalists seized power.[10] Some had no aims other than destruction. The Catalan official Juan Matas found a man preparing to burn the church of Santa María del Mar in Barcelona; when Matas tried to show him his directive from the government to preserve works of art from the flames, the incendiary called such concern "priests' matters" and told Matas, "I'm not interested in your papers; moreover I can't read, nor do I want to. I'm a gravedigger and letters confuse me."[11]

Many were caught up in what André Malraux in *L'Espoir* called *l'illusion lyrique* of the revolution: the spirit of wonderful release, the do-what-you-want, take-what-you-wish, destroy-what-you-will feeling.[12] The legal and social controls had been shattered by the uprising and the expectation of violence. Anyone could do whatever he or she wished with no fear of reprimand.

The anticlerical fury, then, cannot be explained by a single reason. A number of motivations were at work. This is because at least two struggles were going on simultaneously: a war between Republicans and Nationalists—a military struggle being fought in conventional terms—and a revolution in which the left was trying to impose its aims and hopes on the right. Moreover, the struggle occurred within a century's tradition of anticlerical violence. Thus, it seems possible

---

9. See the description of locals joining in the irreverence in W. Stockley's letter in *The Tablet*, September 19, 1936, p. 390.

10. Patricio Escobal, *Death Row: Spain, 1936*, trans. Tana de Gámez (Indianapolis, 1968), p. 248, recognized some of those who later served on Nationalist execution squads in Logroño as being among the church incendiaries of the early spring of 1936 before the war began.

11. As cited in Luis Romero, *Tres días de julio* (Barcelona, 1967), p. 529.

12. Malraux's 1938 work has been translated as *Man's Hope* by S. Gilbert and A. Macdonald (New York, 1979).

to detect three basic motivations based on perceptions of the clergy, with none of them exclusive and all overlapping to a certain extent: 1) the clergy perceived as military enemies in the specific circumstances of the uprising and war; 2) the clergy perceived as part of the old regime, to be destroyed for the aims of the revolution; 3) anticlerical violence perceived as part of Spanish tradition.[13]

Considering the first of these, the least complex motivation for the anticlerical fury was simply that the clergy were enemies of the Republic. The Republicans saw them as having thrown in their lot with the Nationalists and therefore were not to be treated any differently from other warriors for the Nationalist cause. This view carried no implications about the clergy's past or their role as a counter-revolutionary group. It was a matter of military defense. The clergy, it was argued, had been part of the military conspiracy, they had used or allowed to be used their churches and conventos as arsenals and strongholds for the Nationalist forces, they had actually handled weapons and fired on the Republicans, and they had given aid and material comfort to the enemy. They therefore showed themselves as a clear danger to the existence of the Republic.

That this view was not based on reality is another matter. What is important is that the clergy were perceived as such—or perhaps an attempt was made to defend the anticlerical fury on this basis. Thus, the fury was justified: the clergy were the enemy, and the right of self-defense dictated action against them.

It was almost universally believed among the Republicans that the clergy were involved in the military conspiracy, that they had been plotting with army leaders since the overthrow of the monarchy five years before. There is no evidence to support this view.[14] But once the uprising began there is no question that most of the clergy were

---

13. In 1969 the novelist José María Gironella asked 100 of Spain's leading artists, intellectuals, and popular figures, many of whom had lived through the fury of 1936, what each thought was the reason for the persecution of the Church. Among the most frequent responses were: the Church's traditional intolerance of other faiths and other points of view; the clergy's lack of social justice and their support of the wealthy; the immaturity of both the clergy and the people; and the clergy's not practicing what they preached. *Cien españoles y Dios* (Barcelona, 1969).

14. Gabriel Jackson, *The Spanish Republic and the Civil War, 1931–1939* (Princeton, 1965), p. 290, says, "the military had no more taken the Church into confidence on their plans than they had the conservative republican parties." Vicente Cárcel Ortí, "La iglesia durante la II república y la guerra civil (1931–1939)," *Historia de la iglesia en España*, vol. V: *La iglesia en la España contemporánea*, ed. V. Cárcel Ortí (Madrid, 1979), p. 364, says "there is no proof so far to indicate that the Church was involved in the uprising." These statements must be qualified; there is some proof that the lower

favorable toward the Nationalists. Ideology aside, the military had proclaimed against a government that had not been able to stop church arson in the months since the Popular Front's electoral victory in February 1936, a government which had also begun the enforcement of anticlerical legislation passed in 1931. While the original manifesto of the conspirators did not mention religion or the Church, there was a general awareness and knowledge that the military "respected" religion and would abolish the anticlerical laws. And finally, since the left's response to the uprising was a general assumption that the clergy were part of the conspiracy, and on the basis of this belief they began burning churches and killing clergy, it would seem natural for the clergy to gravitate to the side of the conspirators.[15]

In some places the fury was partly provoked or intensified by priests who broadcast anti-Republican sentiments over the radio from Nationalist territory. The Basque priest Iñaki de Azpiazu observed that such broadcasts from Burgos, Vitoria, and Salamanca caused anticlerical extremists to view "every priest as an ally of the rebels."[16]

Some did not support the uprising. Many priests and bishops stayed neutral at first, just as many had played no political role in the past. Many were caught off guard; they had no foreknowledge that the uprising would succeed (General José Sanjurjo's 1932 rebellion had failed), nor did they know how long the fighting would last. Some were genuinely sympathetic to the Republican cause and to nonviolent leftist aims.

But from the first moment of the uprising, rumor and belief combined to paint a picture of a clergy deeply involved with the Nationalists. Rumors were circulated that the clergy were armed and had allowed the use of church buildings as arsenals to store arms for the uprising.[17] In some cases the only arms found were either hunting

---

clergy (but not the bishops) in Navarre were aware of and involved in the conspiracy. See Juan de Iturralde, *El catolicismo y la cruzada de Franco* (Vienne, 1955), I, 447ff.

15. Vicente Palacio Atard, "La guerra de España (1936–1939),"*Diccionario de historia eclesiástica de España* (Madrid, 1972–75), II, 1185, argues that the clergy spontaneously supported the uprising, that the fury was not a factor in those areas where the uprising was immediately successful (chiefly Navarre), and that in fact the clergy there did not even know about the anticlerical violence until much later.

16. Iñaki de Azpiazu, *7 meses y 7 dias in la España de Franco* (Caracas, 1964), p. 13.

17. Elliot Paul, *The Life and Death of a Spanish Town* (New York, 1937), p. 331, claims to have seen such a cache of arms in Ibiza, in a tunnel from the rectory to the church. Joan Manent, the mayor of Baldona (Catalonia), claims to have found 100 rifles and 100,000 rounds of ammunition hidden in the Carthusian monastery in the town; the arms had been hidden there for the defense of the monastery "and the use of right-

pieces or else weapons planted by searchers determined to fix blame upon the clergy. Undoubtedly there were some priests who took up arms and fired along with troops, and some, more understandably, who fired at the mobs advancing on their buildings intent upon arson and murder. But in fact there were few arms stored in church buildings. Most rifles were kept in army-controlled arsenals or barracks. It would have been foolish for the conspirators to have hidden vital arms in churches and conventos which would most likely be the first places attacked by leftist groups.

What gave rise to many of the rumors that the clergy were firing from their churches was that church buildings were used for military purposes by the contending sides, more often by the Nationalists because of the nature of their military tactics. In the smaller towns the churches were usually the strongest structures and frequently commanded the highest points, and in the larger cities church buildings often controlled key intersections. Military units on the defensive, as the Nationalists were in the larger cities, would tend to use such structures.

The evidence, then, is that for the most part the clergy were not involved in the uprising and that if priests did fire from churches, these were isolated cases or else instances of self-defense.[18] But anticlericals would have none of this; there was firing from churches or they were told that there was firing from the churches, and this was enough to corroborate their beliefs.

The anarchist newspaper *Solidaridad Obrero* even claimed that the clergy were firing poison bullets and that the Brothers of San Juan de Dios in the Hospital of San Pablo in Barcelona were killing the working-class wounded with fatal injections.[19] A leader of the young anarchists later commented that rumors of clerical poisonings were rife at the beginning of the uprising: children ill from poverty, dirt,

---

wingers" since before the October 1934 revolution. Cited in Ronald Fraser, *Blood of Spain: An Oral History of the Spanish Civil War* (New York, 1979), pp. 451–52.

18. The bishop of Gerona toward the end of the war denied clerical armed involvement in the uprising: "Did any priests fire from the churches? I never heard of it, and had I been aware of it I would have had no hesitation in taking the steps prescribed by canon law. I can answer for my diocese." Quoted in *The Tablet*, February 18, 1939, p. 207.

19. Cited in Hilari Raguer, *La espada y la cruz (La iglesia 1936–1939)* (Barcelona, 1977), p. 151. This poison claim had become part of the standard repertoire of Spanish anticlericalism; it goes back a century to 1835 when the Jesuits were accused of poisoning the wells of Madrid during the cholera epidemic.

and heat were believed to have been poisoned by clerically contaminated bread, water, and candy.[20]

The press was a chief vehicle for stirring up sentiment against the clergy. Instances were reported of priests firing on the people: among incidents cited was that of a priest arrested for manufacturing hand grenades.[21] Papers in Madrid headlined clerical attacks: "Chauffer attacked by a group of friars." "Large group of friars kill six militiamen."[22] Respectable public figures such as the Catalan Generalidad President Luis Companys and the conservative Republican politician Ángel Ossorio y Gallardo claimed that the clergy had participated in the uprising and therefore deserved their fate. The former minister of education Marcelino Domingo said in a newspaper article on October 5, 1936: "The Government has confirmed that almost all of the churches had been converted into fortresses; that almost all of the sacristies had been converted into arms depots, and most of the priests, curates, and seminarians into sharpshooters of the rebellion. What could the Government do in the face of these circumstances?"[23] These statements and rumors, later proved to be untrue, stirred up the populace.

Probably the best recorded instance of an attack on a church which was used as a fortress and the rumor which surrounded the clergy inside was in Barcelona where the Carmelite church and convento on the corner of the Diagonal and the Calle Lauria were taken by Nationalist troops and turned into a stronghold against Republican forces. The Nationalists set up a machine gun and rifle nest in the bell tower and began firing at their opponents. After a protracted battle the Nationalists were subdued, but not before word was spread throughout Barcelona by radio that the convento was a Nationalist stronghold and that the priests within were firing on the people. Various accounts have since established that the clergy were not involved in the uprising and were forced to stay in the building for protection from the firing outside once it was invaded.[24] The friars were

---

20. Gregorio Gallego, *Madrid, corazón que se desangra* (Madrid, 1976), pp. 46, 47.

21. Montero Moreno, p. 66.

22. Cited in David Jato Miranda, *Madrid, capital republicana* (Barcelona, 1976), p. 212.

23. From *El Pueblo* (Tortosa), cited in Montero Moreno, pp. 65–66.

24. One dissenter from this view is the anti-Franco Catalan priest Josep M. Llorens, who claims that a friend of his was told two months before the uprising by one of the Carmelite friars that weapons were being stored in the convento in anticipation of the uprising: *La iglesia contra la república española* (Vieux, 1968), p. 199.

probably afraid also, for other churches and conventos were by this time being attacked and burned throughout the city. They stayed in the convento and, according to some accounts, fed the Nationalist defenders and cared for the wounded. It is not known how willingly they did this, but it is not surprising that they did so, for they would have been not only following their natural political instincts but their own Christian precepts of charity as well.

Megan Laird, an American resident of Barcelona, described what happened after the Nationalists surrendered and the government forces entered the church to bring out the defeated and the wounded on stretchers:

> One by one they carry them beneath our windows. One man is delirious, and writhes back and forth on the stretcher, trying to get down, to fight again. . . .
>
> They bring out a dead priest, and the mob shouts and dances in the streets; for the priests have sheltered the insurgents in the church. Against the common soldiers the mob bears no malice; they are released at once and even aided to their homes—they were forced to fight, and only acted under orders. But against the priests and officers the hatred of the people is implacable. . . . The guards are powerless to restrain the people now. They are setting fire to the church, shattering the windows with incendiary bombs, and flinging lighted torches into the dark interior. A slender column of black smoke begins to rise, wavering, uncertain, from beside the tower. Next door to the Carmelites is a garage. . . .
>
> The church is burning well now. The black smoke billows up in larger and larger clouds. Someone has pulled down the white flag in the tower and hoisted in its stead the red flag. The smoke and flames lick up toward it. But the mob does not withdraw. The people are waiting for something. All the soldiers and the officers have been taken out. But the mob is waiting— because the priests remain. They must still be in the church. The mob is waiting for the fire to drive them out.
>
> The first one escapes. He emerges suddenly, running, from an unattended side door, and is helped into a car which speeds instantly away. He has been wounded in the head, and his entire face is covered with a gleaming liquid mask of scarlet blood.
>
> And now the other priests come out, one by one. They are dressed in ordinary shirts and trousers, and keep their hands held high above their heads, asking for mercy. The first ones are pro-

tected by the Civil Guards and disappear into side streets. Although the mob is restive and murmurs against them, it lets them pass.

But now the humor changes. The Civil Guards are pushed aside and the mob takes control. A machine gun is placed opposite the church door, and as the priests come out they are shot down one by one against the wall.

Across a bench, in the Diagonal, lies the crumpled body of another priest—one of those the people had at first let pass.

They must be all out now. The mob has begun to disperse. Flames are crackling in high, singing ribbons around the tower of the church. The door opens once again and a Civil Guard comes out, holding up his hands to ward off attack on the priest beside him. This is an old priest, very fat, dressed in a yellow shirt, rolled up at the elbows, and black trousers. He walks close at the side of the guard, his head bent down. He is set upon and beaten with the stock end of a gun, but the guard begs the populace for mercy, and they let the priest go on. They direct him out into the wide stretch of the Diagonal, and make him set off down it, alone, under the arching branches of the trees.

The priest walks slowly, with a staggering, uncertain gait. He is on the point of collapse, but when he tries to lean against a wall to rest himself the people force him on. He staggers slowly down the Diagonal, his palms joined before his breast, praying. When he has covered perhaps a hundred paces they shoot him from behind and he falls down. They let the body lie.[25]

This particular instance may have been atypical because the church in question was indeed being used as a fortress. In most other places the mob attacked the churches on the basis of rumor alone. For example, no proof exists that they were being so used in Madrid, or even other churches in Barcelona. Luis Romero's montage history records a typical answer to the question "What is burning?" A youth with a pistol answered: "The Church of Pueblo Nuevo. The priests were firing on women and children. Let's punish the rabble."[26]

Carlos Vicuña, the Augustinian historian, describes the attack

25. Megan Laird, "A Diary of Revolution," *The Atlantic Monthly* 158 (1936), pp. 522–23. See also the accounts in Arrarás, V, 287ff., and Romero, pp. 519ff. Arrarás is a proclerical source, but he is factual. If there is a lack of balance in these accounts, it is because there are no descriptions by anticlericals; in fact there are few anticlerical accounts of the fury.

26. Luis Romero, p. 394.

on the Augustinian convento of Valverde in Madrid: the mob entered the building and took the monks to the police station, where they were accused of firing on the crowd and were then imprisoned; while in jail, the monks found this to be a common experience of other imprisoned clergy.[27] Nor were such denunciations based on the best of witnesses: Ramón Sender, stalwart Republican and anticlerical, recounts the arrest of a rural priest on the word of the village idiot that the priest had been firing from the church.[28]

Many of the killings were done as reprisals for specific events of the war. For example, 6 Claretian priests and brothers were among 17 prisoners killed in Barcelona in reprisal for the fall of Irún on September 4, 1936. The clerics had been in prison since July 20. In Málaga, which was under Nationalist siege by sea and air, clergy were routinely killed in response to shelling or bombardment, especially in September 1936.[29] After the first month of the war it became commonplace to kill prisoners, including but not exclusively clergy, in response to Nationalist bombardment behind the lines and to news of Nationalist victories or atrocities.

The clergy involved in these reprisals had almost all been arrested in the first few days of the war, and in many instances had been put in makeshift prisons for protection from the mob. These prisons were under the control of local authorities, often nominally government officials. But they were greatly influenced by the mob and the revolutionary committees, and when these latter two wanted to kill prisoners, they usually did so with impunity during the first month of the war. The government decreed the creation of popular tribunals to judge acts against state security and crimes of rebellion, to go into effect on August 24, 1936, in an attempt to prevent mob rule and continued lynchings. In anticipation of this, 74 clergy were killed in Lérida on August 20–21 by more than 200 militiamen who watched the executions with cheering and applause.[30]

The beginning of the siege of Madrid in November 1936 was another event that occasioned numerous reprisals. While Catalonia was an area where local control in the form of regional autonomy was strongest and clerical assassinations were greatest in the first weeks

27. Carlos Vicuña, *Mártires Agustinos del El Escorial* (El Escorial, 1945), pp. 47ff.

28. Ramón Sender, *Counter-Attack in Spain*, trans. P.C. Mitchell (Boston, 1937), pp. 42–43. See also the account of the travails of the Madrid priest Alejandro Martínez from arrest through imprisonment on a prison ship to his eventual release, in Fraser, pp. 419–25.

29. Montero Moreno, pp. 230; 279ff.

30. Ibid., pp. 242–44.

of the war, Madrid had fewer assassinations primarily because it was the seat of the central government. When the siege began, the central government moved to Valencia, leaving Madrid in the hands of local authorities. This action, combined with reprisals for Nationalist bombardment and shelling, along with fear that the prisoners would soon become executioners or would finger their captors as the Nationalists penetrated the city's defenses, led to one of the largest series of executions during the entire war. There were more than 5,000 prisoners in the city. Some 2,400 were taken to large trenches dug near the village of Paracuellos del Jarama on the outskirts of the city where they were shot and buried. Hundreds of clerics were included in the number killed, and the assassinations continued from the first day of the siege on November 7 through the end of the month.[31] There were also killings in the city itself. Twenty-three nuns, members of the order of Adoratrices, were arrested in the apartment they had been living in since they had been forced out of their convento. The cause for the arrest was the killing of a militiaman on the street outside the apartment; it was claimed that the fatal bullet had come from the nuns' window. All 23 were taken to prison and then to a cemetery where they were shot and killed on the morning of November 10, 1936.[32]

Finally, the role played by frustration, anxiety, and the desire to display one's loyalty to the Republic in a wartime situation must not be overlooked. Undoubtedly many persons felt the situation to be uneasy and reacted accordingly. Some wanted to do anything to relieve the frustrations of the war. "Anticlericalism," a sociologist says, "is a form of cheap rebellion"; it costs little and enables one to rebel against authority.[33] Attacks on the clergy, along with anticlerical activity of any sort, were relatively safe and probably satisfying, especially along the eastern seaboard where the field of action was far away once the barracks uprisings were put down. The clergy were demonstrably the enemy and deserved to be attacked. Furthermore, there must have been some uneasiness in the larger cities as the militiamen hunted people for arrest and probably execution. What better way to demonstrate one's loyalty to the Republic and progressive ideals than by a harmless attack on a church, which in any event would probably be burned soon anyway? Or to turn one's head the other way when a priest was arrested or being led to his execution? Certainly one could argue that

---

31. See the account in Montero Moreno, pp. 328–46. Ian Gibson, *Paracuellos: como fue* (Barcelona, 1983), p. 191, has accurate figures in his analysis.

32. Montero Moreno, pp. 496–97.

33. Díaz Mozaz, p. 153.

if the crowds watched these events in silence, they also did so in fear that if they took action to openly protect a cleric or to stop a church arsonist, they would probably become victims also. Simone Weil observes: "I was very nearly present at the execution of a priest. In the minutes of suspense I was asking myself whether I should simply look on or whether I should try to intervene and get myself shot as well. I still don't know which I would have done if a lucky chance had not prevented the execution."[34] Not many Spaniards were fortunate enough to be able to have had such a terrible decision put off so easily.

---

34. Quoted in Sperber, p. 260.

CHAPTER 3

The Revolutionary Attack

The Spanish Civil War was also a revolution. The military-rightist uprising had unleashed the revolution of the left, which for violent anticlericals became the culmination of a process that had begun in the nineteenth century. This revolution does not lend itself to easy analysis because it was both a political and a social upheaval; furthermore, Spanish anticlericalism has always been a complicated ideology with diverse stimuli and aims. One astute observer has delineated the anticlerical conflict as a three-faceted struggle between secular institutions and the clergy competing for political power, between the secular intelligentsia and the clericals competing for educational and intellectual power, and between the secular working-class ideologies and the Church in competition for ideological power, for the ultimate power of faith.[1]

Spaniards of the left had generally opposed the clergy's political aims, which since 1814 had usually supported the right. By 1936 both middle-class liberals and working-class activists had what they considered a solid rationale for attacking clerical political power: they had tried to legislate the Church out of politics since 1931, but they had been successful only in achieving the facade of separation of church and state, and actually their actions, and those of the violent anticlericals, had prompted both the formal entry of the Church into partisan politics, and the waving of the banner of the defense of Church rights by practically all of the parties of the conservative right. The anticlerical attack of 1936 thus came to be aimed not only at the clergy but also against Catholic politicians who supported the rightist parties and identified the Church with those groups. Given the circumstances of 1936, the anticlericalism turned to violence.

Since 1814, when the first political parties appeared in Spain,

---

1. Ullman, "Warp and Woof," p. 150. See also the classification of anticlericals in Díaz Mozaz, pp. 110–21.

the clergy had supported, sponsored, or organized partisan political parties that were clearly identified with the Church. None was totally accepted by all practicing Catholics at any given time as the only officially endorsed Church party, but to anticlericals there was little need for distinction. They saw the Church as involved in politics. After 1830 many churchmen supported the Carlist cause and its political arm, the Traditionalist party, chiefly because the Traditionalists made the defense of religious rights against liberal anticlericals the central concern of their party.

By the turn of the century the Vatican had become concerned that specifically sponsored Catholic political parties inhibited the Church's freedom and caused anticlerical reaction. It began to promote the tactic developed by some Jesuits that Catholics in Spain (and elsewhere) should no longer rely on Catholic-identified parties to protect their rights. Instead they should form organizations that would transcend politics and emphasize the reconstruction of a Christian social order. This approach would be more fruitful in the long run, the Vatican believed, because social changes would be more permanent than political ones; furthermore, such an approach would protect the Church from charges of meddling in partisan politics. One of the most active proponents of this idea in Spain was Ángel Herrera Ória, editor of the moderate Catholic daily *El Debate*. In 1909 he helped found an activist organization for Catholic newsmen, the *Asociación Católica Nacional de Propagandistas* (ACN de P), with the aim of using the press to disseminate Catholic social ideas.[2] Other Catholic lobbyist and pressure groups were organized.

But Herrera Ória was not promoting the passive social Christianity of Francis of Assisi and the medieval mendicant orders. He favored Ignatius Loyola's aggressive grappling with the modern world, so-called Jesuit realism. He got involved in partisan politics. In 1922 he and other Catholic laymen organized the *Partido Social Popular* (PSP), a demo-Christian party with the unstated but obvious support of the Vatican. The papal nuncio, Federico Tedeschini, worked actively to support the party. Primo de Rivera's 1923 coup forestalled a formal testing of the PSP's strength at the polls, but the party was an implicit violation of the Vatican's intention that the Church should avoid identification with political parties.[3] Perhaps Spain's problems were

2. See José R. Montero, *La CEDA: el catolicismo social y política en la II república* (Madrid, 1977), II, 439–539, for an analysis of the ACN de P.

3. See Javier Tusell Gómez, *Historia de la democracia cristiana en España:* vol. I: *Los antecendentes: La CEDA y la II república* (Madrid, 1974), pp. 104ff., on the formation of the PSP.

judged too pressing by the Vatican to allow for the slower but non-partisan social Christian approach; it was a judgment for which many Catholic laymen and clergy paid with their lives in the anticlerical fury of 1936.

In 1932, after the establishment of the Republic and the experience of enacted anticlerical legislation and incendiary violence, the nonpartisan approach was dropped altogether. A new party—actually a group of rightist parties—the *Confederación Española de Derechas Autónomas* (CEDA) was organized with the specific aim of revising the anticlerical legislation and defending the Church's interests.[4] Although neither the Vatican nor the Spanish bishops gave the CEDA official public endorsement, it was common knowledge that they supported the party. In the elections of 1933 four priests were elected as CEDA deputies to the Cortes (and two in the elections of 1936).

Other rightist parties had by 1933 been organized or revitalized, all of them identified (but to a lesser degree than the CEDA) with the defense of the Church. Two dated from the nineteenth century: the *Partido Nacionalista Vasco* (PNV), with a specific regional appeal to the Basques, and the *Comunión Tradicionalista*, heir of the nineteenth-century Traditionalists. There were two new parties: *Renovación Española*, the monarchist party which called for a restoration of Alfonso XIII and which saw Spain as essentially Catholic, although it was less adamant on this point than the Traditionalists; and the *Falange*, the fascist party, which stressed Catholicism as a necessary ingredient of Spanish nationalism.

All of these parties called for abolition of the anticlerical legislation, and all appealed to Catholic voters as defenders of the Church, each in its own way. The CEDA used its plurality in the Cortes of 1933–36 to prevent implementation of the anticlerical legislation. In the elections of February 1936 the Spanish bishops called upon Catholics to vote for those parties that would defend the Church, and they gave permission for cloistered nuns to leave their conventos to vote, presumably for the CEDA. It is therefore not surprising that the clergy and Catholic politicians were attacked in the anticlerical fury as a means of eliminating the clergy's political influence.[5] The fury, in

---

4. Herrera Ória was the CEDA's *eminence grise*, José María Gil Robles its parliamentary leader and tactician, and Luis Lucía was the organizer of the Valencian branch of the party. Montero, *La CEDA*, and Tusell Gómez have the best accounts of the organization of the CEDA.

5. Richard A.H. Robinson, *The Origins of Franco's Spain* (Pittsburgh, 1970), is a good study of the position and development of the parties of the right. Juan J. Linz, "Religion and Politics in Spain from Conflict to Consensus above Cleavage," *Social*

turn, confirmed the spectacular failure of the Vatican's activist socio-
political partisan policy of the 1920s and 1930s.

But there is another dimension to Catholic political involvement. This is the question of whether the various rightist politicians
used the theme of defense of the Church as a means of attracting
Catholic voters to support their parties. Were they using religion to
further partisan political aims? In the case of the CEDA and the Traditionalists this charge seems less likely than with the other parties:
both had been organized with specifically Catholic aims. The other
parties had nonreligious concerns more central to their existence.
The Basque Nationalists wanted regional autonomy, the Falange
wanted the establishment of a fascist state, and *Renovación Española*
wanted a restoration of the monarchy.[6] However, as there were clerics
and clearly identified Catholic laymen who supported each of these
parties, subtle distinctions were lost on anticlericals, who attacked
them all.

The aim of eliminating clerical and Catholic influence in politics, attempted first by legislation, and then by the fury, is much easier
to grasp than the other issue involved in the revolution—the intention of achieving a social turnover. Here the aim of the working-class
parties must be taken into consideration, for they were the chief proponents of the social revolution, and they wanted to destroy not only
the clergy's baneful social influence, they wanted to replace Christianity, or at least the Catholic cultural ethic, with belief in the
socialist revolution. Motives and aims need to be analyzed, for this
question strikes at the heart of the anticlerical fury.

The Socialist party was the most articulate of the working-class
groups. Until the 1920s Socialists had largely followed the dictates
of their founder Pablo Iglesias, who had said that clericalism existed
only because of capitalism, that the clericals derived their power from
the capitalist classes, and that Socialists should not allow the religious issue to deflect them from their true aims. Anticlericalism, he
said, was a middle-class matter: the workers wanted bread, not masses.[7]
Socialists were particularly angry at the hypocrisy of the middle

---

Compass 27 (1980), p. 256, says that the role of the CEDA was an important factor
in the radicalization of the anticlerical left.

6. Indeed, it is interesting to compare *Renovación Española* with the French
monarchist movement *Action Française* which had been condemned by the papacy
in 1926 precisely for using religion to further partisan political aims. See Eugen Weber,
Action Française: Royalism and Reaction in Twentieth-Century France (Stanford, 1962),
pp. 218–55.

7. Quoted in Cárcel Ortí, p. 350.

classes, whom they said mouthed anticlerical slogans but married in the Church, baptized their children, and sent them to religious schools. As for the clergy, the Socialists argued that their counseling humble acceptance of the evils of this world avoided facing the true root of modern problems, namely capitalism.[8]

By the time the Republic was established in 1931, the Socialists had become more overtly anticlerical: the clergy had become more entrenched in power, Iglesias had died in 1925 and his steadying hand was lost, and the party began to expand and draw in more illiterate — and hence cruder—supporters.[9] But the Socialists apparently did not join in the anticlerical incendiarism of the early weeks of the Republic and in fact sent pickets to guard some of the churches because they realized that anticlerical violence would simply react against the Republican-Socialist reformers. By 1934 the Socialists had developed a more specific anticlerical program: they called for the dissolution of all the regular clergy and confiscation of their property and expulsion of those "whose past attitudes made them hostile to the new institutions."[10]

Despite the increasingly radical stance taken by the Socialists as the war approached in 1936, they were still the best disciplined of the working-class parties (except for the miniscule Communist party), and most evidence points to the anarchists as forming the main ranks of the uncontrollables. The anarchists had long been the most violent anticlericals in Spain. Their libertarian views were well known. They lived by the violent deed, and there was little need for them to outline their religious program. The Anarcho-Syndicalist trade union, the CNT, stated as part of its program in May 1936, before the war began, that "Religion, that purely subjective manifestation of the human being, will be recognized in as much as it stays relegated to the sanctuary of the individual conscience, but in no case will it be permitted as a form of public display, nor as a moral and intellectual coercion; individuals will be free to hold whatever moral ideas they find suitable and there will be no need for religious ceremonies."[11]

---

8. There is a good discussion of Socialist anticlerical views in Arbeloa, *Socialismo y anticlericalismo*, pp. 151–59. See also Colin M. Winston, *Workers and the Right in Spain 1900–1936* (Princeton, 1985), for a history of the *sindicatos libres*, an attempt to organize the working classes in Catholic labor organizations.

9. Payne, *Spanish Catholicism*, p. 150.

10. From the party's program as cited in Jackson, *Entre la reforma*, p. 128. This was based, it said, on the fanatical opposition of many Catholics to the religious legislation of 1931.

11. In Jackson, *Entre la reforma*, p. 156, who quotes the entire CNT platform.

Once the uprising began and the revolution was unleashed, violence became commonplace, and the anarchist press talked violence in the broadest terms: "The Church has to disappear forever. . . . The priest, the friar, the Jesuit, have dominated Spain; we must extirpate them. . . . The religious orders must be dissolved; the bishops and cardinals must be shot; and church property must be expropriated."[12] One paper, urging an end to the terror after a month of violence, perhaps came the closest to describing the proletarian goal: "It should not be a question of burning churches or of executing priests, but of destroying the Church as a social institution."[13]

The attack raises the question of the clergy's socioeconomic role in Spain. This role became the justification for the violence that earned the revolutionaries support and sympathy from liberals and workers abroad, and of all the issues involved in the anticlerical violence it is the most complex. The clergy were pictured as social parasites, catering to the rich and ignoring the poor—an attractive picture for foreign anticlerical believers of the black legend. There were, of course, priests who sacrificed for the poor and who were in sympathy with proletarian needs. There were those who preached social justice. But there were not enough of them to change public perceptions.[14]

Perceptions were more important than reality. The clergy were perceived and labeled as social hypocrites. It was easy to do so, especially in a country with such great social needs and with such a large and culturally powerful clerical establishment. Clerics have always found it difficult to practice what they preach. The ethic of Christianity has been demanding: love your neighbor, do good to them that harm you, strive to be humble, the first shall be last—these precepts are difficult to fulfill, and it is little wonder that the clergy were faulted. But beyond this there were more substantial charges made against the clergy.

The Spanish clergy had, for nearly a hundred years before 1936, been criticized for allying themselves with the wealthy in the always-simmering class war. They did so for reasons that have already been

---

See also John Brademas, *Anarcosindicalismo y revolución en España*, trans, J. Romero Maura (Barcelona, 1974), on the anarchists.

12. From the anarchist *Solidaridad Obrero*, August 15, 1936, as cited in Montero Moreno, pp. 55–56.

13. From the POUM (Trotskyist) paper *La Batalla*, August 19, 1936, as cited in Montero Moreno, pp. 55–56.

14. See Jerome R. Mintz, *The Anarchists of Casas Viejas* (Chicago, 1982), pp. 71ff., for a view of a prewar anarchist stronghold in which the priests were generally well-liked.

discussed (see chapter 1), but it is also likely that in the developing bourgeois economy of the early twentieth century with its growing class divisions and class consciousness, the clergy catered to the wealthy because they felt more at ease among those who attended their masses and aided them in their evangelical work. Spanish priests were seldom recruited from among the desperately poor, whose children dropped out of school at an early age, if they went at all. Clerics usually came from pious families of lower middle-class origins whose values tended to identify more with the classes above rather than below them.[15] They can have felt little sympathy with the embittered and anticlerical urban and rural masses. Furthermore, the phenomenon known as the apostasy of the masses was not an exclusively Spanish one: it occurred in Italy, France, and Portugal as well. It is a difficult issue to resolve, and propaganda has obscured the problem. In any event, the clergy were perceived as social hypocrites, preachers but not doers of the word of Christ. It was a scandal of major proportions, and while individual — and important — clerics spoke out against the oppression of the poor, the general support the clergy gave the establishment classes outweighed these individual efforts.[16]

There is a long history of criticism, going back to the latter part of the nineteenth century, of the social attitudes and activities of the clergy. Aside from the obvious faulting of priests' social climbing to wealthy parishes and of catering to the wealthy to the exclusion of the poor, there are the charges laid against those clerics who did minister to the poor, rebuking them for their patronizing attitudes. Nuns especially were criticized for teaching their students and wards that they were not to rise above their social class.[17] Indeed, there were so many deprecations of the pre-1936 clergy that even the priests were concerned and wrote about them.[18]

In the anticlerical fury all of these charges were raised again, along with claims that the clergy possessed large fortunes. The proletarian press published accounts in August 1936 of vast riches and fabulous fortunes found in bishops' residences and in the invaded con-

---

15. For insight into recruitment of the clergy and class distinctions see Lannon, "Modern Spain," pp. 577–78.

16. See statements of the bishops in the 1900s and 1910s in Sánchez, *Reform and Reaction*, pp. 43–48.

17. Constancia de la Mora, *In Place of Splendor* (New York, 1939), pp. 15ff., has examples of this.

18. Two of the most perceptive studies are Gabriel Palau, ed., *Diario íntimo de un cura español (1919–1931)* (Barcelona, 1932), and Franciso Pieró, *El problema religioso-social de España* (Madrid, 1936).

ventos. The bishop of Madrid-Alcalá, for example, was reported to have had 18 million pesetas in his residence (in United States 1936 currency equivalence this amounted to about 2 million dollars). The Little Sisters of the Poor were reported to have had in the vault of the Bank of Credit Lyonnaise over 200 million pesetas (22 million dollars) worth of currency and securities.[19] Although there is no evidence that either the bishop or the sisters used the money to live lives of luxury, the reports served the purpose of whipping up anticlerical sentiment.

In the village of Baena (Córdoba) Ronald Fraser's pseudonymous Manuel Castro, a baker's son, claimed that the poor people knew that the priests needed money from the rich to give alms to the poor, "but the poor always believed that a part of the money, the best part perhaps, remained in the priests' hands. There were many priests who knew nothing of the laborers' lives, who lived aloof from the people."[20] Yet in the 1920s there were priests who had to take on part-time jobs as manual laborers to supplement their meager incomes.[21]

The claim that the clergy sided with the bourgeoisie against the working class has found its way into practically every pro-Republican commentary on the war. Franz Borkenau, who traveled throughout Republican Spain in 1936, remarked upon the greediness of the clergy and captured in a phrase the perception the liberal world had of the Spanish clergy: "The Church of the poor," he said, "has proved very clever at securing the best of the pleasures of this world."[22] And yet Cardinal Pedro Segura, expelled from Spain in 1931 for his anti-Republican activities and seen in leftist mythology as the classic clerical, used the income from his archdiocese to feed and clothe the poor.[23]

---

19. Montero Moreno, who cites these accounts, pp. 64–65, 432, claims that they ring false and do not take into account the large amounts of money necessary for administering a diocese of over a million souls or a large charitable institution such as the sisters operated, or that frequently these were legacies of pious foundations and were not the clergy's personal or disposable income. It is furthermore interesting to note that much of the expropriated wealth was used to finance the revolutionary committees in their terroristic activities. See Pierre Broué and Emile Témime, *The Revolution and the Civil War in Spain,* trans. T. White (Cambridge, Mass., 1972), p. 126.

20. In Fraser, p. 131. This comment from an Andalusian is complemented by the observations of Rafael Abella, *La vida cotidiana durante la guerra civil: La España nacional* (Barcelona, 1973), p. 178, who says that many Catalan clergy who escaped the fury in Catalonia passed over to the Nationalist zone and went to live in Andalusia, where they were astounded by the poverty of the people, and they realized that the Andalusian clergy were accomplices to this misery.

21. See the complaints on the situation addressed to Primo de Rivera, in Ben-Ami, p. 302.

22. Franz Borkenau, *Spanish Cockpit,* p. 82.

23. Carlos Seco Serrano, *Historia de España,* vol. IV: *Epoca contemporánea* (third

In fact, much of the clergy's income was devoted to charitable enterprise: the nineteenth- and early twentieth-century Spanish state spent little for orphanages, asylums, hospitals, unemployment relief, or any of the other social services provided by the modern state (although it was expanding these), and as a consequence the Church had traditionally filled the gap between human need and state aid; and it was expected to do so, partly because it had played such a massive role in the social welfare economy of the eighteenth century, when it had the resources.[24]

Perhaps it was the visibility of the clergy that singled them out for persecution. That very astute observer Jason Gurney says that the peasants never saw the oppressive landlords, but they saw the priests and believed that they supported the landlords.[25] Perception and myth apparently had a great deal to do with the fury. One wonders how much of the fury was manufactured, how much was done in cold blood, how much propaganda was involved, and how much violence was committed by those who were less than pure in their intentions.

Working-class attitudes toward the clergy naturally varied according to the religiosity of the populace. In some parts of northern Spain, where there was a high degree of concern about religious matters, local townspeople helped priests escape the fury; in one area even the Republican committees were concerned with protecting priests, churches, and shrines from outside agitators.[26] In southern Spain there was a greater incidence of home-grown anticlericalism that erupted into violence, and although the originators of the violence may have been few in number, townspeople more frequently joined in. But even in the south there was a general tendency to blame outsiders for the fury.[27]

---

ed., Barcelona, 1971), p. 39, says of Segura that "while he was Archbishop of Toledo, neither rural nor city workers lacked for food in times of crisis or unemployment."

24. See William J. Callahan, "The Origins of the Conservative Church in Spain, 1793–1823," *European Studies Review* 10 (1980), p. 209; and Baldomero Jiménez Duque, "Espiritualidad y apostolado," *Historia de la iglesia en España*, V, 450–56.

25. Jason Gurney, *Crusade in Spain* (London, 1974), p. 60.

26. William A. Christian, Jr., *Person and God in a Spanish Valley* (New York, 1972), p. 82. This work deals with the Rionansa valley in Santander province. Other works which concern northern areas are Carmelo Lisón Tolosana, *Belmonte de los Caballeros* (Oxford, 1966), Richard A. Barrett, *Benabarre* (New York, 1974), and Susan Tax Freeman, "Faith and Fashion in Spanish Religion: Notes on the Observation of Observance," *Peasant Studies* 7 (1978), pp. 101–23.

27. See the sociological studies of Alcalá de la Sierra in Cádiz province in J.A. Pitt-Rivers, *People of the Sierra* (Chicago, 1961), and of Fuenmayor in Seville in David D. Gilmore, *People of the Plain* (New York, 1980). Mintz, p. 170, notes that outsiders

In any event, a chief motivation of the uncontrollables appears to have been that the clergy were perceived to be social hypocrites. It was a cruel dilemma for the clergy. Given the class divisions and the emphasis upon them in the Spain of the late nineteenth and early twentieth centuries, there were few people and no groups who stood above class. The clergy should have, but they did not, not in Spain or elsewhere in the Catholic world. It would have been unrealistic to have expected the Spanish clergy to have reacted otherwise.[28]

The training of the clergy emphasized piety, puritanism, formalism, discipline, and the acceptance of one's station in life, and they taught these values to their parishioners. They preached a great deal of superstition also. Spanish intellectuals from the middle of the nineteenth century on complained about these clerical shortcomings, and in particular they claimed that the clergy ignored the simplicity of the Christian message of love and instead emphasized the mindless formalism of a hierarchical caste.[29]

How great an effect this had upon the working class is difficult to tell. They were not schooled in theological disputation, but they were aware of their parish priest's shortcomings. And there is an interesting point that has not yet been considered: many clerics and laymen who held progressive views on the social question and who were well known to be sympathetic to the poor were attacked and killed along with other clerics.[30] Perhaps the socioeconomic motivation was a smokescreen, albeit an unconscious one, for a more primitive and deeply felt hatred of the clergy and clerical things.

For the anticlerical fury went beyond mere assassination and destruction, acts that might be considered normal in wartime situations. The anticlericals went far beyond this: they tortured, they profaned, they burlesqued sacred ceremonies, they were violently iconoclastic. These acts must have emanated from deep wellsprings within the psyches of those who destroyed and those who applauded them. While there is probably an element of sadism in most destruction of this nature, perhaps much of the violence can be best explained by André

tried to burn the church in Casas Viejas in 1932 but that they were prevented from doing so by the anarchist villagers.

28. José María García Escudero, *Historia política de las dos Españas* (Madrid, 1975), III, 1441–44.

29. Spanish literature is replete with examples, many of which are examined in John Devlin, *Spanish Anticlericalism* (New York, 1966). Díaz Mozaz, p. 33, claims that seminary training tended to separate the clergy from the reality of the world and thereby produced priests estranged from society.

30. Many observers claim this to be true; one of the most reliable is Raguer, *La espada*, p. 151, who notes this to have been the case especially in Barcelona.

Gide's remark that the Spanish anticlericals were like chicks who had to break through their shells in order to be free.[31]

Beyond breaking through the shell of tradition, however, there seems to have been a deeper, more hidden motive: fear and the desire to purge fear. How else can some of the events and acts be explained? Observe what happened in Barcelona. Shortly after the uprising and the iconoclastic fury of church burnings, the cloistered conventos were invaded. In most cases the nuns were "set free,"[32] but the true objective of the mob was to penetrate the cloisters in order to discover their secrets. These included various penetential devices: scourges, hairshirts, sharply studded belts. These instruments of self-inflicted penance—understandable to a more pious folk—were called sexual devices by the anticlerical press and were put on display; in some cases they were labeled as instruments of torture, with the implication that the nuns captured young women and children and tortured them.[33] Worse, the mob desecrated the nuns' tombs. They disinterred the long-dead bodies (usually shelved in wall niches or in catacombs beneath convento chapels) and carried the decomposing remains to the front of the churches and chapels and put them on public display. For days lines of people formed to view the corpses of generations of nuns.[34] It was pointed out in the press that small bodies were found as well, and these were branded as the nuns' illegitimate children, proof of the scandalous immorality that went on behind convent walls, although some observers noted that the corpses appeared to be those of small adults, certainly too well developed to be infants.[35]

The correspondent for the London *Daily Telegraph* in Barcelona described one such scene:

> Lower down, just above the British consulate, a crowd had formed outside the entrance to a convent. I went in with them and found a long wall lined with coffins from which the lids had

---

31. *The Journals of André Gide*, trans. J. O'Brien (New York, 1949), III, 160. Colin Campbell, "Analyzing the Rejection of Religion," *Social Compass* 24 (1977), pp. 339–46, argues that because Catholicism demands total allegiance and jurisdiction, rejection of Catholicism is likewise total and involves rejection of liturgy, clergy, and even the symbols along with the rejection of dogma.

32. This element of the fury hearkens back to the *semana trágica* of 1909 when the agitator Alejandro Lerroux urged his anticlerical followers to liberate nuns and "elevate them to motherhood." See Joan Connelly Ullman, *The Tragic Week: A Study of Anticlericalism in Spain, 1875–1912* (Cambridge, Mass., 1968), p. 88.

33. Montero Moreno, pp. 64, 431–32.

34. Some 40,000 people viewed the corpses outside the Church of the Enseñanza during the three days of July 23–25, 1936. See Pérez de Olaguer, p. 21.

35. Arrarás, V, 318ff.

been stripped. The poor, century-old bodies of the nuns were exposed and what flesh still clung to the bones was slowly blackening in the hot sun. Fresh coffins were being excavated from the convent burial ground and a peseta was being charged for the hire of a long stick with which to strike or insult with unnameable obscenities these sightless, shrunken relics. A charnel-house stench and my own sick horror drove me back into the street.[36]

Nor was this all. People stuck cigarettes in the corpses' mouths and mocked the mummies. Some even performed impromptu dances with the withered corpses. A similar occurrence was noted in a church in Illescas (near Toledo), where bodies had been taken from church crypts and cigarettes placed in the mouths of the better-preserved ones.[37] In the church of San Antonio de Florida in Madrid the mob played soccer with the patron saint's skull.[38]

It can be argued that these macabre profanations were a by-product of the invasion of the cloisters, a desire to expose the secrets of the convent to the modern world.[39] Perhaps it was the desire to be rid of the fear of nuns, the fear of the clergy, of the psychological fear of death. The obsession with mortality and death scenes and with relics and preserved bodies that was so much a part of the Catholic cultural ethic had to be purged if the fear was to be gotten rid of.[40] Despite the presence of nuns in classrooms and hospitals, nuns' ways were not familiar ones and certainly appeared unnatural to many, and the cloister was a place of seclusion. There was a general gloominess about convents, and they were places of mortification and secrecy. What better way to purge the fear than by exposing the corpses to the light of day and then by sticking cigarettes—the ultimate symbol of modern secularism—in the corpses' mouths? But while the anticlericals appear jaunty in the photographs taken of these scenes, the faces

36. Cedric Salter, Try-Out in Spain (New York, 1943), p. 20.
37. As noted by José Llordés Badia, Al dejar el fusil (Barcelona, 1968), pp. 91–92.
38. Jato, p. 95.
39. One-third of all the cloistered nuns in the Catholic world in 1936 lived in Spain. See Federico Bravo Morata, Historia de Madrid (Madrid, 1968), III, 30.
40. See the views of José Jiménez Lozano in Gironella, Cien españoles, p. 294, who says that the profanation of tombs was an attempt to show that the clergy died and their bodies corrupted, as everyone else's did, and resulted from a necrophilia that had to do with the clergy as harbingers of death because of their presence at deathbeds and funerals. Bruce Lincoln, "Revolutionary Exhumations in Spain, July, 1936," Comparative Studies in Society and History 27 (April 1985), pp. 214–260, agrees, arguing that the corruption of the bodies was viewed as a revelation that the Church was an inwardly corrupt institution.

of common people looking at the corpses appear haunted and betray a fear that suggests such things are better kept out of sight and out of mind.[41]

If profanation of tombs reveals a desire to be free of some particular conceptions of Spanish Catholicism, other anticlerical actions had the same aim. Aside from the incendiary anticlericalism (which will be treated in the next chapter) there was the iconoclastic destructions of statues such as that of the Sacred Heart (as related in chapter 1). Religious objects were sought out and destroyed. Searches were conducted in private homes for religious medals, scapulars, holy pictures, statues, rosaries, and other objects.[42] Spaniards were ordered to bring their religious objects to central depots for burning. Confessionals were especially sought out from ruined or transformed churches and were put to use as stalls, newspaper kiosks, bus-waiting stands. Churches themselves, either after being burned out or otherwise gutted, were turned into barracks, warehouses, museums, marketplaces, even butcher shops. The mass was parodied and profaned; burlesques of religious ceremonies were performed in some of the churches.[43]

Finally, some mention should be made of the violent deaths by means other than shooting. The pages of works published during the war describe priests hunted down and tortured with refinements better left to the imagination. It has even been claimed that some priests were crucified: *The New York Times* correspondent Joseph Lee Mason reported, in accompanying the Nationalist army through the town of El Saucejo in Seville province, "as we passed the parish church we saw the body of the priest, Father José de la Cora, crucified, head down on the main door. The body was clad in ceremonial vestments."[44] While this crucifixion was later disputed,[45] there is no question that there were instances of extreme cruelty. The *Daily Telegraph* correspondent described a scene he saw in Barcelona on July 19, 1936:

---

41. See the photographs in Arrarás, V, 319.

42. Juan Gomis, *Testigos de poca edad (1936–1943)* (Barcelona, 1968), p. 29, the child of a Catalan banker, recalled such a search of his home by "gangs of uncontrollables."

43. Montero Moreno, pp. 639ff. See the photos of these in Bernardo Gil Mugarza, *España en llamas, 1936* (Barcelona, 1960), pp. 378–79.

44. *The New York Times*, September 14, 1936, p. 34.

45. Montero Moreno, p. 63, confesses that he could find no proof of any crucifixions. Nor does the official martyrology of the Seville archdiocese list Cora among the martyred; and its description of the death of Salvador Lobato Pérez, pastor of the church of El Saucejo, is quite different. See José Sebastián y Bandarán and Antonio Tineo Lara, *La persecución religiosa en la Archidiócesis de Sevilla* (Sevilla, 1938), pp. 114–20.

On my way down I passed a burning church. The flames had only caught at one end of the building and I pushed my way into the entrance. Flames were licking up round the altar, on which still stood two beautiful wrought silver candlesticks gleaming through the clouds of black smoke. From the high carved stone pulpit an elderly priest swung very slowly to and fro by his sickeningly elongated neck. He had offered resistance, a guardia told me, when they had seized the Sacred Wafer and hurled it into the flames, and had died cursing them. Around the walls the pale painted faces of the Saints slowly distorted into nightmare grimaces as the heat melted the wax of which they were made.[46]

Andrés Nin, Trotskyist leader and councillor of justice in the Catalan government, succinctly summed up the proletarian view of the religious problem. During a press interview two weeks after the war began he stated: "The working class has solved the problem of the Church very simply; it has not left a single one standing."[47]

---

46. Salter, pp. 19–20. Correspondent Edward Knoblaugh, p. 72, claims that he saw dead clergy with scapulars and rosaries jammed into their mouths. See also Cecil D. Eby, *The Siege of the Alcázar* (New York, 1965), pp. 68–71, for a description of the terror in Toledo based on Alberto Risco, *La epopeya del Alcázar de Toledo* (Toledo, 1941), who interviewed survivors right after the event.
47. Quoted in Montero Moreno, p. 55.

CHAPTER 4

Spanish Tradition and the Fury

Political anticlericalism was a phenomenon of nineteenth-century Latin Europe and Latin America, and as such it became a tradition in many countries. Violent—social—anticlericalism was less of a tradition outside of Spain, although outbreaks occurred in France during the Revolution of 1789 and the Paris Commune of 1870 and occasionally in other countries.[1] In Spain violent anticlericalism was the rule rather than the exception.

In Spain there was an intensity to the violence that is difficult to find elsewhere, and there was a variant that was generally unknown in other countries: incendiary anticlericalism, the firing and burning of churches. So much did this incendiarism become a part of Spain's modern history that events and motivations were transcended by tradition. Churches were burned and profaned and priests were killed not only because they were the actual political and social enemies but also because church-burning and priest-killing were part of Spanish tradition, and anticlerical violence had been a part of every liberal/leftist uprising and revolt since the beginning of the nineteenth century.

Or so it was perceived, especially by foreigners. There were, in fact, a number of revolts, uprisings, coups, both successful and not, in which no anticlerical violence was present. But others were so violently anticlerical that they came to constitute a tradition, particularly to the popular mind.

Before the advent of the Second Republic in 1931 there were four periods in which large-scale attacks were made upon the clergy and religious buildings. In 1822 and 1823 during the revolutionary upheaval that began with the abortive revolution of 1820 some 88 clerics were killed, including the bishop of Vich. In 1834 and 1835, shortly after

---

1. See my *Anticlericalism: A Brief History* (Notre Dame, 1972), pp. 79–86, for the distinction between moderate political and violent social anticlericalism.

the First Carlist War began, about a hundred clerics, mainly regulars, were killed in Madrid, Barcelona, Saragossa, and Murcia. During that upheaval churches and conventos were put to the torch for the first time. In 1868, and again in 1873, during the revolutionary chaos that accompanied the overthrow of Isabella II and the establishment of the First Republic, churches were again burned and probably some half-dozen clerics were killed. Finally, in the upheaval of 1909 in Barcelona known as the *semana trágica*, three clerics were killed (one accidentally), while some 50 churches and conventos were set ablaze.[2]

There were sporadic incidents of anticlerical violence not connected with these events; the most serious occurred in July 1923 when, during the upheavals that preceded Primo de Rivera's coup, Cardinal Juan Soldevila Romero, archbishop of Saragossa, was assassinated by anarchists.[3]

In 1931 the anticlerical attacks increased in number and intensity. The proclamation of the Second Republic, the political movements for anticlerical reform, and apparently anarchist attempts to provoke a monarchist reaction led to the burning of over 100 churches and conventos during the incendiary riots of May 11–13, mainly in Madrid and Andalusia. No clerics were killed. There was sporadic incendiarism thereafter. When the electoral results of 1933 were announced, there was more incendiarism, but the new conservative governments increased security measures, and except for the 1934 uprising in the Asturias, no churches were burned until February 1936. In the 1934 uprising, however, 37 clerics were killed.[4] In addition, some 58 religious buildings were set on fire. And more churches were burned after the February 1936 elections; sporadic incendiarism continued until the outbreak of war in July 1936.

If all of these deaths and arsons are added together, the total from 1822 to July 1936 is some 235 clerics killed and probably somewhat

2. See Julio Caro Baroja, *Introducción a una historia contemporánea de anticlericalismo español* (Madrid, 1980), pp. 151ff.; Allison Peers, *Spain, the Church and the Orders* (London, 1945), pp. 65–91; Montero Moreno, pp. 1–4; Payne, *Spanish Catholicism*, pp. 82ff.; and Callahan, *Church, Politics, and Society*, pp. 127, 153–57, 250, for the first three incidents. Ullman, *Tragic Week* (especially the revised Spanish edition, *La semana trágica*, trans. G. Pontón [Barcelona, 1972]); Joaquín Romero Maura, *La Rosa de Fuego* (Barcelona, 1975), pp. 518–35; and Jordi Estivill and Gustau Barbat, "Anticlericalisme populaire en Catalogne au début du siècle," *Social Compass* 27 (1980), pp. 215–30, all have thought-provoking analyses of the *semana trágica*.

3. Paz, p. 58, and Robert W. Korn, *Red Years/Black Years* (Philadelphia, 1978), pp. 60ff.

4. Montero Moreno, p. 44. These deaths, moreover, are included in the 6,832 deaths he calculates for the 1936–39 period.

less than 500 churches burned. The frequency and intensity of these acts, especially as they increased in tempo after 1931, were certainly sufficient to constitute a tradition.

Incendiary anticlericalism was not only a tradition in Spain: it became unique. Occasional incidents of church arson elsewhere should not obscure the fact that nowhere else in the world were churches burned with the degree of regularity and intensity as they were in Spain during revolutionary outbursts.[5] Tradition fed on tradition, and church burning became an expected reaction. People expected churches to be burned, and therefore such episodes became less frightening and more comfortable, and ordinary people who would not have committed violence or arson in other circumstances participated in the destructive acts. Usually authorities did not take action to arrest arsonists. Indeed, in the days following the 1936 uprising participation in anticlerical violence became a way of protecting oneself against charges of counterrevolutionary sympathy. Thus, there were neither civil nor social restraints upon the arsonists. Given these circumstances, it is not surprising that churches were burned; it would have been surprising if they had not.

Fire is, of course, part of the revolutionary ritual everywhere, but only in Spain were churches burned. In other countries the revolutionary mob attacked government buildings, houses of the wealthy, banks — structures they considered the institutions of oppression. In Spain the Church was an oppressive institution. In the early nineteenth century it was the most powerful institution in the peninsula, and after its political power was diminished by the confiscation of clerical lands in the middle third of the century, the churches were attacked because the clergy still retained social and educational power and because it became traditional to do so. Iconoclasm was also an element. The baroque and roccoco Spanish churches with all of their decorative art, ornate woodwork, and the large amount of combustibles — pews, confessionals, altar decorations, wooden statues, cloth hangings and tapestries, and paintings — simply presented an irresistible target to iconoclasts and arsonists.[6]

Provocative parallels could be drawn comparing the Spanish incendiaries with Puritan iconoclasts of the Protestant Reformation of

---

5. There was some incendiarism in France in 1830, in Colombia during the *bogotazo* of 1948, and very occasionally in Italy at the turn of the century.

6. See especially the symbolic meaning attached to statues as described in Christian, p. 100, and in Elias Canetti, *Crowds and Power*, trans. C. Stewart (New York, 1962), pp. 19, 50, 77, 154–58.

the sixteenth century. Then churches in England and Holland were stripped of their decorations, stained glass windows were smashed, statues were destroyed, and walls whitewashed. There may have been similar motives on the part of some of the Spanish incendiaries, but on the whole this does not seem to have been the case. Perhaps on a deeper, even subconscious level, there was an urge to purify by fire. Sufficient example exists in Christian scripture and teaching of the metaphor of fire as a destructive-creative symbol (and this passion can be found in the Bakuninist-anarchist tradition as well) to have provided some degree of motivation.[7] Perhaps it is possible to accept this motive after all of the uncontrollable criminal elements and social suasions are put aside. But to do so would argue a deeply radical Christian feeling on the part of the arsonists. Were they in fact motivated by true Christian anger against the scandal of priests violating the primary principle of Christianity—namely, charity to the oppressed? The Catalan poet Joan Maragall wrote a moving piece after seeing the burned-out chapels of Barcelona in 1909. He envisioned a priest calling from the altar to those who had stormed his church:

> Come in, come in! The door is open; you yourselves have opened it with the fire of hatred; but within you will find the Mystery of Love. . . . In destroying the church you have restored the Church which was founded for you, the poor, the oppressed and the desperate. . . . And we, your ministers, have by your persecution been returned to our former dignity, and your blasphemy has enabled us to speak the Word again, and the Mystery of Blood has been re-invigorated with the new blood which has been shed in the struggle. How strange! The fire has constructed, the blasphemy has purified, and the hatred of Christ has restored Christ to his house.[8]

But this argument raises more questions than it answers, for it must then be asked where the arsonists learned their Christian teaching from, if not from the clergy?

Gerald Brenan, in his classic study of modern Spain, viewed the incendiaries as primitive Christians driven by millennialist visions and suggested that the "anger of the Spanish Anarchists against the

---

7. On the revolutionary metaphor of fire see Melvin J. Lasky, *Utopia and Revolution* (Chicago, 1976), pp. 472–93.

8. Joan Maragall, "La iglesia cremada," *Obres Completes d'en Joan Maragall* (serie Catalana): *Escrits en prosa* (Barcelona, 1912), I, 221–30. Lincoln, p. 256, argues that one reason that iconoclasts destroy the icon is not because they believe in its sacred power but because they want to demonstrate the powerlessness of the icon.

Church is the anger of an intensely religious people who feel they have been deserted and deceived." He further argues that the clergy before the nineteenth century were "the defenders of personal and local liberty against both the encroachments of the State and the arrogance of the upper classes."[9] But there is some reason to believe that it was not the clergy who changed but rather the people, through the forces of industrialization and modernization. How else can one explain the fact that the masses in the early nineteenth century wanted to restore the Inquisition, yet a century later were burning churches?[10] The rationalization of modern life as a result of industrialization and urbanization meant, of necessity, that traditional religion would become less important in the lives of the urban masses. But the need for transcendence was still there. If traditional Catholicism could no longer address working-class needs because it counseled humble acceptance of economic oppression, then it had to be rejected in favor of the secular ideologies of anarchism and socialism; or else traditional Catholicism had to be purified, purged of its unworthy elements.

Did the masses attack the clergy and their symbols because of the threat to their working-class ideologies, or did they burn and kill to purify Christianity of this clerical perversion? Unamuno perceptively noted that the incendiaries destroyed the objects of consolation when they could no longer find consolation.[11] Two contemporary Catholic observers felt the arson and violence justified. Maurici Serrahima, a Catalan lawyer and active Catholic layman and political activist said:

> I always maintained that, deep down, these burnings were an act of faith. That's to say an act of protest because the church was not, in the people's eyes, what it should be. The disappointment of someone who believes and loves and is betrayed. It springs from the idea that the church should be on the side of the poor — and isn't; as indeed it hadn't been for a great number of years,

9. Gerald Brenan, *The Spanish Labyrinth: An Account of the Social and Political Background of the Spanish Civil War* (2nd ed., Cambridge, 1950), pp. 191, 41. The argument is succinctly stated by Carlos Cardó as cited in González-Anleo, p. 439. See also Charles C. Noel, "Missionary Preachers in Spain: Teaching Social Virtue in the Eighteenth Century," *The American Historical Review* 90 (October 1985), pp. 866–92, for an analysis of prerevolutionary clerics' concern with social justice for the poorer classes.

10. See Owen Chadwick, *The Popes and European Revolution* (Oxford, 1981), p. 542.

11. As told to Francisco Ynduráin, "Resentimiento español: Arturo Barea," *Arbor* 24 (January 1953), p. 79.

excepting certain individual churchmen. A protest against the church's submission to the propertied classes.[12]

And, Manuel de Irujo, the Basque Catholic minister of justice in the Republican government of 1937, defended the arsonists to a visiting foreigner: "The burning of churches has nothing to do with anti-religious feeling; it is a protest against the state and if you allow me to say so, a sort of appeal to God against human injustice."[13]

The belief that the Spanish anticlerical masses were deeply religious and in fact more in touch with the true meaning of Christianity than the clergy were became widespread in the years following the war. Perhaps the bizarre fascist Ernesto Giménez Caballero was responsible for popularizing this notion when he said in the early 1930s that anarchism was "the most authentic refuge for popular Catholicism in Spain."[14] It is an explanation of the fury that can satisfy both foreign anticlericals and anticlerical Catholics in Spain, for it maintains that Catholicism was still part of the Spaniard's makeup, indeed that the Spanish masses were so fiercely and truly Catholic that they would not allow their faith to be corrupted by clericalism.[15]

The incendiarism has also been seen as a step forward in human progress. A Republican writer, Eduardo Zamacois, said:

> Those buildings had lasted long enough; their mission was completed; now they were anachronisms, weighty and obstructing, casting a jailhouse stench over the city. The times condemned them to death and the people carried out the execution of justice. These burnings were the *autos da fe* necessary for the progress of civilization.[16]

Stanbury Pearse, a British businessman in Barcelona, watched the looting of a church and was invited by the looters to join them

---

12. Quoted in Fraser, p. 153. See also Serrahima's comments on his experiences in Barcelona on July 20, 1936, in his *Memories de le guerra i de l'exili 1936–1940,* vol. I: *1936–1937* (Barcelona, 1978), pp. 115–42.

13. Quoted in Prince Hubertus of Loewenstein, *A Catholic in Republican Spain* (London, 1937), p. 98.

14. Quoted in Raymond Carr, *Spain, 1808–1939* (Oxford, 1966), p. 647.

15. Gabriel Jackson, *A Concise History of the Spanish Civil War* (New York, 1974), p. 176, idealizes the masses as well; the Spanish war, he says, allowed "at an intuitive level, fulfilling a deeply religious people's conception of what Christianity should really mean." It is also a common theme running throughout the impressions of modern Spaniards as cited in Gironella, *Cien españoles;* however the religious motivation of the anarchists is disputed by Mintz, pp. 3–7, and is the topic of current debate among historians.

16. Quoted in Jato, p. 134.

"in the name of the humanity of the people."[17] The British poet Sylvia Townsend Warner visited a gutted church in Barcelona and commented that the churches "have been cleaned out exactly as sick-rooms are cleaned out after a pestilence. Everything that could preserve the contagion has been destroyed."[18]

There are few contemporary accounts of the church burnings. The arsonists were not likely to write of their experiences. Ronald Fraser interviewed José Robuste, a Barcelona bookkeeper who on July 19, 1936, went with his wife to the church of Santa Madrona when they heard that rebels were firing from the top of the building:

> When we got to the church, we found men dragging out pews and trying to set fire to them. They poured petrol over them twice and each time only the petrol burned, though the wood was old and dry. A priest dressed in civilian clothes arrived. "*Muchachos,* why are you trying to set fire to these? They may come in useful to you—" I turned to my companion. "That man is right, let's have nothing to do with this," and we set off up the Ramblas . . .[19]

The best accounts come from foreign travelers caught in Spain by the outbreak of the war or by observers who went to Spain to examine conditions. Among the former was Professor Walter Cook of New York University, who described a church burning in Barcelona. The arsonists, he said, took mattresses from nearby hotels, soaked them in gasoline, and then threw them in the churches and set them on fire.[20] One of the most perceptive observers was Franz Borkenau, who visited Barcelona and the Catalan countryside during the first weeks of August 1936, some two weeks after the uprising. A sociologist and former Comintern bureaucrat, Borkenau was sympathetic to the Republic.

He arrived in Barcelona on August 5, 1936, and noted that all the churches save the cathedral had been burned and that some were still smoking. Later that day he witnessed the burning of a church:

> On my way home I saw the burning of a church, and again it was a big surprise. I imagined it would be an act of almost

---

17. *The Tablet,* August 15, 1936, p. 203.

18. Quoted in Valentine Cunningham, ed., *The Penguin Book of Spanish Civil War Verse* (Harmondsworth, 1980), p. 140.

19. Quoted in Fraser, pp. 66–67. There is an account of a church burning in Madrid in Arturo Barea's autobiography, *The Forging of a Rebel,* trans. Ilsa Barea (New York, 1946), pp. 512–16.

20. *The New York Times,* August 9, 1936, p. 3.

demoniac excitement of the mob, and it proved to be an administrative business. The burning church stood in a corner of the big Plaza de Cataluña. Flames were devouring it rapidly. A small group of people stood about (it was about 11 p.m.) silently watching, certainly not regretting the burning, but as certainly not very excited about the matter. The fire-brigade did service at the spot, carefully limiting the flames to the church and protecting the surrounding buildings; nobody was allowed to come near the burning church—in order to avoid accidents—and to this regulation people submitted with surprising docility. Earlier church burnings must have been more passionate, I suppose.[21]

On August 11 Borkenau left Barcelona for the Catalan countryside. As he passed through small villages he noted that all the churches had been burned, "mostly by order of the CNT or the passing militia columns."[22] On August 20 he was at Sitges, where he witnessed another aspect of the anticlerical fury:

One afternoon there was a burning of religious objects on the beach, which again was a sad performance. The committee had ordered everybody to deliver objects of worship, such as images, statues, prayerbooks, talismans, to be burned in public. There the women went, carrying their petty objects of devotion, most of them with obvious reluctance, many a one taking a last adieu, with the sad look at what had been, perhaps, an object less of religious value than of family pride, a part of the familiar daily life. There was not the slightest sign that anybody was enjoying the proceeding, with the exception of the children. They looked upon it all as first-rate fun, cutting the noses of the statues before throwing them into the bonfire, and committing all sorts of mischief. It was disgusting, and obviously very unpolitic. Such an act would be likely to awake rather than to destroy the allegiance of people to their Catholic faith.[23]

Peadar O'Donnell, an Irishman with strong working-class and Republican sympathies, was in Sitges a few weeks earlier than Borkenau, when the uprising began. He described the sacking of the village church:

The promenade was noticeably empty, and there was not the same orchestration of sirens on the street. Many people were

---

21. Borkenau, *Spanish Cockpit*, p. 74.
22. Ibid., p. 94.
23. Ibid., pp. 112–13.

standing still gazing fixedly towards the chapel. But nothing was happening there that I could see. And then suddenly the great massing of people on the strand and on the promenade in front of the fishermen's cafe came into view between the trees. We reached the outskirts of the crowd and inquired eagerly. But there was no need for reply, for just then men came out of the church door dragging church furniture after them. The sacking of the church had begun. Not a word from the crowd. Not a murmur. Not a movement. There was an air of unreality about it all. Daylight. The silence. The fishing boats. A crowd of normal workaday people. . . . I made my way easily through the silent crowd and crossed a strip of strand in front of one of the boats. On an upturned box a middle-aged fisherman sat mending a net, pausing now and then to take in the scene before him. Priests' vestments came flying through the air. The monstrance crashed on a flagstone. I was sorry now that any word had been said against burning, for burning would have been better than this. Certainly not more than twenty people were at work—all men; and two of them were of the foreign band I had encountered the evening before. Statues came flying through the air, and little bursts of laughter broke out on and off. St. Patrick got a cheer, for his statue landed snugly into some shavings in a box. The confessional-boxes were flung bodily on to the strand. And still nobody stirred.

A few children ventured near the debris. A boy of ten picked up a vestment. It was a signal—the children of the village swept on to the strand and dressed themselves in any bit of vestment they could see. One raised the monstrance and started a procession. Gales of laughter swept the crowd. The assembled village began moving again along the strand and promenade.[24]

Although there appears to have been a certain reluctance on the part of parishioners to burn their own churches, it did happen. Jason Gurney wrote that everywhere he traveled he saw churches "destroyed or deserted with an extreme of hatred and detestation that was unmistakable and everything that I was able to find out about events led me to the conviction that very few people in any village had not actively participated in the revulsion."[25]

---

24. Peadar O'Donnell, "An Irishman in Spain," *The Nineteenth Century* (December 1936), pp. 704–5. Compare this account with the impossibly idealistic description in Ralph Bates, "Compañero Sagasta Burns a Church," *The New Republic* 88 (October 14, 1936), pp. 274–76. See also John Langdon-Davies, *Behind the Spanish Barricades* (New York, 1936), pp. 161–95, for a sympathetic view of the incendiaries.

25. Gurney, p. 60. Gurney continued about the church in Madrigueras (Murcia)

Whether or not clerics were killed because they were Spaniards is another matter. Some observers have argued that the Spanish clergy somehow earned or at least deserved what they got at the hands of anticlericals because they were radically different from clergy elsewhere, that the Spanish clergy were narrowminded, legalistic, puritanical, sex-obsessed, and above all hypocritical, preaching love and sowing hatred.[26]

It is difficult to see these differences in reality. Clergy were educated alike throughout the world (the standardization of seminary training assured that), and the anticlericals were not killing only priests. Countless laypersons died in the cause of religion, killed because they were known to be militant Catholics or else known to associate with the clergy. Some were killed for their piety and devotion. The common factor was that all were practitioners of a faith that was part of Spain's cultural ethic.[27]

As far as national differences go, what is more likely is that Spanish priests were no more oppressive and obscurantist than priests elsewhere; it was just that they were more militant about it. In no other country had the clergy as much political, social, and economic power as they did in Spain in the first half of the nineteenth century; and nowhere else did they have the degree of social and educational power up to 1936. If the violent anticlericals were killing priests because they were Spanish priests, it was not because the Spanish clergy were radically different from clergy elsewhere; only that they were more militant, more aggressive, and more powerful than their clerical counterparts elsewhere. Instances where non-Spanish clergy were arrested and then released, as was the case of two Argentine novices in Bar-

---

which had been burned out and then converted into a mess hall for the Brigadiers: "I never saw any village people enter it and they seemed to avoid looking at the place, as if they had a sense of guilt about it. I never discovered what actually happened there but it left me with an uneasy feeling that something had occurred which everybody preferred to forget."

26. Borkenau, p. 82, came across an American resident of Barcelona who told him that the Spanish clergy were not like the French, whom he characterized as cultured, devout, sincere, and decent.

27. Unfortunately, the killing of laypersons for their faith is a largely unexamined issue. Montero Moreno, p. 542, says that earlier claims that most of the civilians killed in the terror died for their religious beliefs simply cannot be substantiated. He cites the *Informe diocesano de Albacete* on the examination of 52 laypersons killed in Almansa: "The circumstances of the death of each person involved different factors of partisan politics, social class, class hatred, and even personal animosity. Although all who died were believers in the Faith, the motive of the assassins was not strictly antireligious."

bastro and an Argentine nursing brother at Calafell (Catalonia), may possibly be attributed to fear of creating an international incident (which would assume some degree of sophistication among the assassins); however, in August 1936 seven Colombian nationals, nursing brothers at Ciempozuelos, were killed despite protests from the Colombian consul in Barcelona.[28]

There is another factor in the clerical killings that deserves some mention: the sparing of certain clergy. Who these were depended on circumstances, and there is no clear-cut pattern that emerges. For example, although thirteen bishops were killed, the bishop of Badajoz was allowed to live, first in his episcopal residence and then at his vicar-general's home until the town was captured by the Nationalists in mid-August 1936. The bishop of Menorca was allowed to go to a hospital (he was over 90 and blind), where he stayed unmolested until he died in January 1939. Some clergy were spared because they had led blameless lives; others because of their immorality. Borkenau mentions the villagers at Tosas (Catalonia) who hid and kept from danger a priest who was lax and who had taken liberties with village girls, while they pursued a fanatical and strict priest until he fell and broke his neck.[29] It is tempting to generalize from this incident and argue that Spaniards wanted a less fanatical and more naturalistic clergy, but it is difficult to do so. Priests of all types were killed: strict, loose, moral, immoral, libertines, and ascetics. Hilari Raguer, one of the most reliable observers, says that no distinction was made: the charitable suffered along with the mean-spirited, and that, in fact, some priests who were social activists and had actively opposed the uprising were also killed.[30]

It should be noted that among all the terrible instances of torture and cruelty no nuns were sexually violated during the entire period by any anticlerical. Montero Moreno (who would be naturally sympathetic to recounting such stories if they existed) contradicts statements made during the first months of the war that naked nuns were forced to dance in public and that there were wholesale rapes by Republican militiamen.[31] In his exhaustive examination he says

28. And the Republican government later paid an indemnity to the families of these Colombian clerics. Montero Moreno, pp. 211, 226, 227, and Carreras, p. 94.

29. Borkenau, p. 113.

30. Hilari Raguer, *La espada*, p. 151.

31. A story published in *The Daily Mail* (London), August 15, 1936, p. 12, cites Réné Lignac, special correspondent for *Le Jour* (Paris), who says an Assumptionist nun from a convent "between Harabel and Barcelona" told him that 30 nuns were forced to undress and walk single file out of the convent, where they were then shown the

that Spaniards have an inherent respect for women, and especially for virgins consecrated to God, and that when nuns were arrested and sexually threatened "and there appeared no cause for hope, among the members of the committees or soldiers there would appear a spontaneous defender who would protect the nuns."[32]

If tradition defended nuns' honors in Spain, still it was not tradition that nuns should die, and the 283 nuns assassinated marked the first time in the nation's anticlerical history that nuns were actually killed by anticlericals. This fact reveals the extent of the fury: nuns were spared sexual assault but were killed anyway. Tradition nurtures expectation, and anticlericalism was a tradition in Spain. "Martyrdom," one observer said, "is simply a professional risk for a Spanish priest."[33]

Hundreds of cases of clergy and laymen have been presented to Rome for canonization. Only a few have formally been accepted. Pius XI stated in 1936, at the height of the fury, that the assassinated clergy were "true martyrs in all of the sacred and glorious meaning of the word"; and both Pius XII in April 1939 and John XXIII in January 1959 referred to the dead clergy as martyrs.[34] But none has yet been so individually named or determined to be numbered among the martyrs of the Roman Catholic Church.[35]

In his final comment on the anticlerical fury Montero Moreno says that we must temper our revulsion and resentment against the killers with the knowledge that the deaths of the martyr-priests compensate for "all of the evils of History," and is for the Church a victory of light over darkness: "The history of religious persecution in Spain . . . is a glowing page in the life of the Church."[36]

---

severed heads of priests on tea trays. See also the stories cited in Félix Restrepo, *España mártir* (Bogota, n.d.), pp. 59–60.

32. Montero Moreno, p. 433.

33. Frank Jellineck, *The Civil War in Spain* (London, 1938), p. 322. Perhaps not so curiously, given the Catholic emphasis on the glory of a martyr's death, some Spanish clerics courted martyrdom. A correspondent for the Dutch paper *Tyd* interviewed a Spanish priest after the fury who said, "There were many genuine martyrs among them. . . . There were also many who were anything but discreet in their desire for martyrdom and without meaning it of course, or being aware of it, only embittered feelings and did our cause more harm than good." Cited in *The Tablet*, February 11, 1939, p. 174.

34. In Montero Moreno, pp. 741, 744, 747.

35. It should be pointed out that only one person who has died since 1936 has been beatified and canonized: Maximilian Kolbe, who took the place of another prisoner at Auschwitz and was starved to death.

36. Montero Moreno, p. 653.

Perhaps so, but the glory and compensation were bought at a terrible price, not only from the clergy and laity but also from the common people of Spain who, both numerically and chronologically, suffered the greatest agony of all.

CHAPTER 5

The Clandestine Church

How the clergy and laity responded to the anticlerical fury and the issues raised by the war depended to a large extent upon where they were. In Nationalist Spain the clergy gathered their pastoral ammunition and responded with thunderous support for the Nationalists, claiming that the uprising was a crusade in the most religious sense of the word. In Republican Spain there were two responses: there were those Catholics who, despite the fury and its attendant bloodshed, supported the Republican government, or in the Basque provinces supported the autonomous Basque regime which was allied with the Republic; and there were those Catholics who organized the clandestine Church.

These latter included the many priests who found themselves behind Republican lines and who decided neither to find a way to escape to Nationalist Spain nor to simply lie low until the war was over. Some were hidden by friends and relatives, some put on secular garb and melded into the general populace, but most were determined to exercise their priestly ministries by bringing the consolation of the sacraments to the laity, who they felt needed them now more than ever.

They formed the core of the clandestine Church, the hub of a network of laypersons who aided, supported, fed, and cared for the priests who ministered to them. They heard confessions, said masses, baptized, witnessed marriages, anointed the sick and dying, and consoled and counseled the faithful. They were few in number, of necessity, and for six months—through the remainder of 1936—clergy and laity alike lived in secrecy on the edge of fear as the terror and the fury took their toll.[1]

---

1. For the best survey of the activities and problems of the clandestine Church see Montero Moreno, pp. 81–205; there is a brief account in Carreras, pp. 126–41; see also the articles by Constantino Bayle, SJ, "La cárcel de mujeres in Madrid," *Razón y*

The Republican government had opposed the terror and fury and had tried to defend the clergy by arresting priests and protecting them in its own prisons, a not always successful maneuver. But in its initial anger, and perhaps to prove its own anticlerical bona fides, and maybe even to dampen the fury, the government ordered the nationalization of that clerical property and those religious buildings "which had a direct or indirect relation to the uprising."[2] In Catalonia the Generalidad—the autonomous regional government—authorized the nationalization of all church buildings. This action followed by two days the saying of the last public mass in Republican Spain, on July 25, 1936 (excepting those in the Basque provinces or under Basque auspices) until the end of the war in 1939.[3] At first the government would not allow public masses for fear of provoking the proletarian anticlericals, nor could it guarantee the safety of the clergy, and then, once the ecclesiastical hierarchy took its stand against the Republic, the bishops themselves would not allow public masses, believing that these would be interpreted as a sign that the Republic was no longer persecuting the clergy, and this the bishops refused to acknowledge.

The clandestine Church operated in secrecy during the fury. Discovery of hidden priests or secret masses could mean arrest and imprisonment and often death, not only for the priests but for the laity as well.[4] There are numerous instances of priests arrested in private homes and killed along with the laypersons found with them. The organization of the clandestine Church was secret and hidden, so well that the normally percipient investigator Franz Borkenau, traveling in Catalonia in early 1937, commented that there were "no secret masses said, no priests going to give the blessings of religion to the faithful at the danger of their lives."[5] At the time he made this observation thousands of secret masses were being said daily by priests who continually risked their lives to do so.

Fe 113 (April 1938), pp. 435–50; "El culto a la eucarística en la España roja," Razón y Fe 115 (December 1938), pp. 378–85; "Los comuniones en la España roja," Razón y Fe 117 (May 1939), pp. 72–85. There is a good first-hand account of the fear felt by practicing Catholics in Republican Spain in Concha Espina's work, Esclavitud y libertad: diario de una prisionera (Valladolid, 1938).

  2. Montero Moreno, p. 66.

  3. Jaume Miravitlles described a sermon at a "public" mass he attended as a representative of the Generalidad in Barcelona, "a few months" after the war began; the mass was held in a basement near the Plaza de Catalunya. In Gironella, Cien españoles, p. 430.

  4. In the village of Valdealgorfa (Teruel) the municipality decreed the death penalty for those who hid priests. See Montero Moreno, p. 222.

  5. Borkenau, p. 201.

The clandestine Church functioned on three different levels: in the prisons, in the embassies, and among the general populace. Each called for different responses and tactics.

In the prisons there was little need for clandestine activity. The priests who had been arrested were, of course, known to be priests, and they could say mass and hear confessions where physically possible with some degree of impunity. The prison authorities tolerated such activity because it was not illegal, it offered the consolations of religion to the other prisoners, and this made for a less volatile prison population. Almost every prison had its resident priest-inmate (often each cell block had a priest) who ministered to the other prisoners, heard confessions, said mass when wine could be smuggled in, and in rare instances anointed those about to be executed when sacred oils could be found. In many instances the priests were well known to the other prisoners from prewar times, and some of the teaching clergy often found themselves sharing cells with former pupils.[6]

Women prisoners, frequently nuns, were not as fortunate as the men, because prisoners were separated by sex and the women were thus unable to hear mass or receive the sacraments. A common practice in these women's prisons was the recitation of a dry mass (misa seca), a mass without a priest and without a consecration. Sometimes when men and women prisoners were penned close together, as on the prison ships moored off the coast of Republican Spain, priest prisoners were able to hear women's confessions through the holes in connecting walls.[7]

At the second level in which the clandestine Church operated— the embassies—religious life was both more and less constrained. Thousands of Spaniards had sought refuge from the terror in the foreign embassies in Madrid and in consulates elsewhere. Pressed by space needs, some of the embassies rented apartments and placed them under the protection of their diplomatic immunity. This enabled the diplomats to give some 15,000 persons refuge during the course of the war. Among them were some priests and a large number of laity, although religious refugees were in the minority. Generally life in the

---

6. For a general survey of life in the prisons see Montero Moreno, pp. 145–97; see Vicuña, pp. 95ff. for a description of life in the cárcel modelo in Madrid; see also the personal recollections of Manuel Casanova, Se prorroga el estado de alarma (memorias de un prisionero) (Toledo, 1941), pp. 177–83; for life in another prison see Leopoldo Huidobro Pardo, Memorias de un finlandés (Madrid, 1939), pp. 147–77; and Javier Martín Artajo, No me cuente Ud su casa (Madrid, 1955), trans. by D. Crabb as The Embattled (Westminster, MD, 1956).

7. Montero Moreno, p. 196.

embassies was protected, although there were some instances of militiamen entering diplomatically immune buildings and arresting refugees.[8] The religious life of the refugees depended upon the personal and political sympathies of the particular embassy staff. Those sympathetic to the Nationalist cause were more likely to allow free religious practices. Others did not wish to offend the Republicans, and some were motivated by the anticlerical attitudes of their own native country (Mexico was officially more anticlerical than most other nations). In some embassies clandestine priests from the outside visited daily to say mass and hear confessions, and sometimes to preside at marriages and to baptize.[9]

Conditions of imprisonment or refuge dictated the structure and ministry of the clandestine Church in the prisons and embassies. Outside, among the general populace, different circumstances prevailed. Priests were not always available. Clergy were unprotected and constantly feared detection and arrest. These circumstances dictated the need for some form of organization.

The regular ecclesiastical organization could no longer function. Most of the bishops had fled Republican Spain, or else were in prison or had been killed. In most cases the vicars-general became the leaders and chief organizers of the clandestine Church in their dioceses. Where the vicar-general had also been killed, a new one was named. These men supervised, as best they could, the regulation of religious life; but, of course, it was difficult to establish any sort of regularity, and the structures they devised were largely makeshift. Some wrote pastoral letters and instructions regarding the dispensation of the sacraments.

The regulation of the dispensation of the sacraments raised questions of a legalistic nature that had to be settled. Canon law made no provision for the necessities of wartime. Ordinarily a priest has to obtain permission from the bishop of the diocese to exercise his faculties (dispense the sacraments) within that diocese. Could a priest escaping from his home diocese hear confessions while traveling through another diocese? Regulations regarding consecrated commu-

---

8. Montero Moreno, p. 198.

9. While most refugees were receptive to the clergy, Fraser, p. 300, recounts the experiences of one refugee priest—an exemplary holy man—who was disliked by conservative anticlerical refugees in the Paraguayan embassy and usually said mass in private, attended only by those few who accepted him. See also the description of refugee life in the Chilean embassy by the ambassador, Aurelio Núñez Morgado, *Los sucesos de España vistos por un diplomático* (Buenos Aires, 1941), and the general description in Montero Moreno, pp. 197–205.

nion wafers raised other questions: Could a layperson consume large numbers of these, even without fasting, to prevent profanation? Could mass be said with unconsecrated vessels and without altar stones? The answers to these questions were not given immediately—indeed, the bishops and the Vatican were not even aware of these problems immediately—but over the course of 1936 and 1937 various episcopal and pontifical statements authorized the widest possible latitude on these questions, recognizing that the conditions of wartime and persecution required the suspension of normal formalities.[10]

Even while these questions were being raised, the clandestine Church was being organized. A network of houses and apartments was established where priests could seek refuge or be sent on to another place, and where they could dispense the sacraments. Consecrated communion wafers were distributed to households so that altars could be set up for worship. There were 3,000 of these in Barcelona alone in 1937. Nuns, expelled from their conventos, rented apartments and lived a communal life while wearing secular garb. Some continued to manufacture communion wafers, which were then distributed by children to homes where priests hid. Priests heard confessions while dressed in secular clothes and walking along the streets with penitents, appearing to outsiders as if they were conversing. In Barcelona a confessional was established in a grocery shop. Some priests were disguised as physicians and, with the connivance of medical staffs, visited the sick and dying in hospitals, dispensing the last sacraments. Some Jesuits in Barcelona established a bicycle brigade, traveling outside the city to bring the sacraments to rural areas. Marriages were celebrated, children were baptized, even secret registries of these events were kept. Catholics were given permission to marry without a priest in attendance by the cardinal-primate in a concession broadcast into Republican Spain.[11] So extensive was this religious life that some private homes were churches in everything but name.[12]

This vast enterprise required more than good will and desire. Money was necessary, and this was collected and dispensed through an organization called *Socorro Blanco* (White Relief). A clearing house was set up in Barcelona as a transit point so that priests traveling

10. Montero Moreno, pp. 99–103, and *Espasa Calpe Encyclopedia*, p. 1567.

11. Anastasio Granados, *El Cardenal Gomá, Primado de España* (Madrid, 1971), p. 211.

12. Rafael Abella, *La vida cotidiana durante la guerra civil: la España republicana* (Barcelona, 1975), p. 269.

through could get instructions and be sent to where they were needed most. There was even a priest who carried out a ministry within the ranks of the Republican army: Jerónimo Fábregas Cami served in the army and dispensed the sacraments when he could with the knowledge of a lenient commander.[13]

Cardinal Francesc Vidal i Barraquer of Tarragona (Catalonia), who escaped into exile in Italy, begged funds from foreign bishops to aid clandestine priests in his archdiocese, especially for those who had fled rural parishes to the relative anonymity of Barcelona. He collected funds from the Holy See as well, and an organization was established in Barcelona to distribute the funds. Vidal tried to get French priests who spoke Catalan and who would be acceptable to the Republic to be exchanged for Catalan priests in prison, but there was little Vatican interest in the plan and it fell through.[14]

There exists a first-hand description of the workings of the clandestine Church in the memoirs of one of its functionaries, Florindo de Miguel.[15] A more mature person by most priestly standards, Miguel had studied law before entering the seminary, where he was ordained at age 39 in June 1936. He was assigned to the small village of Sevilleja in Extremadura in the archdiocese of Toledo and had just settled in when the war began. The townspeople were not anticlerical, but militiamen passing through the village on the way to the front asked them why their priest had not yet been killed. On July 26 the townspeople, fearful of violence and under pressure from transients, asked him to leave.

He made his way to Madrid disguised as a peasant. In towns along the way he visited local churches and consumed the sacred wafers to prevent profanation. He found that there was a spontaneous underground network of folk willing to harbor him and to provide him with contacts in other towns. In Madrid he found the same network and stayed with various families and individuals, but he found this risky, as searches of homes were frequently made, and on at least two occasions those who had harbored him were taken to prison and probably killed. The safest place he found was in the apartment of a *portero* who could warn him of impending searches. He spent his days in the National Library disguised as a scholar.

Miguel faced the problem of canon law when he refused to hear

13. Montero Moreno, p. 89.
14. See Raguer, *La espada*, pp. 194–96, and the documents cited in Ramón Muntanyola, *Vidal i Barraquer: el cardenal de la paz* (Barcelona, 1971), pp. 357ff.
15. Florindo de Miguel, *Un cura en zona roja* (Barcelona, 1956).

the confession of one of his hosts because he had no faculties in the Madrid diocese. When his benefactor was arrested and led off to prison, Miguel decided that the formalism of canon law had to give way, and he began to devote his clandestine life to hearing confessions and offering solace. Through contacts within the network he visited homes and apartments daily and set up a schedule in certain apartments to hear confessions regularly. He also visited embassies to hear confessions and say masses, and he baptized and officiated at marriages. He described how he heard the confession of a woman who was the mother of two committee officials who had authorized the killing of priests and who could not reconcile their anticlericalism with their mother's desire to receive the sacraments.

He carried his ministry into the hospitals when he accidentally broke his leg. There he heard confessions from his hospital bed and discovered how the clandestine Church operated in the hospitals through sympathetic physicians and nurses. Then he was arrested and spent the remainder of the war in various prisons throughout Spain. In prison he said mass, heard confessions, and organized religious services.

One is struck, reading Miguel's memoirs, by how many persons were willing to help him, hide him, and provide for him. These people were not always practicing Catholics. Many were Republicans; some, staunch anticlericals who were repelled by the fury and helped the clergy. Luis Companys, the president of the Catalan Generalidad, was instrumental in securing the release of Cardinal Vidal i Barraquer from the hands of militiamen. In September 1936, when the fury was at its peak, the Communist leader *La Pasionaria* (Dolores Ibarruri) placed a community of 25 nuns under the party's protection against the anarchists and provided them with fabric to make clothes for orphans and abandoned children.[16] The Catalan minister of culture, Buenaventura Gassol, saved hundreds of priests with safe-conduct passes.[17] The president of the Republic, Manuel Azaña, recorded in his diary for September 6, 1937 (after the fury had ended) how one of his former teachers, an Augustinian from El Escorial, came to visit him; the priest said that he had been saved from death during the fury by a letter Azaña had written to him years before. Azaña then offered the priest a safe-conduct pass to wherever he wanted to go.[18]

---

16. Dolores Ibarruri, *El único camino,* trans. as *They Shall Not Pass* (New York, 1966), pp. 239–41.

17. Raguer, *La espada,* p. 172.

18. Azaña, IV, 763–66. It is a rather touching incident: the former teacher proud of his now-famous student, even if he was the head of an anticlerical Republic.

The Basques were able to secure the release of hundreds of clergy. Any cleric who could travel to Vizcaya while the Basque autonomous government was in authority was given a safe-conduct to France, and in Madrid the Basque legation was a haven for clergy and laity escaping the fury.[19]

And then there were those Catholics who supported the Republic. Clergy and laity both, most of them felt that other issues of the war were more important than the religious issue; or rather they conceived of the religious issue in broader terms than the clerical-anticlerical struggle. Many of them felt that the social issues of the war and the working-class struggles, placed in the context of the teachings of modern social Catholicism, transcended the attacks upon the clergy and clerical Catholics; and, further, that the authoritarian and fascist tendencies of the Nationalist forces were more threatening to the future of the Church than what they considered justified anarchist violence or momentary communist atheism. Among these prominent supporters of the Republic were the priests Leocadio Lobo, professor at the Madrid seminary;[20] José Manuel Gallegos Rocaful, lectoral canon of Córdoba; Maximiliano Arboleya Martínez, canon from Asturias and tireless worker among the poor;[21] the Catalan priest Josep Maria Llorens i Ventura; and Joan Vilar i Costa, an ex-Jesuit (but still a priest) who authored, edited, and organized most of the pro-Republican religious propaganda.[22] Among prominent laymen were José Bergamín, editor of the review *Cruz y Raya*; José María Semprún Gurrea; Ángel Ossorio y Gallardo, one of the organizers of the demo-Christian PSP in 1922; and the two Catalans, Pere Bosch i Gimpera and Luis Nicolau d'Olwer.[23] Two of the Republic's most famous generals, José Miaja and Vicente Rojo, were both practicing Catholics: the former kept a Jesuit in his home to teach his daughters.[24]

Significantly, most of the clergy and laity who supported the Re-

---

19. See Jesús de Galíndez, *Los vascos en el Madrid sitiado* (Buenos Aires, 1945), pp. 28ff.

20. See his polemic against Cardinal Gomá, *Primate and Priest* (London, 1937).

21. See his biography, Domingo Benavides, *El fracaso social del catolicismo español: Arboleya Martínez (1870–1951)* (Barcelona, 1973).

22. See Raguer, *La espada*, pp. 177–86, for potted biographies of most of these priests.

23. See Raguer, *La espada*, pp. 186–87, for a sympathetic view, and García Escudero, pp. 1459–60, for a critical view. Tusell Gómez, II, 265–302, claims that Catholic supporters of the Republic came from demo-Christian backgrounds or else were tied to the Basque and Catalan Catholic parties. On the latter see the authoritative study of Hilari Raguer i Suñer, *La Unió Democràtica de Catalunya i el seu temps (1931–1939)* (Montserrat, 1976), esp. pp. 293–338.

24. Cárcel Ortí, V, 366.

public were Catalans and were protected by the Generalidad, or else they did not make their views known until after the fury had subsided. And by the beginning of 1937 this had happened. The number of clerical assassinations dropped significantly, and the clandestine Church began to function with greater visibility. On June 30, 1937, it was announced that a public mass (but one not approved by the hierarchy) had been held in Madrid sometime during that month.[25] By August of that same year the position of Catholics and clergy in Republican Spain changed dramatically. A practicing Catholic, Manuel de Irujo, was named minister of justice in the Republican government, and he persuaded the other members of the ministry to authorize private religious services (August 7, 1937) and punishment for those who denounced priests (August 9, 1937); his influence carried over after he left the ministry later in 1937, so that in 1938 decrees ordered that conscripted priests were to be placed in noncombat positions (March 1, 1938), Republican soldiers were to be given the sacraments if they wished (June 5, 1938), and a military chaplaincy was established in the Republican army (October 23, 1938).[26]

But these decrees went largely unfulfilled because the bishops, in Nationalist Spain, refused to allow the clergy in Republican Spain to say mass publicly. Although some seminary students in Barcelona gathered freely to undertake religious studies and some Jesuit schools were quietly opened in Madrid and Barcelona, these were isolated cases.[27] The government allowed these practices and gave Irujo some degree of freedom to normalize religious practices because it needed to conciliate moderate opinion abroad so as to secure military and economic aid. By mid-1937 the bishops in Nationalist Spain had taken a strong stand against the Republic and were getting a great deal of sympathy abroad. Furthermore, the momentum in the military struggle had clearly shifted to the Nationalists. What these facts meant was that the clergy now had the upper hand in their dealings with the Republican government, and the events which followed—attempts to obtain Vatican diplomatic representation to the Republic and the desperate efforts by some Republicans to secure the reopening of churches and to get public masses said again—were doomed from the beginning. The clergy had persevered, and they had protected and served the Church in its moment of greatest peril. They did not have to compromise with their persecutors now. But the fury had struck

25. *Espasa Calpe Encyclopedia*, p. 1565.
26. Montero Moreno, pp. 120–23.
27. Ibid.

such fear into the clergy that they threw themselves completely into the arms of the Nationalists, and they did not respond to the cries of the innocent and those caught in the web of circumstance when the clergy's protectors carried out reprisals and retributions against the Republicans. In this way did the fury lead to the scandal.

CHAPTER 6

The Basque Problem

The Spanish bishops could afford to ignore the relatively few Catalan Catholics who supported the Republic, and they would write off as apostates the handful of priests in Barcelona and Madrid who lectured and wrote for and otherwise gave aid to the anticlerical enemy. What the hierarchy could not ignore were the Basques. In northern Spain, in the provinces of Guipúzcoa and Vizcaya, a large number of the priests and laity refused to join with the Nationalist cause and instead backed the Republic which supported them in their autonomist aspirations. These Basque clergy and laity were considered by everyone—and especially by the bishops themselves—to be the very best Catholics in Spain: they were socially aware, charitable, theologically knowledgeable, educated men and women with the highest rate of practicing Catholicism in all of Spain. As long as the Basques aligned themselves with the Republic, the bishops could not label the conflict a religious war nor could they appeal for foreign support for the Nationalist faction with the claim that it represented Catholic Spain.

To explain the Basque problem illustrates perfectly the historical axiom that to describe is to interpret. The facts have not been disputed: what emphasis one puts on them has been hotly debated, and the problem itself became a most important catalyst in dividing Catholic opinion on the war, both in Spain and abroad.[1]

---

1. Objective surveys of the Basque problem can be found in Stanley G. Payne, *Basque Nationalism* (Reno, 1975), pp. 157–225, and in Juan Ruíz Rico, *El papel político de la iglesia católica en la España de Franco (1936–1971)* (Madrid, 1977), pp. 28–44. Pro-autonomist accounts are in Iturralde (all three volumes) and Lizarra. Pro-Nationalist accounts are in J. Estelrich, "La cuestión vasca y la guerra civil española," *La Ciencia Tomista* 56 (1937), pp. 319–48; Centro de Información Católica Internacional, *El clero y los católicos vascos-separatistas y el movimiento nacional* (Madrid, 1940); García Escudero, pp. 1470–75; and more mildly, Montero Moreno, pp. 75–81; and Maximiano García Venero, *Historia del nacionalismo vasco* (Madrid, 1969), pp. 571–625.

70

The three Basque provinces of Guipúzcoa, Vizcaya, and Álava, along with their eastern neighbor province of Navarre, had developed differently from the other areas of Spain during the centuries-long struggles for national unification and centralization, and by 1800 they had established special economic and tributary arrangements with the Spanish Crown. Two nineteenth-century developments sharpened their sense of distinctness. One of these was the Carlist struggle which began in the 1830s and renewed again in the 1870s; this was a conflict between the two Spains—progressive, urban, and anticlerical on the one hand; traditional, clerical, and rural-pastoral on the other. The Basque-Navarre provinces were the stronghold of the latter—the Carlist cause—and when they lost to the liberal forces, their self-governing economic arrangements were taken from them, and they were absorbed into the rest of the nation. But they did not lose their clerical spirit, and both areas remained Catholic strongholds, providing the Church with missionaries, theologians, large numbers of clergy, and the peninsula's highest rate of practicing Catholics: even in 1936 the small diocese of Vitoria (which incorporated the three Basque provinces; the diocese of Pamplona incorporated Navarre) had nearly twice as many priests as the much larger dioceses of Barcelona and Madrid-Alcalá combined.[2]

The other nineteenth-century event that shaped Basque uniqueness and caused a split between the Basques and the Navarrese was the development of ethnic and cultural nationalism. This was a common phenomenon in the world in general, which emphasized a people's common ethnic, linguistic, and cultural roots and traditions. Nationalism in Spain developed much as it did in multiethnic Austria-Hungary: centrifugal and divisive rather than centripetal and unifying. It worked to develop two strong strains of minority nationalism —Catalan and Basque. Thus, the ancient Basque tongue was cultivated, literary and linguistic traditions were developed, and cultural traditions revived, while the clergy were in the forefront of Basque cultural nationalism. The issue divided the Basques and the Navarrese (who opted for Spanish nationalism), and it was symptomatic of a larger problem, namely, the inability of the Crown to solve Spain's problems. The Basques and Catalans began to urge regional autonomy as a solution to their problems. The Crown could not ignore them because Vizcaya and Guipúzcoa, along with Catalonia, had developed into the most prosperous industrial areas in the nation. The Basques

---

2. Fourteen of the nation's sixty-one dioceses were headed by Basque-born bishops. Lannon, "Modern Spain," p. 582.

and Catalans saw the Madrid government as inefficient and corrupt, and the Basques came to feel that if the government in Madrid could not solve Spain's problems, then the Basques in Bilbao could deal with their own. As national problems became more insoluble, Basque desires for autonomy grew.

Nowhere was this dissatisfaction with the rest of Spain more evident than in religious and politico-religious affairs. While the rest of Spain underwent anticlerical convulsions, as Barcelona's churches burned in 1909, as the cardinal-archbishop of Saragossa was gunned down in 1923, as the level of practicing Catholics in southern Spain dropped to less than 15 percent, as the governments made attempts to cope with the clerical problem by regulating the number of regular clergy, the Basque church thrived. It maintained and strengthened Catholic traditions and developed a strong sense of social responsibility that differed from the Catholic cultural ethic's lack of appeal to the masses. The number of practicing Catholics in the Basque provinces was nearly 100 percent in the rural areas and over 50 percent in the industrial centers.[3] A new seminary had to be built in 1930 to accommodate increasing numbers of seminarians — 800 by 1936 (in a diocese of less than a million inhabitants).[4]

Despite this strong religious life there were conflicts with church leaders elsewhere in Spain. Catholic Basques had founded a political party in the 1880s, the *Partido Nacionalista Vasco* (PNV), devoted to securing autonomy for the region. The Church hierarchy saw this as a divisive attempt that would weaken their efforts to regenerate the Church in its struggle against modern secularism, and they took steps to dampen Basque autonomist aims.[5]

This conflict, combined with the vitality of church life in the diocese of Vitoria and the anticlerical confrontations elsewhere, especially during the 1931–36 period, increased Basque autonomist de-

---

3. There had been a large influx of migrants from other parts of Spain into Guipúzcoa and Vizcaya since the turn of the century; these folk tended toward anticlericalism.

4. These statistics are from the bishop of Vitoria's report of 1936 and can be found in *Le Clerge Basque: Rapports présentés par des pretres basques aux autorites ecclésiastiques* (Paris, 1938), pp. 11–19.

5. Thus, until the 1930s there had not been a native Basque occupant of the sees of Vitoria or Pamplona for over a century. See Lannon, "Modern Spain," pp. 580–85, and Payne, *Spanish Catholicism*, pp. 111–12. On the development of the PNV see Tusell Gómez, II, 11–119, 284–88. Although the Basque autonomists called themselves Basque Nationalists, I have used the term "autonomist" to refer to them; this is done solely to avoid confusion with the word "Nationalist," which I have been using to indicate the groups supporting the uprising.

sires, particularly since the new Republican constitution provided the legislative machinery for obtaining regional autonomy. But the Navarrese would not agree to an autonomy statute, and Basque hopes were frustrated.

The Basques had wanted separate diplomatic relations with the Vatican as part of their autonomy statute. One politician called this an attempt to create a "vaticanist Gibraltar";[6] it illustrates how far removed the Basques felt from the rest of Spain on religious issues. And it was at this point that their relations with Spain's other Catholics became a vital issue. By 1933, in the face of the political anticlericalism of the Republican governments, the Church leaders tried to develop a common political front so as to win power and reverse the anticlerical trend. The PNV joined with the CEDA, but after 1933 politicians of the CEDA refused to support the Basques' autonomist aspirations, and the PNV leaders became convinced that they could do more for their region and their Church by pursuing an independent centrist role between the anticlerical left and their natural partners, the Catholic right.

If any one immediate issue poisoned relations between the Basques and the rest of Spain's Catholics, it was the unwillingness of the PNV to join the anti-Popular Front electoral coalition in the elections of February 1936. A month before the election a group of PNV delegates went to Rome to discuss political and religious matters with Cardinal Eugenio Pacelli, the papal secretary of state. Upon entering the Vatican they were lectured by Pacelli's assistant, Giuseppe Pizzardo, on the need for them to join the anti-Popular Front bloc. Allegations were made belittling the Basques' Catholicity, and the visit ended abruptly when the Basques left before they saw Pacelli.[7]

In the electoral campaign there was such intense pressure from the right to disqualify the PNV as a Catholic party that the bishop of Vitoria authorized his vicar-general to state publicly that Catholics were free to vote for PNV candidates, who, he said, were as Catholic as the other candidates.[8] The vote in the three Basque provinces split almost evenly among the right, the left, and the PNV.

After the election the PNV leaders saw neutrality between right and left as the best solution to the problem of obtaining autonomy

6. Indalecio Prieto, as cited in Payne, *Basque Nationalism*, p. 130. See also the scholarly study by Juan Pablo Fusi Aizpurúa, *El problema vasco en la II república* (Madrid, 1979), on the period from 1931 to 1936.

7. Iturralde, I, 394–97.

8. Ibid., I, 257–58. See also Manuel de Irujo, *La guerra civil en Euzkadi antes del estatuto* (Madrid, 1978), pp. 27–29, on the PNV's prewar religious policy.

for the region and for avoiding the kinds of confrontations that would lead to violence. They believed that the Popular Front government would be more amenable to arranging an autonomy statute; at the same time they heard rumors that the radical left was plotting a coup against the Republic, and in fear they began to arm themselves. It was at this point that they were surprised by the uprising of July 1936.

Thus, by the time the war broke out, sufficient controversy had already been generated over Basque issues. The war created more controversy because the Basque autonomists took their stand with the Republic. In October 1936 the Republican Cortes passed a Basque autonomy statute (which was effective only in Vizcaya, as Álava and Guipúzcoa had been taken by the Nationalists by that time), and a Basque government was formed with the PNV as the controlling party.

Five controversies in particular deserve examination: the extent of the anticlerical fury; the pastoral instruction of August 1936; the Nationalist terror against the Basques, particularly the killing of Basque priests; the exile of the bishop of Vitoria; and the positions of the Basque president and the cardinal-primate of Spain.

The Anticlerical Fury

There was no anticlerical fury in Navarre or Álava; both provinces were won for the Nationalists on the first day of the uprising. In Guipúzcoa, in the cities of San Sebastián and Irún, gangs of uncontrollables carried out a terror. Some priests were killed and churches were burned. Basque autonomists, who were actually in the minority, tried to prevent these acts of violence, but they were unsuccessful. In Vizcaya the Basque autonomists had much greater control, and they were able to prevent anticlerical violence, although some rightists were arrested in Bilbao. Within two weeks after the uprising, however, priests were able to carry out their activities and to say mass publicly.[9]

As the PNV did not take effective political control of Vizcaya until October 7, 1936, they were unable to prevent further anticlerical violence until that time. Furthermore, there were anticlericals in Bilbao who agitated continuously, even after the PNV took power. On the eve of the PNV's assumption of control there occurred two mas-

---

9. Nationalists later claimed that only priests sympathetic to the PNV were free to exercise their ministries. See Centro de Información Católica Internacional, pp. 105–17.

sacres that included clergy. Rightist prisoners from Santander and Asturias had been boarded onto two prison ships, the *Altuna Mendi* and the *Cabo Quilates* and sent into the harbor at Bilbao. On September 25 a mob attacked both ships in reprisal for a Nationalist air raid on the city. Some clergy were killed. On October 2 a group of anticlerical sailors from the battleship *Jaime I*, moored in Bilbao harbor, boarded the *Cabo Quilates* and killed 50 persons, including 15 priests.

Once the PNV took over there were no more massacres through the rest of 1936. On January 4, 1937, however, a mob attacked four prisons in Bilbao after a Nationalist air attack on the city. Two hundred and nine persons, including 10 priests, were killed before troops were able to gain control of the prison and stop further killings.[10]

The total of all killings of clergy by the left in all three of the Basque provinces numbers 46.[11] It is difficult to say whether fewer or more priests would have been killed if the Basques had thrown in their lot with the Nationalists at the time of the uprising; certainly more of the laity would have been killed.

The Basque autonomists' decision to support the Republic was probably the most controversial of the entire war. Two of the conditions they stipulated for joining the Republicans were that they be granted regional autonomy and that their freedom of religion be respected. Nationalists accused them of selling their common interests and the defense of the Faith for a mess of autonomy. The Basques replied that although they deplored the violent anticlericalism, they liked a fascist-military dictatorship even less, and furthermore that they did not believe the circumstances of July 1936 justified a rebellion against the constituted powers. The rebellion, they said, was not a just war. All these reasons may have been valid, yet the overriding one was sheer survival. Whatever their ideological affinities with the Republic in the sphere of social and political justice, the dominant issue was one of security.[12] If the Basque autonomists had supported the uprising, they would have been slaughtered by the radical leftists

---

10. For descriptions of the incidents see G.L. Steer, *The Tree of Gernika: A Field Study of Modern War* (London, 1938), pp. 113ff., and Montero Moreno, pp. 357–62.

11. Montero Moreno, p. 77. Nationalist historians argue that the Basques deserve some of the responsibility for these deaths. The Basques' partisans deplore the killings but point out that most of the clergy killed were either from other provinces or were arrested for some degree of complicity in the uprising (although this is difficult to prove).

12. However, Tusell Gómez, II, 284, says that autonomy aside, the PNV would have supported the Republic on the basis of its economic and social policy.

in Bilbao: not immediately, but each day they hesitated made it more likely. They had wanted to remain neutral in the struggle but soon found that they could not, and to have gone with their common interest group—conservative Catholics—would have been suicidal. As it was, they could at least protect their property and their religious rights.

The Bishops' Pastoral Instruction

The anticlerical fury was uncontrollable and unpredictable, and criticism of the Basque autonomists has more to do with their reaction than anything else. However, their approach and answer to their bishops' counsels is a more debatable issue, although to a certain extent the autonomists' freedom of action was considerably circumscribed in this issue also.

The points of dispute involve three of the most controversial churchmen of the period: the archbishop of Toledo and the bishops of Vitoria and Pamplona.

Isidro Gomá y Tomás, cardinal-archbishop of Toledo and primate of Spain, was in Pamplona when the uprising began. Troubled by kidney ailments, he had gone there to take the baths and thus by coincidence found himself in the most actively Catholic pro-Nationalist part of Spain. Had he been in his see city of Toledo he probably would have been assassinated, as so many of his clergy were, a thought that must have loomed large in his reaction to events.[13] Cardinal Gomá saw the need for a plea to bring the Basque autonomists over to support the Nationalists. Such a move would unify all Catholics against the Republicans and, if done quickly enough, would avoid a military struggle for the Basque provinces, thereby shortening the war and saving lives. He hoped to accomplish this by appealing to the Basques in the names of their bishops; he therefore wrote what was called the pastoral instruction and presented it to the bishops for their signatures.[14]

---

13. Forty-eight percent of the secular clergy in Toledo were killed in the fury. Anastasio Granados, Gomá's personal secretary, has written a sympathetic biography, based largely on Gomá's archives, El Cardenal Gomá, Primado de España (Madrid, 1971). More recently there is the heavily documented study of María Luisa Rodríguez Aisa, El Cardenal Gomá y la guerra de España: aspectos de la gestión pública del Primado, 1936–1939 (Madrid, 1981).
14. The pro-Republican Basque priest Juan de Iturralde, II, 292, says that Gomá did not want to commit himself publicly to support of the Nationalists at that time

It was a clearly worded document that appealed to the Basques and Navarrese from their bishops, both of them native Basques. It stated the issues involved: that Spain was undergoing her worst suffering in centuries and, worse, that Catholics (i.e., the Basques) were killing other Catholics (i.e., the Navarrese) even while they both received "God's holy communion." Thus, the bishops wished to speak clearly and authoritatively: "with all the authority we can command, we say categorically *non licet!* It is not permissible to divide Catholic forces in the face of a common enemy. . . . It is even less permissible to join with the enemy to fight one's own brother . . . especially so when the enemy is Marxism or Communism, the seven-headed hydra, synthesis of all heresies, which is diametrically opposed to the political, social, economic, and religious doctrines of Christianity." The instruction went on to condemn the idea that one could do evil to serve a greater good (i.e., support the Republicans to prevent attacks on the Church) and stated that politics could not be put before religion.[15]

The instruction did not allow much room for interpretation: it was a straightforward condemnation of the Basque autonomists' unwillingness to join the Nationalist cause and a warning against joining the Republican cause (it was issued before the PNV had decided upon a definite course of action).

There is dispute over the facts of the two bishops' acceptance of Cardinal Gomá's construction. The Basque autonomist priest Juan de Iturralde says that Marcelino Olaechea, the bishop of Pamplona, was pressured to accept the document. Olaechea, he says, had already shown his disapproval of the Nationalists' tactics by refusing to preside at a public mass for them on July 25; furthermore, he would not bless the troops, and he counseled the Nationalists to show mercy to their working-class enemies (as the son of a worker himself). He made some amendments to the instruction but was surprised to see it published over his name without these. Furthermore, Iturralde says, Olaechea confessed that he was not made of the stuff of martyrs, and he therefore accepted the publication of the instruction without further protest.[16]

---

for fear that he would compromise himself if they failed. So, with apparent neutrality he could accomplish his aims by writing a plea and then issuing it over the names of the bishops of Vitoria and Pamplona. Gomá himself said in a report to the Holy See (August 13, 1936), in Rodríguez Aisa, pp. 371–78, that the two bishops asked him to write the document for them.

15. The document is in Montero Moreno, pp. 682–86.

16. Iturralde, II, 299–302.

As for the bishop of Vitoria, Iturralde says that Mateo Múgica was not opposed to the essence of the instruction, only that he wanted to consult with autonomist leaders before it was published, arguing that if it were done without their prior knowledge, the instruction would be counterproductive; but before he could do so, the instruction was released over his name.[17]

Gomá said that he discussed the main points of the instruction with Olaechea and the vicar-general of Vitoria (Múgica did not want to leave his residence for fear of assassination), and both totally agreed with all of the points, although Múgica, he said, later made a very minor amendment "of no importance."[18]

Both Olaechea and Múgica later confirmed that they agreed with the instruction and neither ever protested the issue. It may very well be that Iturralde's arguments are valid and that both bishops simply came to an acceptance of the circumstances.

But the Basques refused to accept the instruction. The document was not immediately published but was instead broadcast by radio to Vizcaya and Guipúzcoa. The autonomists argued, therefore, that it had not been properly promulgated.[19] The priest Alberto de Onaindía, traveling throughout Vizcaya and Guipúzcoa in August and early September, claimed that he learned about the instruction only by accident on September 14.[20] A more telling argument against acceptance was advanced by Juan Ajuriguerra, a PNV leader. He said that neither bishop was in Guipúzcoa or Vizcaya (both towns of Vitoria and Pamplona were in Nationalist hands) and hence lacked valid knowledge of what the actual circumstances were, and they were therefore commanding without sufficient knowledge.[21]

As the instruction did not have its desired effect, Gomá wrote Múgica (August 21, 1936) to ask whether he thought the clergy should be ordered to read the instruction to the faithful at mass. Múgica replied that such an order would expose the clergy to danger from vio-

---

17. Ibid., II, 302–3.
18. In a report to the Holy See (August 13, 1936) in Rodríguez Aisa, pp. 371–78, and in a later letter to a priest, a Father Conesa, cited in Granados, pp. 125–26.
19. Even the cleric Antonio Pérez Ormazábal, who later was Gomá's choice as vicar-general of Vitoria to act in Múgica's absence, declared that as the instruction was not published but rather broadcast by the enemy, it lacked authority; this according to Azpiazu, p. 14.
20. Alberto de Onaindía, Hombre de paz en la guerra (Buenos Aires, 1973), p. 34.
21. Cited in Fraser, p. 417.

lent anticlericals, but that army leaders had suggested that copies be dropped by airplane over the towns of the provinces, and he thought this a good idea.[22]

As confirmation of his support of the instruction, Múgica wrote a clarification on September 8, 1936. In it he castigated those who believed the instruction was not authentic and noted that it had been published in the diocesan bulletin on September 1 and that copies had been sent to parishes where possible. He then repeated the message of the instruction in even more authoritative terms, praised the Nationalist army and its auxiliaries, and appealed to the Basques' love of country and support of the Nationalists as the only way to secure peace.[23]

This document had no effect either, because in fact the Basques could not support the Nationalists—with whom they had much in common—without exposing themselves to attack by uncontrollables in the province and to Republican armed groups as well. As it was, the churches stayed open, priests walked the streets unmolested, and mass was said publicly, despite the occasional moments of terror. These religious rights—and property rights as well—would be lost if they supported the Nationalists because the Nationalists could not aid them at that time. It was a decision of fear and practicality.

The Execution of Basque Autonomist Clergy

When the Nationalists conquered Guipúzcoa in September 1936, they carried out reprisals against those who had been fighting them or who had supported the autonomist cause. They had done this against autonomist adherents in Álava earlier, right after the uprising. In these northern provinces, because of the traditional identification of religious and political values, the reprisals took on a religious bent. The Navarrese felt intense anger against the Basque autonomists, their brothers in religion, whom they felt had deserted a holy cause (a crusade, as shall be seen later).[24]

But the issue that caused the greatest amount of controversy was

---

22. The letters are in Granados, pp. 131–33.

23. The document is in Montero Moreno, pp. 686–87.

24. Autonomist adherents were imprisoned and their wives mishandled; Iturralde, II, 71–72, says that in Tolosa a socialist was shaved bald, dressed in a spotted paper gown, and forced to walk through the streets, shouting "Viva Cristo Rey!" Apparently blasphemy was not limited to anticlerical Republicans.

the arrest and execution of priests suspected of autonomist sympathies.[25] The executions by the Nationalists began in late October and continued into November 1936. Fourteen priests, along with many laymen, were judged, sentenced, and executed for the crime of treason, specifically for helping to organize the PNV or giving aid to the organization. The executions, it was reported to Cardinal Gomá, were carried out with proper consideration: the condemned priests were dressed in secular clothes, were taken out at night "to avoid publicity," and were allowed to confess before being shot.[26]

When Gomá first heard of these executions, he went to Burgos to complain to General Francisco Franco (the head of the Nationalists by this time); Franco told him that he knew nothing about the executions but that he would investigate and he assured Gomá that they would be immediately stopped, and Gomá so informed the Holy See.[27]

The executions were stopped, but priests continued to be arrested and imprisoned. There were still large numbers of these clerics in prison, and more were arrested after the fall of Bilbao in the summer of 1937. Each was classified according to his degree of support for the autonomist cause, and individual dispositions of their cases were made. Some remained in prison, others were sent to different parishes within the diocese of Vitoria, still others were sent to parishes in other parts of Spain, and the rest were exiled from the country. For the regular clergy involved this task was made easier, as most orders had missions abroad where the clergy could be sent to avoid Nationalist reprisals. Some 283 secular and 131 regular clergy were imprisoned, exiled, or sent out of the diocese.[28]

---

25. Iturralde, I, 120, claims that a hit-list of names of those to be executed was composed before the February elections—some six months before the war broke out— and the autonomist priest Iñaki de Azpiazu, pp. 16ff., confirms that his name was on such a list, and he was in fact arrested shortly after the Nationalists entered his village in September.

26. From a description by one of the sentencing judges, quoted in Granados, p. 147. Most of the accounts do not differ substantially from this, although Azpiazu (who was there) describes some brutalities when they were arrested (pp. 17ff.), and Iturralde, II, 396, cites Jean Pelletier, a French journalist arrested with one of the executed priests, who said the priest was beaten. See also the accounts in *Le Clergé Basque*, pp. 33ff. The Nationalist view is in Centro de Información Católica Internacional, pp. 203–11.

27. The letter is in Granados, pp. 145–47; see also Rodríguez Aisa, pp. 61–65.

28. *Le Clergé Basque*, pp. 110ff. See also Dr. de Azpilikoeta, *The Basque Problem as Seen by Cardinal Gomá and President Aguirre* (New York, 1938), pp. 132–37,

The fact of the executions, and later the imprisonments, was publicized throughout the world, and Republican partisans balanced them off against the assassinations in the anticlerical fury (without mentioning the disproportionate figures: 6,832 to 14). If it is argued, as Nationalist partisans did, that the Basque clergy were killed for political rather than religious reasons,[29] the argument raises disturbing questions about the nature of the anticlerical fury and in the end demonstrates just how thin was the line dividing religion from politics in all of Spain.

The Case of Bishop Múgica

The actions, endorsements, retractions, and musings of Bishop Mateo Múgica of Vitoria are probably the most difficult to make any sense of. He was persecuted and threatened by the Nationalists, yet he stoutly defended their cause; he was a Basque and he defended his clergy and laity, yet he criticized their political decisions.

Múgica was the highest ecclesiastical authority in his diocese (which included the three Basque provinces), and it was there that all of these controversial events occurred. Cardinal Gomá was primate of Spain but was only an equal with Múgica as a bishop, and it was as a bishop—a shepherd of souls—that Múgica viewed himself. Indeed, throughout his letters and writings the concept of shepherd and flock is the most used metaphor.

He was no stranger to controversy; he thrived on it. When municipal elections were held in Spain in April 1931 as a referendum on the monarchy, Múgica, alone among all the bishops, told his diocesan faithful that they would be placing their souls in mortal danger if they voted for any but monarchist candidates.[30] After the Republic was proclaimed, he was expelled from Spain as a threat to the Repub-

---

and Azpiazu, pp. 21ff. There is a more recent account in Luis María and Juan Carlos Jiménez de Aberásturi, eds., *La guerra en Euzkadi* (Barcelona, 1978), p. 197.

29. Montero Moreno, p. 78, says that anyone who examines the issues would agree that the passions of war made the sentences harsher than otherwise; that whether the priests were sentenced justly or not, the fact is that they were not killed for religious reasons (as priests were so killed in Republican Spain); and that the bishops played a moderating role in preventing further deaths. In short, he says, the priests were executed in the heat of war for political activities; that they happened to be priests was beside the point.

30. Sánchez, *Reform and Reaction*, p. 76.

lic, and he settled into French exile. By 1933 he had been allowed to return to his see, and he had become a supporter of the Basque autonomy statute.[31]

What we can make of Múgica by the time the war began is that he was a devoted monarchist who eagerly desired the return of Alfonso XIII, and he was also a strong supporter of Basque cultural traditions—two not opposed ideals. But the Nationalist leaders were angry with him for his support of the autonomists, his toleration of autonomist clergy (many of whom had important positions in the diocese), and they believed that he had played an important role in the PNV's decision to stand against the Nationalists.[32] In fact, Múgica criticized the PNV's support of the Republic and firmly believed in the principles enunciated in the pastoral instruction of August 6, 1936. But he disagreed on the question of distribution. He did not want his clergy to have to read it in public and thereby expose themselves to violence. But neither the instruction nor his clarifying letter of September 8 were forced from him; he later affirmed this in vehement terms to a Republican priest.[33]

What is generally not known and what must have contributed to Múgica's thinking at the time was the fact that he had just lost a brother to the anticlerical fury; Juan Múgica, an Augustinian priest, was assassinated in Madrid on July 29, 1936. The Bishop probably knew this with certainty by the beginning of September. In all of his published correspondence and writings he alluded to this death only once, nine years later.[34] The shock he must have felt might help to explain some of the apparently contradictory actions he took.

The Nationalists wanted him out and in fact plotted to kidnap and assassinate him, a deed it would have been easy to get away with in the violent atmosphere of the early days of the war. It was fear of such an attempt that kept Múgica from leaving his episcopal residence to consult with Gomá about the pastoral instruction of August 6. An attempt was plotted for August 18, but Múgica was forewarned and took precautions.[35] By early September the Nationalist leaders had contacted Gomá and demanded that Múgica leave Spain. Gomá pro-

---

31. *Euskera*, the Basque language, continued to be taught in the diocesan seminary, and Basque cultural traditions were promoted. See Frances Lannon, "A Basque Challenge to the pre-Civil War Spanish Church," *European Studies Review* 9 (1979), pp. 29–48.
32. Rodríguez Aisa, p. 43.
33. Quoted in Iturralde, II, 327–28.
34. Mateo Múgica, *Imperativos de me conciencia* (Buenos Aires, 1945), p. 21.
35. Iturralde, II, 278–89.

tested that whatever support Múgica had given the Basque autonomists in the past was more than offset by his present support of the
Nationalist cause. He suggested a compromise: that Múgica go to
Rome for a visit and that while he was gone, the Nationalist army
could launch an offensive and capture Vizcaya and Guipúzcoa. But
Múgica refused to leave his flock, and he feared that his exit would
be interpreted as a political success for the Nationalists. The Nationalists were adamant, and after a report to the Holy See, Gomá was
finally able to persuade Múgica to go to Rome at the behest of Pope
Pius XI on the pretext of attending a missionary congress.[36]

Múgica left for Rome on October 14, 1936, and, while no longer
a problem to the Nationalists, became a problem to Gomá and the
Holy See. He was able to see the Pope and Pacelli, the papal secretary
of state, and to give them his view of the Basque situation. And, even
though exiled, he still considered himself the bishop of Vitoria and
the shepherd of his flock, particularly his priestly flock. When news
of the killing of autonomist priests by the Nationalists filtered into
Rome and when he heard of the plan to send some of the Basque priests
into exile, he wrote Gomá in protest and continued to complain about
actions taken against his priests.[37] He argued that while some of his
clergy were guilty of political excesses, killing them was unjustified;
and furthermore, most of the executed clergy were "model priests."
Yet, despite everything, he stated that he still desired a Nationalist
victory for the sake of security of religion.[38]

Shortly after Bilbao fell in the summer of 1937, Múgica resigned
his see and settled into exile. Eight years later, in 1945, he published
a statement in response to a letter from the vice-rector of the seminary of Vitoria. This statement, *Imperativos de me conciencia*, contains the final justification of his seemingly contradictory actions. It
also reveals an intensely political bishop who was so devoted to his

---

36. Letters of September 4 and 5, 1936, quoted in Granados, pp. 134–41. A new
vicar-general, Antonio Pérez Ormazábal, was named to administer the diocese in Múgica's
absence. The circumstances surrounding the entire event are described in Rodríguez
Aisa, pp. 41–53.

37. He wrote again after Gomá's open letter to President Aguirre (January 10,
1937), in which the Cardinal said that the Basque clergy were killed "for a reason which
there is no need to be mentioned in this letter." Gomá answered Múgica's protest, telling him that the unmentioned reason was the abuse of authority by those who ordered
the priests killed, and stated, "How could I pick a quarrel with those in a position of
power? It would be most imprudent." After making this astonishing and revealing confession, Gomá asked Múgica to keep it an absolute secret. The letters are quoted in
Granados, pp. 147–50.

38. In Granados, pp. 151–52.

faith that all matters—even clearly political ones—became matters of religion. Thus, he could openly support the monarchy, the Nationalists, and the autonomists because the alternative in each case was an attack upon the clergy and the faithful.

In his statement he makes a concession to ignorance by saying that he really did not have much information about what was happening in Spain at large or even in the rest of his diocese in the early days of the war (interestingly, the identical point argued by the autonomists at the time), but at the same time some action was necessary to avoid bloodshed. Hence he signed the pastoral instruction. Then he saw that there were those on both sides who did wrong: "Some did evil to serve the aims of anarchism; others did the same under the pretext of working in the name of Christ."[39] He discovered that there was no formal collaboration between the autonomists and the "communists": "not the unity of a common goal, but rather the unity of being attacked by a common enemy."[40] Thus, it was natural that many of his clergy did not support the Nationalists. He denied allegations that the autonomists placed their ethnic and cultural interests above those of religion, that the seminary was a hotbed of autonomism, and he said that "none of the 2,020 priests in the diocese of Vitoria ever put politics before religion."[41]

Why did he not speak out at the time? He says that he protested to the Pope, but he did not make his protest public "because a person I could not ignore begged me not to, and I agreed because I feared that my protests would be used against innocent persons by the Nationalists."[42]

Múgica was a complex person, a bishop who took a more active political role than most clerics, yet denied that he put politics before religion. To his own way of thinking he was right. Religion touched everything: thus when he told his faithful how to vote or whom to support, he was thinking only of the interests of their souls. He ended his 1945 statement by referring to himself as "the shepherd of the best diocese in the entire world, and now the least of the Bishops of the Holy Church of Jesus Christ."[43]

---

39. Múgica, p. 10.
40. Ibid., p. 12.
41. Ibid., p. 16.
42. Ibid., p. 15. Múgica did not identify this person. Alberto de Onaindía, p. 335, says that Múgica told him in 1949 that "neither Pope Pius XI, Pacelli, nor Pizzardo ever told me to keep silent about these matters." Was it Cardinal Gomá?
43. Ibid., p. 30. Onaindía, p. 317, says that his impression of Múgica after talking to him in July 1937 was that the Bishop's chief weakness was in his being too deferen-

Gomá and Aguirre

While all these events—the execution of the clergy, the exile of Bishop Múgica, and the military struggle—were taking place, the Basque autonomous government—Euzkadi—came into being on October 1, 1936. Two prominent Catholics were leaders in this government: the president, José Antonio de Aguirre, a Jesuit-schooled 32-year-old lawyer and active Catholic layman;[44] and Manuel de Irujo, who on September 26 joined the Republican ministry in Madrid. As practicing Catholics, both men lent immense prestige and propaganda value to the Republican government.

Aguirre took his oath of office in Guernica on October 7, 1936, after attending a public mass, an act which both the Republican government and the Basque autonomists used for its propaganda value. Yet if the anticlerical Republicans could point to this act as an example of the freedom of worship in Republican Spain, Aguirre could counter with a more telling symbolism: the mass was said by Pedro Errasti, a traditionalist (nonautonomist) priest who had secretly made his way across the lines to Guernica with communion wafers smuggled out of anticlerical Madrid, and Aguirre communicated with a smuggled wafer. Hence the message: the Church was free in Euzkadi—even free for a cleric opposed to the autonomists—while it was persecuted in the rest of Spain.[45]

Euzkadi thus became an island of religious normality in a sea of Republican anticlericalism. In the army units raised in Euzkadi 82 priests served as chaplains, and public military masses were said daily at the same time that priests were being hunted down in the rest of Republican Spain.[46]

At the end of the year, on December 22, 1936, Aguirre delivered a speech summing up his policy and commenting on the progress of his government. He talked about freedom of worship in Euzkadi and defended his aims against the conservative classes, whom he accused of "indefensible excesses," arguing that his regime was based on principles of Christian social justice. He said that the war was not a religious struggle. He addressed the bishops and asked why they had remained silent in the face of the executions of priests murdered "for

---

tial to his superiors in not wanting to annoy them with his qualms about the Nationalists or his later doubts about the pastoral instruction of 1936.

44. He had achieved popularity as a soccer star as well. Seco Serrano, p. 35.
45. Iturralde, II, 233.
46. Ibid., II, 248.

the simple reason that they loved their Basque Fatherland," and asked why the bishops had not protested the exiling of Basque clerics from "invaded Basque territory." He appealed to "the Father of Christianity to put an end to this silence."[47]

Cardinal Gomá responded in an open letter on January 10, 1937. He said that Aguirre's speech "left on my soul the impression that I was listening to the voice of a convinced Catholic" and admitted that "social injustice is at bottom one of the remote causes of the disaster, but we categorically deny that this war is a class war." The war he said "is at bottom one of love or hatred toward religion. It is the love of the God of our fathers that has armed one half of Spain, even if it should be granted that less spiritual motives are operating in this war; it is hatred that has ranged the other half against God."

Gomá deplored not only the execution of Basque priests but also "the aberration of certain priests which brought them in front of a firing party, because a priest should not descend from that level of holiness, both ontological and moral." He assured Aguirre that the hierarchy had not been silent and that the executions had stopped. He then asked Aguirre why the President had been silent in the face of the many more executions of priests in Republican Spain and then went on to condemn Aguirre's alliance with the "godless communists."[48]

Aguirre responded two months later to Cardinal Gomá's assertions, saying that he had made a public protest in the Spanish Cortes against the anticlerical violence, but that none of the bishops had made a public protest against the execution of the Basque clergy. Aguirre condemned the bishops' stand as "a scandal and profound disturbance in Christian ethics." He deplored the persecution of the clergy but asked "God with all my strength to give us a persecuted Church rather than a protected Church."[49]

This letter ended the public polemic, and the two corresponded no more. The Nationalist invasion of Euzkadi began in late March 1937, and more immediate problems came up. The Basque towns of Durango and Guernica were bombed, and churches were hit and priests and laity killed while attending mass. Some 20,000 Basque children

---

47. The speech is in Azpilikoeta, pp. 17–47.
48. The letter is in Azpilikoeta, pp. 93–112. See also the gloss on Gomá's letter in Ángel de Zumeta, *Un cardenal español y los católicos vascos* (Bilbao, 1937), pp. 60ff. Gomá sent a private letter along with the open letter in which he said that the purpose of the open letter was "to clarify a few points in your speech which, though it was certainly not your intention, left the ecclesiastical hierarchy in a doubtful situation," and stated that "I should regret with all my heart if my letter should contain a single idea that might hurt you." In Azpilikoeta, pp. 152–53.
49. The letter is in Azpilikoeta, pp. 158–69.

were evacuated to foster homes abroad (including nearly 1,500 to Soviet Russia). Many of these children were accompanied by Basque
priests to look after their spiritual welfare.[50] Gomá wanted to be
assured that they would be placed in Catholic foster homes.[51] He wrote
to the primates of other Catholic nations to ask them to ensure that
the children be given a Catholic education.[52]

Even before the Nationalist offensive began, Gomá and the Vatican tried to find a way to mediate an end to the war against the Basques.
Franco wanted a papal condemnation of the autonomists for their support of the anticlerical Republicans. Pacelli responded that the Pope
would do so only if the Nationalist leader would offer concessions
to the autonomists and be lenient in the treatment of their leaders.
Franco rejected this as impractical and difficult.[53] As the war continued, Gomá came to believe that the autonomists would not fight a
hopeless struggle and that they would surrender if offered favorable
terms. The Vatican agreed and, along with the Italian government,
attempted mediation again. Cardinal Pacelli offered a plan for a con-
ditional surrender and appealed to the Nationalists to be moderate
in their treatment of the conquered Basques. But mediation aims were
not realized. Bilbao surrendered in June, and the Basque forces capitu-
lated in August.[54] When the victorious Nationalist army entered
Euzkadi, they arrested autonomists, both clergy and laity, and imprisoned many of them. (See chapter 9 for more details on the Vatican's
role.)[55]

The Basque problem, more than any other, raised the religious
issues of the war abroad. It divided foreign Catholics over the war and
confirmed in their opposition those who had opposed the Nationalists from the beginning. But the Spanish bishops were prepared for
this, and the defeat of the Catholic Basque autonomists now enabled
them to make their plea to the world. The bishops now represented
a solid Catholic front in Spain for the support of the Nationalist forces.

50. See Dorothy Legarreta, *The Guernica Generation: Basque Refugee Children
of the Spanish Civil War* (Reno, 1984), for a survey of the emigration, acceptance elsewhere, and, after 1939, repatriation of these children.
51. An impossibility in the Soviet Union; only children so designated by their
parents were sent there. See Pedro P. Altabella Gracia, *El catolicismo de los nacionalistas vascas* (Madrid, 1939), pp. 125–55.
52. See Isidro Gomá y Tomás, *Por Dios y por España* (Barcelona, 1940), pp.
549–50.
53. The letters, in January 1937, are in Rodríguez Aisa, pp. 403–10.
54. See Iturralde, III, 203–9, and Granados, pp. 158–65, for the surrender negotiations.
55. Iturralde, III, 286–318, and Azpiazu, pp. 45ff., have details on the occupation. See also Rodríguez Aisa, pp. 203–31, on the role of Gomá.

CHAPTER 7

The Bishops' Collective Letter
of 1937

In the late summer of 1937 the Spanish bishops published a collective letter addressed to their fellow bishops throughout the world. The stated purpose of the letter was to correct certain false impressions about the war that had been circulated abroad, particularly by some segments of the foreign Catholic press; it was designed, they said, to spread the truth about the war. This letter and the publicity given the Basque struggle made the religious issues of the war known in other countries and contributed greatly to making the Spanish war the decisive religious event it became.

Foreigners tended to stereotype the Spanish clergy and particularly the bishops as scheming prelates, machinating with—or being manipulated by—the generals, with both castes intent upon preserving their favored status at the expense of the downtrodden poor. Photographs of dyspeptic-looking bishops with hands raised in fascist salutes did little to dispel the image.[1] These impressions contributed to confusion about the role of the bishops and the collective letter itself. To understand the letter, first the bishops must be understood.

Ordinarily a bishop, unlike a politician, has no power over unbelievers. But when the state is officially Catholic, as Spain was before 1931 and as Nationalist Spain became after 1936, a bishop's power over unbelievers increases, but only to the extent that the state allows. The Nationalists, although there were unbelievers and anticlericals among them, allowed the bishops to exercise power in educational, social, and cultural affairs in order to get their support and the support of believing Catholics. Given the fact of the anticlerical fury, this

---

1. See Gil Mugarza, p. 377, for the most widely reproduced one, featuring the archbishop of Santiago.

bid for support was unnecessary; the clergy and most Catholics would have supported anyone who did *not* persecute them. But this perception was not clear at the time.

The bishops were thus cast into a political role whether they liked it or not. This role probably gave them an exaggerated sense of their own power. They were asked to preside at military and civil functions, to preach to troops, to serve on political committees. They had the educational system of Nationalist Spain turned over to them, and they could influence social legislation. But these powers were given to them, and they could be taken away. The only inherent power they had was that of spiritual direction, and this was useful only to influence believers. This distinction was not easily made, and probably some of the bishops believed that their new-found powers were intrinsic to their roles. And with power went responsibility, a theme the bishops stressed consistently throughout their public pronouncements on the war.

A bishop is the supreme spiritual director of the believers in his diocese; he is subordinate only to the pope, but his is the main responsibility for his flock. In Spain in 1936 there were 61 dioceses, but there were not 61 bishops, owing to the vacancies that always existed, caused by death or resignation. After the anticlerical fury had passed, by December 1936 there were 49 bishops (excluding auxiliaries) left. Nine had been assassinated by that time. Three of the remaining bishops were cardinals: the primate and archbishop of Toledo, Isidro Gomá y Tomás; the archbishop of Tarragona (Catalonia), Francesc Vidal i Barraquer; and the archbishop of Seville, Eustaquio Ilundáin y Esteban. There was a fourth Spanish cardinal, Pedro Segura y Sáenz, former primate and archbishop of Toledo, now resident in Rome after having resigned his see in 1931, following his expulsion by the Republican government.[2] Of all these men three achieved some degree of fame for their roles in the war: Gomá, Vidal, and Mateo Múgica of Vitoria (whose role has been discussed on the Basque problem in the preceding chapter). Two achieved lesser fame: Marcelino Olaechea of Pamplona, cosigner with Múgica of the pastoral instruction of August 1936, and Segura, who was appointed archbishop of Seville in September 1937 after Ilundáin died, and who thereafter became a constant critic of the Falange. Gomá and Vidal provide the greatest interest and the

---

2. Most of the bishops were over 60: Gomá was 67, Vidal 68; only four were younger than 50. See José Manuel Cuenca Toribio, *Sociología de una élite de poder de España e Hispanoamérica contemporáneas: la jerarquía eclesiástica (1789–1965)* (Córdoba, 1976), pp. 290–355, which lists all of the bishops and their backgrounds.

greatest contrast because one was the author of the collective letter and the other refused to sign it.

Isidro Gomá y Tomás was a Catalan from Tarragona. A scholar with earned doctorates in theology and philosophy, possessor of a florid preaching and writing style, he had been rector of the Tarragona seminary for twenty years before he became bishop of Tarrazona in 1927. In 1933 he was named to succeed Segura in Spain's most important see, primatial Toledo. It is difficult to tell why he was selected for the key ecclesiastical post in Spain; perhaps his style had made an impression, for he now became the chief spokesman for the Church. He had exhibited no political leanings before this time. In 1935 he was named a cardinal. By 1936 he was playing an active political role. In the campaign leading to the February 1936 elections he issued a pastoral letter calling for Catholics to support rightist candidates and unite in the face of the anticlerical enemy.[3] Thus, when the uprising began, he was clearly sympathetic to the Nationalists, and the anticlerical fury made him one of their principal supporters.

From Pamplona where he had been recuperating from a kidney ailment when the uprising began, Gomá saw his responsibility clearly: to unite Spain's Catholics against the anticlerical horde, which he viewed in simplistic terms as part of the international Marxist conspiracy. He wrote reports, sometimes weekly, to the Holy See (specifically to the secretary of state, Cardinal Eugenio Pacelli); he wrote the August 1936 pastoral instruction signed by Múgica and Olaechea; and he began to write pastoral letters over his own signature. One was written to answer foreign criticism of the Nationalists and of the stand taken by Gomá and the other bishops; it foreshadowed the collective letter of 1937 in its intent. In it Gomá said that the civil war was not a political struggle in the strict sense of the word; rather it was a conflict between two concepts of civilization, a war, he said, between Christianity and Marxist materialism.[4]

Within a month after the uprising Gomá was clearly the spokesman for the Spanish Church. Vidal was in exile, and Ilundáin was mortally ill. There were no other bishops of comparable status or talent. Pacelli and the Pope placed their trust in him, and in December 1936 Gomá was named confidential and semiofficial representative of the Holy See to the Nationalist government (see chapter 9). Thus, Gomá

---

3. The letter is in Granados, pp. 72–73.

4. "El caso de España," (November 23, 1936), in Gomá, *Por Dios*, pp. 17–39. He enlarged on these themes in his open letter to Basque President Aguirre and in a Lenten pastoral, "La cuaresma de España" (January 1937), in ibid., pp. 85–127.

came to represent not only the Spanish bishops to the world but also the Holy See to General Franco. Gomá's support of the Nationalists was echoed—and in many cases amplified—by his fellow bishops. Almost to a man the episcopal survivors of the fury issued pastoral letters and made other public statements condemning the anticlerical enemies, calling them a "conglomeration of atheists, masons, jews, and enemies of God" (archbishop of Burgos), "international communist savages" (bishop of Palencia), and "satanic revolutionaries" (bishop of Madrid-Alcalá). The bishops clearly indicated their support of the Nationalist armies in what they called a "religious and patriotic war on the same scale and importance as the reconquest of Spain from the Muslims" (archbishop of Santiago), and some used the term *cruzada* (crusade), a theme developed in great detail by Bishop Enrique Pla y Deniel of Salamanca.[5]

Whatever a bishop's feelings may have been before the war, no matter how moderate or conciliatory he may have appeared toward the prewar anticlerical Republican regime, all (save Vidal) were turned into open supporters of the Nationalists by the fury. Even Ilundáin, a political moderate in his relations with prewar Republicans, participated in well-publicized religious and civil ceremonies with Generals Franco and Gonzalo Quiepo de Llano in Seville a few weeks after the uprising.[6] None of the bishops—not even the two who refused to sign the collective letter—wanted a Republican victory in the war.

They were following a time-honored tradition. Spanish bishops had seldom shirked from pronouncements on war; after all, most of Spain's nineteenth-century wars had been, at least in part, clerical-anticlerical struggles.[7] Certainly there was ample precedent of clerical involvement in wars, and it would have been unusual if the bishops had said nothing about the most violent attack on their clergy in all of history.

Given this tradition and Gomá's earlier pastorals, the publication of the collective letter of 1937 was not initially unusual in any way. It became controversial because it raised the issues of the war formally, because it was unique—addressed to those outside the nation —and because of the circumstances behind its writing and publication.

---

5. These statements are collected and analyzed in Arbeloa, "Anticlericalismo y guerra civil."

6. See Antonio Bahamonde y Sánchez de Castro, *Memoirs of a Spanish Nationalist* (London, 1939), pp. 37, 56–57. In his pastoral on the war Ilundáin called the anticlericals "hordes of hell" (Arbeloa, "Anticlericalismo y guerra civil," p. 167).

7. See Manuel Revuelta González, "La iglesia española ante la crises del antiguo régimen (1808–33)," in Cárcel Ortí, ed., *Historia de la iglesia en España,* V, 11–14.

Apparently Cardinal Pacelli was the first to suggest such a document. After he rejected Franco's request for a papal condemnation of the Basques, Pacelli suggested to Gomá that the Spanish bishops collectively "outline the truth concerning cooperation between Catholics and communists."[8] Gomá consulted some of the bishops, but they answered that a joint pastoral letter would have little effect, no more than the pastoral instruction of August 1936. Furthermore, they said that Gomá's open letter to Aguirre had sufficient references to the Basque problem. Gomá thus responded to Pacelli (February 23, 1937) his estimation that a joint pastoral would be counterproductive in the case of the Basques but that a collective pastoral on the general situation might be in order.[9] Pacelli responded that Gomá could proceed with such a letter whenever he wished and that the Holy See trusted his tact and prudence in the matter.[10]

The matter rested there until mid-May 1937. Gomá reported to Pacelli that in a discussion with Franco on May 10 the Nationalist leader had requested an episcopal letter with the aim of dispelling false information abroad.[11] Gomá said he had taken this initiative to send the outline of such a letter to all the Spanish bishops, and all except Vidal had responded favorably. Gomá pointed out to Pacelli that such a letter would not be solely in response to Franco's request but that the other bishops and numerous Catholics in Spain had asked for it, and an episcopal statement would be an act of true patriotism.[12]

Why did Franco want a letter at this time? Probably because the Basque issue was dividing Catholics abroad, and by this time Franco had come to realize that the war would not easily be won and would be decided only by an unconditional military victory. A negotiated peace would be unlikely. Therefore, foreign aid and support would be crucial to the outcome of the war. An episcopal statement would have an effect upon foreign Catholic opinion to the purpose of preventing the democracies from coming to the support of the Republic.[13]

Gomá wrote the letter and sent it to each of the bishops for his approval. It was published without any major corrections.[14]

---

8. Letter from Pacelli to Gomá, February 10, 1937, in Rodríguez Aisa, p. 411. See also her discussion on pp. 233–69 on the origins and writing of the letter, and the comment in Hilari Raguer, "Los obispos españoles y la guerra civil," *Arbor* 62 (July–August 1982), pp. 7–32.

9. In Rodríguez Aisa, pp. 415–18.

10. Letter of March 10, 1937, in Rodríguez Aisa, p. 418.

11. Letter of May 12, 1937, in Rodríguez Aisa, pp. 442–45.

12. Letter of June 8, 1937, in Rodríguez Aisa, pp. 453–54.

13. This is the suggestion of Cárcel Ortí, p. 376.

14. The collective letter is in Montero Moreno, pp. 726–41, among many other

The collective letter is a lengthy work—over nine thousand words in all—written in Gomá's forceful style. The document stated at the beginning that it was addressed to the bishops of the world as a response to their messages of condolence on the anticlerical fury, to warn them about the forces and ideologies "that aspire to conquer the world," and most importantly to ask them to help spread the truth about the war. It said that the Spanish bishops were particularly concerned that the foreign Catholic press was spreading false notions about the Church and the war, especially claims that the Spanish clergy possessed vast amounts of landed wealth and that they favored the wealthy, that they had provoked the anticlerical fury by firing on people from their churches, and that they supported the Nationalists because they were faced with a dilemma and had no alternative to siding with Franco's forces.

The collective letter said that these falsehoods were the result of ignorance of the Spanish situation and due to the malicious intent of anti-Christian forces, "hidden international forces," and the anti-patriotism of misguided Spaniards who called themselves Catholics. The bishops, it stated, were particularly indignant that for foreigners the voice of the prelates was being equated with vulgar pamphleteers on Spanish issues.

The letter defended the clergy against the charge of possessing vast amounts of wealth, noting correctly that their landholdings were sparse. It cited statistics to prove that the clergy were drawn almost entirely from the ranks of the poorer segments of the population. It pointed out that the Church had been the victim of anticlerical violence since 1931. The bishops' prewar conduct was defended: they had given the "highest examples of apostolic and civic moderation" despite the anticlerical laws and violence.

The collective letter gave a studied defense of the legitimacy of the "civic-military" uprising, admitting that the causes of the war were not simple, claiming that the Church "neither wished for the war nor provoked it." The causes of the war were listed as the mistakes and "maybe the malice and cowardice" of those who governed, the passage of secularist legislation which was an attack upon the national conscience, the corrupt elections of February 1936, the government's surrendering of power to the populace, and, above all, the existence of a communist conspiracy aimed at seizing power. Thus, the letter concluded, there was no alternative but a revolt against the government.

places. The authorized English translation is in The New York Times, September 3, 1937, pp. 4–5, and can also be found in Luis Aguirre Prado, The Church and the Spanish War (Madrid, 1965), pp. 26–49.

It defended this judgment by citing St. Thomas Aquinas on the justice of rebellion and argued that the rebellion met his criteria: namely, that the common good was compromised, that social authorities and prudent men recognized the public danger, and as for the probability of success, this was left "to the judgment of history."[15] The war, it said, thus became "an armed plebiscite," "a struggle between irreconcilable ideologies," and "a conflict between Bolshevism and Christian civilization."

This characterization of the war as an anti-Christian movement led to the argument that the revolution unleashed by the uprising was chiefly a communist-directed conspiracy organized by the Comintern and that these "hidden forces" had been plotting the destruction of the Spanish nation since 1931. The revolution, it said, was preconceived, cruel to persons, barbarous to art, anti-Spanish, and, above all, anti-Christian, aimed "directly at the abolition of the Catholic religion in Spain." The clergy were the primary targets of the revolutionaries and were marked for assassination even before the war began. In answer to those who claimed that the anticlerical violence was a reaction to clerical despotism, the letter stated that the violence was promoted by Russians and "exported by Orientals of perverse spirit"; Spaniards were simply the instruments of this hatred, and as proof, statistics were cited to show that most of the assassins ("our Communists") were reconciled to Catholicism before they were executed.[16]

Having defended the uprising as just and shown the revolutionaries to be directed by foreign conspirators, the collective letter announced the bishops' support of the Nationalists, who it said represented the Spanish nation and had established a regime of law, order, and justice and had even "released a current of love for the fatherland." The defense of the rights of religion, it said, was a primary motive for many who fought for the Nationalists. As for the charges that the Nationalists were barbarous in their treatment of captured Republicans, the letter did not defend these "excesses" but said that there was no comparison between the "outrages against justice" on the Republican side and the orderly administration of justice by the Nationalists.

But the collective letter took great pains to defend the bishops' independence and freedom to criticize; the Church, it said, was not

---

15. Significantly, the letter did not cite all of Aquinas' criteria, omitting the judgment of proportionality. See chapter 11.

16. "In Majorca only 2% have died unrepentent; in the south no more than 20%; and in the north they do not reach, maybe, 10%."

tied to the Nationalists but rather accepted their protection. And the bishops were concerned about the future: they wanted a government "with roots in the nation" and rejected foreign models (which was a veiled objection to fascism). The "witness of blood" of the martyred clergy would serve as a reminder of the political responsibility of those who would reconstruct the new state of the future.

A common theme running throughout the letter was the forgiveness of the persecutors. It referred to them as "our sons" and generously admitted that not all Republicans were fighting for communism and that the government leaders were not malicious. It extended the bishops' sympathy to the defeated Basques but also reproved them for not listening to their bishops. Thus, except for the acceptance of the communist conspiracy theory, the letter was neither simplistic, ungenerous, nor unsympathetic: it admitted the complexity of the war, the good will of many Republicans, and the "human defects" of the Nationalists. But the collective letter made clear on which side the bishops stood.

The collective letter contained no surprises in the context of what the bishops had already been saying individually: indeed, it was milder than most of their earlier statements, milder even than Gomá's earlier pastorals. The term *cruzada* was not used in the letter;[17] however, in fact it established the concept for foreign Catholics that the Nationalist uprising was indeed a crusade and that most Spaniards were fighting the war for religious (or antireligious) reasons.[18]

Gomá sent a draft copy of the letter to all the bishops, save two, for their approval: the bishop of Orihuela, Francisco Javier de Irastorza Loinaz, was in London on canonical leave, and he was not approached;

---

17. Gomá's critic, Raguer, *La espada*, p. 119, wonders if this was omitted at the request of the Holy See.

18. The conservative historian García Escudero, pp. 1454–55, says that the document's main argument is simply that the bishops were prudent in their support of the prewar Republican governments despite the weaknesses and attacks of those governments, that this prudence was insufficient, and that, finally, war was inevitable, especially given the determination of international communism. The political scientist Ruíz Rico, p. 52, says that two characteristics stand out in the letter: the importance given the role of communism, although the bishops' perception of that role was faulty (and García Escudero agrees that the bishops were simplistic on this point), and the priority of religious motivation in the war.

Franco's supporter Ricardo de la Cierva, *Los documentos de la primavera trágica* (Madrid, 1967), pp. 608–9, defends the bishops' approach: "The Bishops' reaction was perfectly professional: the letter is the work of shepherds who defend their flocks with perhaps rudimentary, but efficacious arms. . . . It is not strange that shepherds use shepherds' tools."

and Juan Torres y Ribas, the aged and infirm bishop of Menorca, was not contacted because he was still in Republican hands and not free to act. All the bishops contacted responded affirmatively to Gomá except for two. Mateo Múgica, the bishop of Vitoria, was in Rome in Nationalist-imposed exile (see chapter 6), and he wrote Gomá on June 28 that he could not sign the letter on the technicality that he was not in possession of his see but that he prayed for a Nationalist victory. Múgica then wrote the Holy See and explained his refusal in different terms. He said that the collective letter stated that the Church was free in Franco's Spain, and this was not true: "the Church is enslaved"; furthermore, the letter stated that justice was administered fairly in Franco's Spain, and this was not true: he knew of many fervent Christians and exemplary priests who had been executed by the Nationalists without any formal trial; and, finally, the collective letter's position on the Basques was an offense against their bishop.[19]

The other churchman who did not sign was the most controversial of all the Spanish bishops, Cardinal Francesc Vidal i Barraquer, archbishop of Tarragona, in exile in Italy. Vidal has been cast as a supporter of the Republic, a martyr to democratic ideals, a man whose ecumenical outlook predated the Second Vatican Council. He was some of those things; he was not others. Vidal attracts interest partly because he was so different from the other bishops. He was the opposite of Gomá. Their temperaments and approaches were different: Gomá was a leader; Vidal a persuader.[20] Even their looks clashed: Gomá appeared the very picture of the traditionalist spokesman—large, florid, and stern—while Vidal looked slight, spare, and taciturn.

Vidal was a Catalan (like Gomá; both men were born a year apart in the province of Tarragona). He came from a family of lawyers, politicians, and priests. Unlike most clerics, he waited until he was 28 to enter the seminary, and by the time he made that decision he had already acquired a law degree from the University of Barcelona and was a practicing lawyer. He was ordained after three years of study and then began a rapid rise through ecclesiastical ranks. By the age of forty-five he was consecrated bishop of Solsona. Four years later he was offered the archbishopric of Tarragona, the metropolitan see of Catalonia, and two years after that he was created a cardinal by

---

19. Both letters are in Iturralde, III, 348–49.

20. Ramón Comas, *Isidro Gomá—Francesc Vidal i Barraquer: dos visiones antagónicas de la iglesia española de 1939* (Salamanca, 1977), p. 12, says Gomá was the supporter of an ecclesiastical tradition that rejected modern European culture, while Vidal tried to incorporate the new currents of thinking into his outlook.

Pope Benedict XV in 1921. He was an amiable churchman, with friends from all walks of life, royalty and anticlerical working-class folk included.[21]

Without wanting to, Vidal became a champion of Catalan cultural nationalism when he became the focal point of Primo de Rivera's campaign against the Catalans during the 1923–30 dictatorship. Vidal defended the use of the Catalan language in preaching and teaching; Primo suppressed use of the language. Vidal protested and became the symbol of resistance to Primo's centralizing activities; he also found himself to be a political figure for his stand. He was not a political autonomist and took great care to avoid political activity, but he felt it his episcopal obligation to defend his flock's right to hear sermons in their native language. But Primo persevered and got concessions from the Holy See on the issue. Vidal was outraged against the Vatican bureaucrats who bowed to Primo.[22]

By the time the monarchy was overthrown in 1931 Vidal was seen as the most liberal churchman in Spain. After Segura was expelled, he became the de facto primate, and he led the hierarchy to a policy of moderate conciliation with the anticlerical government.[23] He was offered the see of Toledo, but he rejected it, preferring to stay in his native Catalonia. By 1936 he was certainly the cleric most respected in the country by middle-class Republicans.

Vidal was in Catalonia in July 1936 when the war began; because of the anticlerical fury representatives of the Generalidad feared for his life, and they asked him to leave his episcopal residence and flee to safety. Vidal agreed only after it became obvious that the Generalidad could not protect the lives of his clergy. He went to the monastery of Poblet with his auxiliary, Bishop Manuel Borràs, and both were arrested by a group of anarchist uncontrollables. Vidal asked that a foreign power be notified so that he could request diplomatic protection, but the anarchists refused and took him to Montblanc, where his life was threatened several times. Generalidad representatives working on the initiative of Catalan President Luis Companys and Catalan Minister of Culture Ventura Gassol managed to rescue him, and they secured passage on an Italian ship (Borràs, his auxiliary, was not allowed to leave by the anarchists, and he was assassinated the fol-

---

21. Muntanyola, pp. 39–50, recounts many anecdotes of his friendships.

22. There is a good discussion of the conflict, which extended beyond Vidal to include all the Catalan bishops against Primo, in Ben-Ami, pp. 199–202.

23. See his collected papers, Arxiu Vidal i Barraquer, *Esglesia i Estat durant la Segonya República Espanyola 1931–1936*, ed. M. Batllori and V.M. Arbeloa (Montserrat, 1971, 1977).

lowing month). On July 29 Vidal and the bishops of Tortosa and Gerona left Barcelona harbor and sailed for Italy. Vidal settled into exile
at a Carthusian monastery in Lucca.

Vidal felt helpless in Italy. Reports of massacres of his clergy increased his sense of helplessness. He came to believe that much of
the anticlerical violence was caused by perceptions of clerical political activity and that the only way to prevent further violence was for
the clergy to play an absolutely neutral political role; a political stance,
any public support for the Nationalists, would simply cause reprisals
and more anticlerical violence. He maintained this attitude stead-
fastly throughout the war even though he foresaw a Nationalist victory and probably wanted it as a means of ending the violence.[24]

Vidal wrote Pacelli and the Pope frequently, urging neutrality
and clarifying his position. In early September 1936, when the Italian
press announced that the Pope was receiving Spanish refugees in a
special audience, Vidal wrote Pacelli that the publicity would have
an adverse effect upon Catholics in Republican Spain and might lead
to more persecution.[25] He made no public statements on the war while
his fellow bishops were issuing pastorals condemning the Republicans and extolling the Nationalists. In early 1937 he corroborated this
position in a letter to Pacelli in which he said that some of the refugee bishops' statements were causing reprisals against Catholics in
their dioceses within Republican Spain.[26]

Given this attitude and background, it is not surprising that Vidal
rejected the idea of a collective letter, as he made clear in his first
response to Gomá's query to all the bishops on the need for such a
letter. Vidal responded, "I do not consider it opportune at this time,"
citing the fear of reprisals; besides, he said, there was no need for such
a letter, as papal and episcopal statements had already given Catholics adequate direction.[27]

After Gomá heard Franco's request in May for a letter, he solicited
the bishops again. Vidal responded to the primate's urgings: "We should
not allow ourselves to be manipulated by persons outside the hier-

---

24. Hilari Raguer, an admirer of Vidal and no partisan of the Nationalist cause,
emphasizes this point: "It is clear—Vidal said it unambiguously in more than one letter —that although he had not wanted the war and had tried to avoid it, once it had
begun and once he saw what the situation was, he sincerely wanted and foresaw Franco's victory; but he did not believe that a bishop, much less the official Church, should
publicly manifest those sympathies" (*La espada*, p. 111).

25. Letter of September 2, 1936, in Muntanyola, p. 308.

26. Letter of February 21, 1937, in ibid., p. 314.

27. Letter of March 26, 1937, in ibid., pp. 315–16.

archy," he said, and while he agreed that the foreign press was not telling the truth about Spain, he did not think that a collective letter would be the best way to correct the situation; he said that it could be handled more discreetly.[28] After Gomá sent him a draft copy of the collective letter, Vidal said that the bishops should stay completely out of partisan politics, especially as an example to the other clergy. He suggested that a conference of bishops should meet so that everyone could give his point of view rather than accept a dictated letter from the primate, and he argued that the Holy See would be compromised; the collective letter would confirm the impression that the Spanish clergy were constantly involved in politics. He said that "we should love our country and work with the civil power to establish the common good, but we should do so as priests and bishops . . . within our mission of peace, charity, and harmony." He said that private letters sent to bishops abroad would be more productive. Finally, he stated about the collective letter: "I cannot accept it in conscience. I think about my poor flock. I am frightened at the repercussions this will have in our land."[29] Gomá informed the Holy See of Vidal's refusal and noted that other bishops had agreed with the collective letter but that some had urged caution to prevent reprisals.[30]

As pressure mounted, Vidal wrote Pacelli and said that if the Holy See approved the letter and wanted him to sign, he would be the first to do so, but he believed that such matters were better approached by a conference of bishops.[31] Neither the Pope nor Pacelli ordered Vidal to sign.[32]

The collective letter was dated July 1, 1937, but Gomá did not want to publish it without Vidal's signature. He held off publication while he made a last request, which he sent to Vidal along with the galley proofs of the letter. Vidal again rejected Gomá's request.[33] Other

---

28. Letter of May 30, 1937, in ibid., pp. 319–20.

29. Letter of June 23, 1937, in ibid., pp. 323–24.

30. Letter of June 25, 1937, in Rodríguez Aisa, pp. 461–62.

31. Letter of June 29, 1937, in Muntanyola, p. 325.

32. This has been interpreted as part of the Vatican's policy of caution so that Vidal could be used as a trump card should the Republicans win the war, a point denied by Muntanyola, p. 306.

33. Letter of July 9, 1937, in Muntanyola, pp. 325–26. In prefacing his refusal to sign he said, "I find the letter excellent in substance and form" (lo encuentro admirable de fondo y de forma). Gomá's biographer, Granados, p. 177, says that this indicates that Vidal did not oppose the content or thesis of the letter, only the method of publication (i.e., that a public letter would lead to reprisals); therefore Gomá believed that Vidal supported the substance of the letter. Vidal's biographer, Muntanyola, p. 326, argues that all the letters that Vidal wrote are opposed to this interpretation and that

bishops tried to get Vidal to sign, among them his fellow passenger into exile, José Cartaña e Ingles, bishop of Gerona. Vidal repeated his refusal to Cartaña, and in another letter to Gomá he said that he would be sorry if his not signing the letter "should be attributed to a lack of confidence or confraternity" with his fellow bishops, but it was rather the fear of reprisals against the large number of priests still under Republican domination in his diocese.[34] Vidal communicated this refusal to Pacelli, saying, "the hierarchy should follow the examples of the early Christians and recent popes on the doctrine of respect and obedience to constituted authority; they should not confuse the fact of authority with the abuses of those in power."[35]

Vidal's final refusal sealed his fate into permanent exile. He was never allowed to return to Spain; the Nationalist government after 1939 refused all his appeals. But he believed that he had been right, and before his death in 1943 he said that he would take the same stance on the letter if he had to do it over again.[36]

The collective letter was translated into other languages and released to the press in late August 1937, still carrying the July 1 date. The response was immediate and widespread: over five hundred bishops throughout the world answered sympathetically and favorably. Those who opposed the collective letter presumably kept silent. Neither the letter nor even the fact of its existence was published in *L'Osservatore Romano*, a curious omission considering the amount of ecclesiastical trivia published in the Vatican newspaper; this led to speculation that the Pope disapproved of the letter. However, a year later Pacelli wrote a laudatory introduction to a compilation of favorable episcopal responses to the letter from throughout

---

the *fondo y forma* phrase was simply a polite protocolary introduction. García Escudero, p. 1454, no partisan of Vidal, agrees with Muntanyola.

34. Letter of August 3, 1937, in Muntanyola, p. 329.

35. Letter of September 10, 1937, in ibid., pp. 334–35.

36. Muntanyola, p. 329. Also missing from the signatures was that of Cardinal Segura. Technically he would not have been asked to sign because he was not in possession of a see at the time the letter was published. On August 10, after the letter was written—but before it was published—Cardinal Ilundáin of Seville died. Three weeks after the letter was released for publication Segura was appointed to the see of Seville. It would not have been difficult for Gomá to have justified Segura's signature on the letter, but it is doubtful if Segura could have been persuaded to sign. His biographer, Ramón Garriga, *El cardenal Segura y el nacional-catolicismo* (Barcelona, 1977), p. 249, says that Segura returned to Spain in early May 1937 for his brother's funeral and he could have been approached by Gomá at that time, but that Segura would never have signed the letter because he was too opposed to the Falange and its influence on the Franco regime.

the world.[37] There was some controversy when it was revealed that the letter had been written at Franco's request,[38] and hostile reporters made much of the fact that there were two bishops who did not sign, but Catholics responded vigorously in defense.[39]

Evaluations on the collective letter are as divided as positions on the war in general.[40] Was the letter necessary? Cardinal Vidal had argued that its publication would lead to reprisals, but there is no evidence that it did. In fact, the anticlerical fury was over by the time the letter was published, and it had no effect upon the level of anticlerical violence. It may have played a role in the assassination of Bishop Anselmo Polanco of Teruel (see chapter 10), but it is difficult to find any other deaths caused by it. Did it compromise the clergy? Unquestionably yes, and without necessity. The Nationalists depended upon reaction to the anticlerical fury to keep the clergy and Catholics on their side. They could not afford to alienate this group, who were without any doubt the strongest supporters of the Nationalists. Within the country the letter was useless and compromising, and it changed no one's attitude.

But the letter was not intended for domestic consumption: it was aimed at foreign bishops who might influence opinion in their own countries to prevent aid to the Republic. Even though all sided with their Spanish brethren, it is questionable how much influence the let-

37. *El mundo católico y la carta colectiva del episcopado español* (Burgos, 1938), pp. 5–6.

38. Ángel de Zumeta, a Basque priest, made this fact public soon after the letter was published; apparently Bishop Múgica told him so. See Rodríguez Aisa, pp. 251–53.

39. Ricardo de la Cierva, *La historia se confiesa: España 1930–1976* (Barcelona, 1976), IV, 23, points out that the letter was "an absolutely logical document" for the Church to have produced against an enemy determined to liquidate it; furthermore, he says, "the most visible absences among the bishops were not the three [sic] who refused to sign it but the twelve assassinated and one in prison who could *not* sign it."

40. One of the most interesting commentaries is that of the former Jesuit Joan Vilar i Costa (J.V.C.), *Montserrat: glosas a la carta colectiva de los obispos españoles* (Barcelona, 1938), a 389-page work analyzing the letter line by line, purporting to show its variance from accepted Christian opinion; it is probably the longest single-volume polemic published during the war. Among modern commentators Pierre Broué and Emile Témime, p. 434, note that the letter "was one of the few texts that tried to justify the Nationalist movement in a rational and intelligent way." Cárcel Ortí, p. 379, says that the letter allowed the Nationalists to do as they pleased without fear of reproach from the bishops. Azpiazu, p. 53, agrees that the letter meant that the Church would suppress information about the Franco regime's criminal atrocities. Rafael Abella, *La España nacional*, p. 179, says that many Spanish Catholics opposed the bishops' stance but kept silent because of wartime conditions.

ter had.[41] Only Mexico and the Soviet Union were openly aiding the Republic: one was officially anticlerical and the other officially atheist, and the letter had no effect on either. As for swaying opinion in the democracies, particularly France, the United States, and Great Britain, by 1937 opinion had already hardened, and it is doubtful that the letter had much effect there (See chapters 12, 13, and 14).

In fact, the collective letter was only one of a number of compromising positions taken by the clergy in support of the Nationalists. But the letter was useful to the Nationalists in that it provided, among other things, a characterization of the Republicans as being communist directed (and communism was a doctrine upon which the Church had a clear and precise doctrine), and the letter downplayed the political and social aspects of the war and its origins to emphasize that the war was primarily a religious conflict.[42] This fact alone made the Nationalists' task infinitely easier.

It is tempting today, half a century after the event, to argue that the bishops sacrificed their ideals for institutional survival. The problem is not that simple. They clearly saw that the Church could not perform its functions, could not act as leaven in the hearts of men if it did not survive. And they believed that they were not simply fighting the inroads of secularism—as were all the Christian churches in the world—but that they were engaged in a mortal struggle with the personification of the Antichrist. There is little wonder that they rallied so strongly against the apocalyptic enemy and compromised themselves with a friendly regime, no matter what its defects. Indeed, it is easier to wonder at Vidal's stance. The tragic effect of the collective letter and the bishops' position was that it compromised the Church in ways not intended. The bishops had hoped to sway foreign opinion; they instead compromised themselves with a regime that had already begun to commit wartime and reprisal atrocities that no Christian—and especially no cleric—should allow. Thus, the tragedy was compounded: nearly one-eighth of the Spanish clergy were killed by violent anticlericals; the other seven-eighths found themselves compromised by a violent and barbarous regime. They did not protest their protectors' cruel ways, and the fury came to be compounded by the scandal of silence.

---

41. Caro Baroja, p. 238, comments, "the letter convinced, as always, those who were already convinced."

42. Ruíz Rico, p. 46.

CHAPTER 8

The Clergy's Support
of the Nationalists

The clergy and practicing Catholics generally supported the Nationalist cause, openly in Nationalist Spain, secretly in Republican Spain. On the surface it appears predictable. They had been the targets of anticlerical legislation before the war and anticlerical violence after the war began. It was to be expected that they would defend both their persons and their institutions under mortal attack by supporting those who were fighting Republican anticlericals.[1]

But this response was not based solely on the anticlerical fury. There were some clergy and laity who saw the war as an opportunity firmly to establish in all of Spain the Catholic cultural ethic that was under attack.[2] Many other clergy and laity supported the Nationalists because they also agreed with the political positions of the Nationalists' component groups. They believed that not only would the Church be better protected under a restoration of the monarchy or the establishment of a fascist state but also Spain would be better off under a more conservative, authoritarian, antiliberal, antidemocratic state. It is difficult to separate these religious and political convictions, and in fact both were frequently involved in decisions of support.[3]

---

1. Although the manifesto of the uprising did not mention either religion or the Church (the document is in Iturralde, II, 22–26), the clerical writer Ángel García, *La iglesia española y el 18 de julio* (Barcelona, 1977), p. 299, says that only a fool would ask why the clergy did not remain impartial during the war.

2. Lannon, "Modern Spain," p. 586, says "Official ecclesiastical support for the rising did not find its origin . . . in horror at the murder of priests and nuns. . . . It originated in persistent patterns of Catholic thinking which upheld the ideal of a totally Catholic society and state from which heterodox elements should be expunged."

3. Gomá, in a report to the Holy See, October 24, 1936, commented that the war and the fury had created a revival of the practice of Catholicism. In Antonio Marquina Barrio, *La diplomacia Vaticana y la España de Franco (1936–1945)* (Madrid, 1983), p. 46.

The single most important group of Catholics who supported the Nationalists without regard to the fury were the Carlists. Their party, the *Comunión Tradicionalista*, had opposed the anticlerical legislation in the Cortes since 1931, and individual Carlist leaders had been involved in the conspiracy behind the uprising of 1936. They were committed ideologues who believed that the Republic, because it rejected Catholic monarchist principles, was intrinsically wrong.[4]

These were the most exalted Catholics of all. Ideologically committed to the establishment of a clerically dominated state and society even before the war began, they saw the war as an opportunity to realize their dreams. They were from the regions of Spain where there was little or no anticlericalism, where the people tended, in the main, to be solidly behind the clergy. They were convinced that religion was the cement of society and that Spain could be Spain only if it was totally and exclusively Catholic. Their ancestors had fought the liberals in the nineteenth century; defeated in numerous battles over the years, they had nonetheless remained devoted to their hopes. Just as the uprising offered the anticlericals the opportunity of realizing their dream of a priestless Spain, so also did it offer the Carlists the possibility of realizing theirs of a totally Catholic Spain, monarchical, traditionalist, and clerical.[5] The young men of Navarre flocked to the cities to join the *requetés* (the Carlist military units), and their priests went with them to serve as their chaplains and to shrive them before they left for the front. For the Carlists the war was nothing less than a religious crusade, and especially so after news of the anticlerical fury came through. But while they were ideologues who could justify any action in the name of religion, they tended to be more merciful to conquered enemy troops and thus were constantly at odds with Falangists and others on the question of reprisals taken against both enemy soldiers and the civilian population. Above all they demanded that any enemy be allowed to confess (receive the sacrament of penance) to a priest before execution.[6] The Carlist requetés

---

4. Palacio Atard, "La guerra," p. 1179, claims that they did not even take the fury into their calculations.

5. In a letter to Franco on October 7, 1936, in Marquina Barrio, *La diplomacia Vaticana*, p. 47, the leaders of the Comunión Tradicionalista expressed their opposition to the Nationalist leader's broadcast that although the new Spanish state was not a confessional state, it gave full liberty and recognition to the Church; the Carlists argued that Catholicism was in fact the essence of Spain.

6. See Martin Blinkhorn, *Carlism and Crisis in Spain, 1931–1939* (Cambridge, 1975), pp. 261ff.; Jaime del Burgo, *Conspiración y guerra civil* (Madrid, 1970), pp. 76ff.; and the memoirs of Juan Urra Lusarreta, *En la trincheras del frente de Madrid (memo-*

themselves heard mass and confessed before they went into battle; their courage and idealism were remarkable, confirming the folk saying that "there is no animal in all creation more ferocious than a newly confessed requeté."[7]

A second group of clergy and laity who supported the Nationalists were Catholic moderates who had formed the ranks of the CEDA before the uprising. They were neither anti-Republican nor antidemocratic, but they were opposed to the anticlerical laws and violence, and by the time the war broke out they had come to realize that the Republic as it was then constituted could never command the allegiance of Catholics.[8] Many were neutral at first or gave the uprising grudging support, but this attitude could not be maintained long, for they became liable to assassination as any cleric during the fury. Some 20 percent of the CEDA Cortes deputies of 1933–36 were assassinated during the terror, a higher proportion than the clergy.[9] Most became disillusioned, rather than fervid, supporters of the Nationalists; they supported Franco less out of conviction than necessity. Their leader, José María Gil Robles, sought exile in Portugal when the war broke out, but before the end of 1936 he came out in support of the Nationalists.[10] The only significant faction among the Cedists to give fervid support to the Nationalists was their youth group under the leadership of Ramón Serrano Suñer (who later became Franco's foreign minister and brother-in-law).[11]

The other group of monarchists, Alfonso's supporters, also joined the Nationalists, but their primary aim was a restoration of the monarchy, although they believed that the Church was an essential part of any Spanish monarchy. Numerous clerics supported these monarchists, including most of the bishops, practically all of them appointees of Alfonso before 1931.

---

rias de un capellán de requetés, herido de guerra) (Madrid, 1967), who joined the Carlists as a chaplain and captures the essence of the crusade feeling.

7. Abella, La España nacional, p. 172.

8. Indeed, their willingness to support any form of government that protected church rights had led to division among the rightists and bitter opposition from the monarchists against the CEDA. See Robinson, pp. 105ff., 242ff.

9. Tusell Gómez, II, 269.

10. Ángel Herrera Ória, one of the founders of the CEDA, by 1936 was studying for the priesthood in Switzerland and sent a commendatory wire to Gil Robles immediately after the uprising in the mistaken belief that Gil Robles was remaining neutral. Ibid., II, 269.

11. The other party leader, Luis Lucía, was arrested first by the Republicans, and after he was released, by the Nationalists, and spent most of his remaining years in a Nationalist prison.

The Falange attracted many younger Catholics. Its leader, José Antonio Primo de Rivera, stressed the party's Hispanic identity and rejected the paganism of the Nazis and Italian fascists, so that Catholics could view it as an authoritarian Catholic movement. There were also some priests who admired the Falange's ideals and saw it as the hope of a renewed and regenerated Spain.[12]

Many clergy and laity did, of course, support the Nationalists because they viewed them as their protectors against the anticlerical fury. Some were opposed to the Nationalists' aims; some saw the Falange as an unchristian organization; some were wary of the political and social oppressions that might occur in a military state; but whatever their reservations, they were all fearful of the fury. They wanted a restoration of law and order and protection for their lives, and if the Nationalists offered this at a price, the alternative was so frightening that they were willing to pay it.[13]

There was another factor in determining Catholic support for the Nationalists, although of less importance. This was the Nationalist regime's willingness to support demands for the restoration of a clerical state. Indeed, the restoration of clerical privileges was a matter of primary importance to the Nationalists in order to win and keep the support of the clergy and the faithful, although in fact nothing more than protection from the fury was necessary. As early as August 19, 1936, a month after the uprising, the Nationalist regime ordered teachers to use Catholic religious and moral principles as the basis of their teaching and by late September had banned "laic" schools completely. In the following years the anticlerical laws were abolished; the Jesuits were restored and religious education was established as the norm, not the exception.[14]

There was also a process of mutual advantage between generals and bishops that had repercussions beyond simple support. The generals denounced the anticlerical fury, and the bishops supported the uprising; in turn, this support served the anticlericals as justification for the fury and made it more difficult for the Republican officials

---

12. Among the more publicized was Fermín Yzurdiaga, who became an official of the party and the editor of the Falange's newspaper in Pamplona. See Abella, *La España nacional*, p. 122.

13. Cárcel Ortí, pp. 365–67, says that most responsible clergy did not support the uprising but that they, and most Catholics, soon came to support the Nationalists, but not the Falange or the Carlists. Their argument was similar to that of the Basque autonomists who said that they were not supporting the communists and socialists but rather they were fighting alongside them against a common enemy.

14. For most of the new laws see Cárcel Ortí, pp. 377–78, 386.

to halt it; and this continuation of the fury led to increased clerical support for the Nationalists.[15]

Beyond support there is the more important question of responsibility, particularly for the clergy. How responsible were they for the Nationalist atrocities, for the reprisals, the executions of innocent people, the imprisonment and suffering of those whose only crime was holding political office under the Republic, even before the war began, or who had openly supported Republican political parties? The answers to these questions depend to a great extent upon how much influence the clergy had, and in these instances support and influence were tied together.

The clergy supported the Nationalists at several different levels. Some kinds of support were more publicized than others, and some were more influential than others. Part of the problem of assessing clerical responsibility arises from the confusion over these different kinds of support. Much of both the domestic and foreign anticlerical propaganda stems from the inability to distinguish among these different levels.

At the most primitive and emotional level were priests who actively engaged in combat. They went with the armies as chaplains, but once in battle they fought alongside the soldiers. Two Carlist priests captured while fighting, when asked by their captors why they violated God's commandment against killing, responded: "That has nothing to do with the present situation. Today it is not a matter of fulfilling God's commandments; rather it is a question of wanting God to live in the souls of the people."[16] A chaplain who wore a pistol in his belt and boasted that he had killed "over a hundred marxists" described killing one who had hidden in a confessional in the Badajoz cathedral.[17] There was a priest in Majorca who accompanied execution squads with a pistol.[18] Some chaplains urged the troops on while not actively engaging in combat themselves. One soldier, in battle near Madrid, described a Jesuit who "advanced in front of us carrying a cross, and urging us on. . . . What bravery he displayed—with-

---

15. Hilari Raguer, "El Vaticano y la guerra civil española (1936–1939)," *Cristianesimo nella Storia* 3 (April 1982), p. 143, says that through this process of acceleration "the uprising acquired a religious character it did not originally have."

16. Enrique Castro Delgado, *Hombres made in Moscú* (Barcelona, 1965), p. 273.

17. Bahamonde, pp. 65–67.

18. According to Georges Bernanos, *A Diary of My Times*, trans. P. Morris (London, 1938), p. 104. Azpiazu, p. 49, describes Carlist priests bearing arms, and the historian of Carlism, Martin Blinkhorn, p. 259, claims that when Carlist commanders were killed in battle, chaplains sometimes took over command in the field.

out touching a rifle."[19] A foreign volunteer who joined the Carlists described the company chaplain who gave the last sacraments to wounded and dying soldiers and then began to urge the men to fire at the fleeing enemy: "he kept pointing out targets to me urging me shrilly to shoot them down."[20]

These instances of men caught up in the emotion of war are isolated, and taken by themselves they have no more importance to the general picture than do the handful of priests who supported the Republic. Furthermore, they were condemned by the bishops to the extent that any army veteran who entered a seminary after the war (or any seminarian who had volunteered for active duty) had to delay ordination for two years, so concerned were the bishops that the clergy not have blood on their hands.[21] Nor were the Nationalist leaders pleased to have such priests fighting for them in an army whose strength was its discipline.[22]

Still at a fairly primitive level was the support the clergy gave in the form of a military chaplaincy. This was a traditional form of support that extended beyond the issues of the war. Every modern army had its chaplaincy corps, and as any clergy supports its government in wartime, so the Spanish clergy in the Nationalist zone supported the regime. That it was technically in rebellion against a legitimate government made no difference, for the clergy believed that the Republican government had forfeited its rights. So traditional was this kind of support that the Republicans themselves established a military chaplaincy, albeit in the final days of the war.

Along with the military chaplaincy went all the symbolism of support: clergy in attendance at military parades and functions, military presence in processions and masses, neither of them unexceptional in wartime, but nevertheless widely publicized.[23] Another form of typically Spanish symbolism was the use of semiscapular medals called *detentes*, small patches of cloth portraying the Sacred Heart of Jesus, issued to soldiers to be sewn on uniforms, preferably over the heart, which were supposed to stop bullets.[24] These detentes were eagerly sought by the Moorish legions that Franco brought over from

---

19. Francisco Gutiérrez del Castillo, as cited in Fraser, p. 116.

20. Peter Kemp, *Mine Were of Trouble* (London, 1957), p. 80.

21. Montero Moreno, p. 74.

22. Abella, *La España nacional*, p. 170.

23. Iturralde, II, 457, claims that no public military function in Burgos took place without the presence of Archbishop Manuel García Castro Alonso.

24. *Detente* means "stop." The typical detente pictured a bleeding heart surmounted by a cross with the words "Stop bullet! The Sacred Heart of Jesus is with me!" printed around the edge. There is a photograph of one in Raymond Aldecoa, *Le Christ*

Africa to fight for the Nationalists, thereby creating the irony of Moslem Moors using Christian symbols to protect themselves.

But the symbols and the chaplaincy are relatively unimportant in assessing the clergy's responsibility in the war, chiefly because they were not that influential. Spaniards on either side probably did not pay much attention to these actions, or else viewed them as mere formalities, dictated by tradition. For, what Western army in any war in recent history has lacked chaplains and religiomilitary symbolism? There are more substantial actions upon which influence and responsibility can be based.

One of the least publicized, because of the scarcity of documentation, is the fiscal contribution of the clergy to the Nationalist war effort; this was particularly important because of the desperate need for foreign exchange. Among the few documents there is one particularly revealing episode. In September 1937 Cardinal Vidal, in exile, received a letter from Cardinal Joseph MacRory of Armagh, the primate of Ireland, apologizing because he could not answer Vidal's appeal for funds to be used to help clerical relief organizations in Republican Spain. He noted that he had sent 44,000 pounds sterling, collected in 1936 from Irish Catholics for the "ruined churches of Spain," to Cardinal Gomá, and said, "I believe that most of the money deposited in Cardinal Gomá's account was spent on munitions. I assume that when General Franco was told about our collection, his Eminence could not refuse him the money to be spent on munitions in spite of the fact that it was to be devoted to Catholic relief."

Vidal responded that he did not believe the money had been spent on war materiel; instead, he believed that MacRory had been confused over a banking transaction in which the funds offered to Gomá were withdrawn by Franco's agents in Ireland, while Franco transferred an equal amount of money in Spain to Gomá.

But Vidal's charitable view was rudely challenged by a letter he received from the Vatican in November 1937, two months later. He was told that Gomá had, after consulting with other bishops, informed MacRory and was now telling the Vatican that "in view of the greater needs of the military" and with the "hope that it would contribute to the Church's prestige," Gomá had given 32,000 pounds (of the original 44,000) to Franco to be spent on medical aid for the Nationalist army.[25] MacRory believed that the Irish contribution was spent on munitions. Gomá said he was donating it for medical aid. Whatever

---

Chez Franco, trans. Rolland-Simon (Paris, 1938), p. 128. Callahan, *Church, Politics, and Society,* p. 267, says detentes were first used by Carlists in 1873.

25. All of the documents are in Muntanyola, p. 361.

form it took, it was a sizable contribution to the Nationalist war effort at a crucial time.[26]

On the other hand, the most highly publicized, but not the most important, form of support was the ideological justification for the war. Bishops and other clerics devoted reams of paper to moral, ethical, and theological arguments in support of the Nationalists. The argument is examined in chapter 11: suffice it to say that if there were any Spaniards in doubt, the clergy provided the ideological justification for the Nationalist uprising.[27]

Yet, one gets the impression that these intellectual and ideological arguments were not very important, that it was at the personal level that the clergy had the greatest amount of influence. Rafael Abella fought in the Nationalist army, and he points out a great truth: for many Spaniards the ultimate decision to kill or to sacrifice one's life could be made only with some degree of religious commitment, religious persuasion, or religious justification.[28] On the great matters of life and death Spaniards—anticlerical or not—were conditioned by education and culture to consider these as religious questions. It is in making these decisions that the clergy's influence was felt at the deepest, most personal, and hence most responsible level. Nationalist troops who had to fight, soldiers who had to kill, men who had to serve on firing squads, human beings who had to sacrifice their lives for a cause, all expected spiritual direction in these matters; and they got it, for the clergy did not shirk their task. They preached sermons; they counseled and confessed the troops.

We have a record of what some said. The priest Justo Pérez de Urbel assured General Millán Astray that he had the secure knowledge of salvation because he was a crusader rescuing Spain for God.[29] But for the most part we must rely on soldiers' actions as proof of the clergy's counsel. It can be presumed that if they had any doubts or questions, they were counseled to fight and serve, for the clergy, certainly if they followed their bishops' statements and pastorals, considered the war a crusade.

If the bishops condemned the Republicans and their allies as communists, hordes of the antichrist, or as diabolically inspired, they also urged that the enemy be treated with mercy. This did not mean

---

26. Gomá's letter to Franco donating the money was made public at the time, November 7, 1936. See Gomá, *Por Dios,* pp. 533–35.

27. See Ruíz Rico, p. 46. Lannon, "Modern Spain," p. 588, says "the rhetoric of national catholicism clothed the ideological nakedness of the military rising."

28. Rafael Abella, *La España nacional,* pp. 171–72.

29. Cited in Raguer, *La Unio Democratica,* p. 309.

that the bishops proposed that their lives be spared, but rather that they be treated with dignity and above all that they be allowed to confess if captured and executed. Marino Ayerra Redín, a Navarrese priest who was forced into exile by the Nationalists before the war ended, described some of the sermons he heard as proposing biblical injunctions as justification for killing the enemy.[30] Dionisio Ridruejo, the Falangist leader in Segovia, heard a sermon in which the priest called for death to the enemy: "This is no time for scruples!"[31] Antonio Ruíz Vilaplana, a magistrate in Burgos, described a sermon he heard in the Burgos cathedral calling for revenge against the Republican enemy and claims that he heard of another priest who became overcome with emotion while distributing communion and cried out for revenge, saying that destroyers of churches and murderers of priests should not be pardoned.[32]

The clergy's greatest scandal occurred in their involvement with reprisals against both Republican soldiers and militiamen and against civilians arrested by the purge committees in those areas which the Nationalists had conquered.[33]

The purge committees were set up to investigate and recommend for trial or release those persons who were believed to have been leftists before the war began, or to have supported leftists, or to have committed criminal acts after the war began. Within this wide net could be found politicians and civil servants who had supported or worked for left Republican and working-class parties as well as violent anticlericals, executioners, and members of revolutionary committees (which were the purge committees' opposite number). Highly placed persons were usually executed immediately; others were taken to makeshift prisons, often the same seminary buildings which the revolutionary committees had used to house prisoners, and then tried and sentenced. In many cases the same procedures of denunciation were used in these trials as were used in the revolutionary tribunals that tried rightists. Frequently the prisoners were executed at night

---

30. Marino Ayerra Redín, *No me avergoncé del evangelio (desde me parroquia)* (2nd ed., Buenos Aires, 1959), p. 52.

31. In Fraser, p. 166.

32. Antonio Ruíz Vilaplana, *Burgos Justice*, trans. W.H. Carter (New York, 1938), pp. 177–78. The original Spanish edition is titled *Doy fe*. Bahamonde, pp. 61–73, describes similar sermons at Rota and Badajoz.

33. Salas Larrázabal, pp. 428–29, estimates that some 35,000 civilians were executed by the Nationalists during the war and 23,000 civilians and soldiers after 1939. Jackson, *Entre la reforma*, p. 392, claims between 150,000 and 200,000 executions from 1936 to 1944.

near cemeteries in much the same way that rightists were killed by the uncontrollables.[34] In fact, it could be argued that there were rightist uncontrollables; probably the Nationalist authorities allowed the white terror as a way of relieving the frustration of war and the immense passions of revenge built up by the red terror.[35]

The clergy were involved. Sometimes they were members of local purge committees, along with other prominent rightists; more often they were chaplains in prisons where the accused and convicted were held. They were confessors to the executed. They were also close to those in authority, so that they were in a position to plead for clemency, leniency, and mercy. Whether the authorities listened to them is another matter. But there were clerics who worked behind the scenes to mitigate the white terror. In Medina Sidonia (Andalusia) the local priest saved the Republican schoolmaster from execution; another priest refused to sanction the reprisals by hearing the condemneds' confessions.[36] Cardinal Gomá congratulated Joaquín Baleztena, the Carlist chief in Pamplona, for his orders after the uprising that Carlists were to avoid reprisals and were to prevent them where possible.[37] The Jesuit Fernando Huidobro called upon the military authorities to establish norms for execution, arguing that persons should not be condemned to death simply for belonging to leftist organizations or even for fighting for their ideals.[38]

Bishop Marcelino Olaechea of Pamplona was troubled by the war and repression. He was a native Basque, the bishop of the province of Navarre, the spiritual leader of the most aggressive and religiously exalted troops on the Nationalist side. As the son of a worker, he was sympathetic to the downtrodden, but he did not condone the violent anticlericalism. Two anti-Nationalist priests, Iñaki de Azpiazu and Marino Ayerra Redín, found him to be most sympathetic to their problems. To the former, fleeing from the anti-Basque persecution,

---

34. Bahamonde, pp. 58ff., witnessed some of the executions in his capacity as Quiepo de Llano's propaganda chief, and the similarities to anticlerical assassinations are striking.

35. Ayerra, p. 88, denies attributing reprisals to uncontrollables, because, he says, there was regimentation and order on the Nationalist side.

36. Mintz, pp. 284, 288. Abella, *La España nacional*, p. 173, claims that such priests were in a minority.

37. In Fraser, p. 169.

38. See Rafael M. Sanz de Diego, S.J., "Actitud del P. Huidobro, S.J., ante la ejecución de prisioneros en la guerra civil. Nuevos datos," *Estudios Eclesiásticos* 60 (Oct.–Nov., 1985), pp. 443–84. Bahamonde, pp. 67–68, reports that he knew of at least one instance of a priest who was assassinated by Falangists for complaining about the reprisals. Iturralde, II, 427–28, cites the case of two Franciscan priests killed for supporting oppressed peasants.

Olaechea promised refuge.[39] Olaechea purposely sent the latter to the parish of Alsasua, a left Republican town in the midst of Carlist Navarre, because the Bishop knew that Ayerra would be sympathetic to the townspeople.[40]

When the war broke out, Olaechea at first refused to lend himself to Nationalist propaganda or even to bless the troops.[41] Then, within a few weeks he was persuaded to sign the pastoral instruction of August 6, written by Cardinal Gomá (see chapter 6). While there was no combat in his diocese, there was repression of leftists, and as the war progressed, his faithful were fighting over all Spain for the Nationalists.

On August 15, 1936, a notorious reprisal occurred. According to Ayerra, who says he was told the story by Antonio Añoveros (later bishop of Cádiz, and then Bilbao), who was an eyewitness to the event, some fifty leftists were executed in Pamplona, shot after being allowed to confess (although Falangists and Carlists argued with each other over the time allotted for confession); at the same time a procession celebrating the feast of the Assumption wound its way through the streets of Pamplona and into the cathedral, and some of the Carlists who had participated in the executions joined in the procession.[42] Olaechea, who was not aware of the reprisal at the time, gave a sermon at the mass which followed the procession in which he said, "This is not war! This is a crusade! And the Church, while she asks God for peace and the sparing of bloodshed among all of her children—those who love her and fight to defend her as well as those who hate her and want to destroy her—cannot do less than put herself on the side of the crusaders."[43]

Three months later, after hearing reports of numerous reprisals including the executions of the Basque autonomist priests, Olaechea gave a memorable sermon. To a group of Catholic Actionists in Pamplona he urged pardon and forgiveness of the enemy. He especially urged that no more blood be shed by special tribunals charged with trying leftists: "No more bloodshed!" he urged. "If your son or brother or companion is killed, do not swear vengeance. True Christians do not swear vengeance."[44]

Except for this particular sermon there is no recorded public con-

---

39. Azpiazu, pp. 23ff.
40. Ayerra, pp. 10–12.
41. Iturralde, II, 299–300.
42. Ayerra, pp. 80–85. The Carlist leader Jaime del Burgo, p. 88, denies that the reprisal happened on that day.
43. In Ayerra, p. 83.
44. In Raguer, *La espada*, pp. 163–65.

demnation of the reprisals. Manuel Azaña, from his presidential palace, noted in September 1937 that since the beginning of the war he had not heard anyone in authority in the Church speak words of peace, charity, or pardon.[45] Azaña had not read or else he had ignored papal and episcopal statements, even the controversial collective letter of 1937, all of which had called for forgiveness for the persecutors of the clergy. Perhaps what he meant was that there was no vigorous addressing of the injustice and inhumanity of the reprisals; and, indeed, that was a scandal. Cardinal Gomá did not speak out: he commented privately on European reaction to the reprisals in a letter to Cardinal Pizzardo in Rome, noting that while the reprisals should be condemned as sins against charity and humanity, other Europeans did not understand the extent or horror of the Republican crimes: "What happens in this war cannot be judged by the same criteria as in an ordinary war."[46]

The clergy also had an important role in the political prisons of Nationalist Spain. As prison chaplains they had the opportunity to intervene with the authorities and also to serve as contacts with the prisoners' families. Most were charitable and kind, but some took advantage of their positions to berate the prisoners for their support of the Republic.[47] Prisoners were forced to attend weekly mass; many received communion out of fear of reprisals rather than out of feelings of sincere worship. Father Martín Torrent, a chaplain in the Nationalist prisons, pointed out the problems faced by the clergy with the large numbers of prisoners who wanted to confess and receive communion, and the clergy's fear that these prisoners might be doing so to impress the authorities so as to win early release. This problem was solved, he said, by ingeniously distributing communion in the prison galleries before mass was said and without the attendance of the authorities so that the prisoners would know that their reception of the sacrament would impress no one. As this resulted in no decline in numbers, Martín Torrent believed that all communicants were sincere. He further determined that in the Barcelona prison where he

---

45. Azaña, IV, 767.

46. Letter of May 25, 1937, in Rodríguez Aisa, pp. 451–52.

47. Escobal, p. 103, describes lectures by priests on morality during his two-year prison term and comments that "kindness and compassion have become such crimes that anyone moved to exercise them is immediately suspect and risks his life. Only the priests can express themselves freely without jeopardizing their personal security. But with some exceptions, the angels of peace, messengers of the Divine Word, are too busy kindling the flames of fratricidal fires from their very pulpits and with all their strength" (p. 7).

served after 1939, one-third of the prisoners complied with their Easter duty (to confess and commune once a year) and four percent communed weekly.[48]

In some areas "certificates of catholicity" were issued by priests; these were necessary to obtain employment or even to use as a protection against the white terror squads and official reprisals. The documents certified that a person had completed his Easter duty; lack of one could place a job in jeopardy.[49] The archbishop of Santiago issued a circular to his clergy forbidding them to give such certificates to known communists and marxists out of a misguided sense of charity to protect them against arrest and possible execution.[50] Such activity prompted many laymen and women to attend church services so that when the clergy commented that the war had brought people back to the Church, this was less from conviction than it was from the fact that it was politically and socially useful to do so.

In the final analysis, given all of the circumstances of the war and its background, Catholic support for the Nationalists was natural and logical. But was it necessary? Probably not. The Nationalists could never have afforded to antagonize or alienate the clergy and Catholics, who, after all, were their main base of support. But to infer from this that the clergy had the upper hand and could have remained neutral in the struggle ignores human nature. After the fury the clergy and the faithful were probably emotionally incapable of neutrality; they were committed to their protectors.

But the clergy could have moderated the violence. They supported the Nationalists, but this did not mean that they had to agree with everything the Nationalists did. While the clergy and the faithful depended on the protection of the regime in the early part of the war, from mid-1937 on this need lessened and at the end of the war disappeared altogether. After 1939 the regime was more depen-

---

48. Martín Torrent, *¿Qué me dice usted de los presos?* (Alcalá, 1942), pp. 15–18, 46–47, 67–69. Although Martín Torrent had great sympathy for the condemned, he argued that one who knows when he is going to die is much better off than one who does not, because he can prepare his soul, for the moment of death determines salvation or damnation. Despite such theological indulgences the fact was that in most cases the solace of confession was allowed, and this was more than the anticlericals allowed their victims.

49. Abella, *La España nacional*, p. 173. Abella also claims that parish clergy were asked to judge a person's degree of support for the Nationalist cause, and this fact was entered on his identification card. See "Daily Life, Nationalist Zone," *Historical Dictionary of the Spanish Civil War, 1936–1939*, ed. James W. Cortada (Westport, Conn., 1982), p. 159.

50. Cited in Raguer, *La espada*, p. 175.

dent on the clergy and the laity than they were on the regime. In this situation the clergy could have condemned the Nationalist reprisals and purges (which continued after the war ended), probably to great effect.[51]

It is this lack of a public condemnation that constitutes the great scandal of silence to which the clergy can be held accountable. Undoubtedly many felt that they could achieve more lasting good by working behind the scenes and that a vociferous condemnation of the Nationalists might prevent the opportunity to mitigate the reprisals; also they may have feared that a public condemnation might work to the advantage of a Republican victory or might bring down the Franco regime after the war, in both cases unleashing another anticlerical fury. But the argument is weak. Nationalist Spain was led by a practicing Catholic who used Catholicism as the ideological cement of the coalition he had forged. A condemnation would most likely have forced Franco to pressure his followers to stop the reprisals; certainly it would have had a powerful effect. Why, then, did the clergy not speak out?

It takes a certain amount of introspection and humility to see what the essentials of such complex situations are. Not all clerics—indeed, not all people—are capable of looking beyond their own needs to understand others'. In the case of the clergy it was enough that they understood institutional needs (which coincided with their own personal needs in 1936); to have asked them to understand humanity's needs would have been asking a great deal—as much as asking the anticlericals of 1936 to understand humanity's needs as well.

Religious wars are ideological wars. The enemy must not only be defeated but his ideas must also, and the enemy must be transformed. It was not enough that Republicans surrendered on the field of battle or that a dictatorial regime was imposed on them. Their ideas must be stamped out as well. Christian ideals were thus compromised for personal and institutional survival; and worse, for it became a positive good to kill for Christ's sake. This warping of Christ's message is what makes the clergy's support of the Nationalists and their silence in the face of the reprisals so reprehensible, and it makes the anticlerical fury seem justifiable (although in fact the fury in most cases preceded the support; yet the anticlericals were protesting years of Christian neglect). While there were countless good and merciful

---

51. Cárcel Ortí, pp. 379–80, one of the most insightful students of these matters, claims that a strong protest by the bishops would have moderated the reprisals considerably.

priests who tried to live the Christian ideals of love and brotherhood, it was the ecclesiastical hierarchy that attracted attention by their scandal of silence, and good men everywhere suffered because of it. Therein lies one of the great tragedies of the war.

CHAPTER 9

The Vatican and the
Nationalist Government

There is a mystique about the papacy that seduces Catholics. The pomp and ceremony, the emphatic declarations couched in the imperial plural, the infallible pronouncements, the majesty of being the Vicar of Christ—all of these lead believers to expect more from the pope than he can deliver. For whatever the pretensions of papal power, the fact is that the pope is a human being, the Vatican is a state, the Holy See is a diplomatic institution, and all of them are subject to the limitations inherent in their condition. The Church teaches that the pope is infallible only in matters of faith and morals and only when the pronouncement is delivered according to a ritual formula.[1] Otherwise the pope's decisions are only as good as the information he receives, and they are effective only to the extent that the faithful accepts them. These two limitations of knowledge and influence weigh heavily on any decision the pope makes: he must ask himself if his sources are reliable and he must act with the constant apprehension that his words will not be heeded; or worse, that he will be disobeyed and the disobedience itself may lead to schism.

Catholics who expect great things from the papacy, then, are usually disappointed. Most popes act prudently and cautiously when faced with any sort of crisis that has effects outside of religion, and more so when actual lives and fortunes are at stake. It is one thing to condemn ideas and ideologies; it is quite another to condemn specific men and actions. And wherein does a pope's power lie? Like the bishops, he has power and influence only over believers; and believers can

---

1. This has happened only twice in modern history: the proclamation of the Immaculate Conception by Pius IX in 1854 and the proclamation of the Assumption in 1950 by Pius XII; three times if the proclamation of papal infallibility itself by Pius IX in 1870 is included.

quickly become unbelievers if pressed to do something to which they object. Thus it was simple and easy for the pope to condemn anticlerical violence in Spain, for it was unlikely that the anticlericals would pay much attention to him, and no believer would object to such a condemnation. But it was more difficult to condemn Catholic Nationalists for atrocities; the condemnation might alienate them from the Church, might even be counterproductive, and might expose the Church itself to danger. There is a fine line between justice and prudence, and the popes have usually erred on the side of prudence.

Nor was Spain the pope's only concern. While it is true that the Church there was undergoing the most violent attack in its long history, the potential danger to the Church in Fascist Italy and Nazi Germany was also important, as well as the danger of Communist Russia to the Church in Eastern Europe. In Mexico the Church had been under attack from anticlerical governments for nearly two decades. In fact, not since the French Revolution of 1789 had the Church been faced with such worldwide potential for harm. In addition the Western world was attempting to recover from two great shattering crises—World War I and the Great Depression—while tottering on the brink of another world war. The pope could hardly devote most or even much of his time to Spain, especially when his options were limited by the circumstances of the war.

In two nonreligious areas, however, the papacy had influence over unbelievers and therefore greater hope of success. These were in providing the structure of a relief organization for war victims and of serving as a mediator in peace negotiations. In order to carry out these tasks (as it had done in other conflicts) the papacy had to observe a scrupulous neutrality. It could not be suspected by either side of partiality. In such cases the papacy acted simply as any secular organization (the International Red Cross, for example, or the disinterested party to a war); but of course it always had to be concerned with its own institutional survival, so that in the final analysis its effectiveness was limited when a national church was under attack.

Each pope has his own style. Achille Ratti, who became Pope Pius XI in 1922, was one of the most volatile and temperamental of modern popes. His early career was as a librarian and bibliographer, and then as a papal diplomat in wartime Poland, where he reportedly learned of the threat of Soviet Communism at first hand; thereafter a rigid anticommunism dominated his views.[2] As pope he was warm and affectionate with friends and with those who had suffered

---

2. Anthony Rhodes, *The Vatican in the Age of the Dictators, 1922–1945* (New

persecution, but he could just as easily lose his temper over trivial matters.[3] These outbursts of affection and irritation characterized his personal relations; yet public papal statements were more careful considerations, worked out in advance with the help of his aides and carefully worded following consultation with the papal secretary of state, Eugenio Pacelli. The temperamental antithesis of Pius XI, Pacelli was not given to displays of affection or irritation. He was intelligent, but he tended to overestimate the willingness of Catholics to forego political opinions for religious beliefs.[4]

Both the Pope and his Secretary of State were subject to the limitations of their information. Pacelli, as chief diplomat, had wider sources, and he was the filter through whom reports were sent to the Pope. His sources included reports from papal nuncios, bishops visiting Rome, foreign statesmen occasionally, and sometimes ordinary clerics petitioning or informing the Holy See. Once the Spanish war began, there came into being a Spanish Nationalist lobby in Rome composed of emigré aristocrats and clergy, including some of the bishops who had fled the fury. The exiled monarch, Alfonso XIII, was also in Rome. To counter these there were the reports of Cardinal Vidal i Barraquer in exile in Lucca but in touch with his Catalan see; Bishop Múgica, in exile in Rome and in touch with Basque Catholics; and other occasional priests and laymen. On the whole there were many more pro-Nationalist sources of information, and papal actions reflected these. There was also a powerful pro-Nationalist Jesuit lobby led by the Jesuit General in Rome, Wladimir Ledochowski. The Dominican superior in Rome, Martin Gillet, was less supportive of the Nationalists.[5]

Undoubtedly all of these people had an effect on the Pope, who was apparently more open to suggestion than was Pacelli, and who was correspondingly more disappointed by his sources when they proved wrong.[6] But in the end there was little he could do on a public level. On the private and personal level more could be accomplished,

---

York, 1973), p. 18. See also Carlo Falconi, *The Popes in the Twentieth Century* (Boston, 1967), pp. 151–233.

3. Llorens, p. 230, gives examples.

4. Cárcel Ortí, p. 353, claims that Pacelli was more sensitive to Spanish problems than Pius XI, but he never understood why Spanish Catholics of differing political opinions—fascist, monarchist, Carlist, Republican, autonomist—were unable to form a common front against communism. The Nationalist diplomats, on the other hand, found that Pacelli lacked confidence in Franco, and they said that he did not understand Spanish problems; this from Marquina Barrio, *La diplomacia Vaticana*, p. 158.

5. Raguer, "El Vaticano," p. 147.

6. Rhodes, p. 214, citing D.F. Binchey.

but here there is only sparse record of the Vatican's accomplishments, great or small.

The Pope and his advisors, while surprised by the intensity of the anticlerical fury, had for some time seen the possibility of conflict in Spain. And they had dealt with the anticlerical Republic for five years before the war. The Holy See's policy had been cautious and prudent. In the face of Republican anticlerical legislation the Holy See made numerous public and private protests (which were so routine as to be expected in any case), but it never broke off relations with Madrid, although it refused to accept the anticlerical Luis de Zulueta, the Republic's ambassadorial nominee during the Republic's first year. During the years of rightist government in 1933–35 the Holy See accepted Leandro Pita Romero as Spain's ambassador. Aside from shorter protests, the Pope had condemned the anticlerical legislation in a major encyclical, *Dilectissima Nobis* (June 1933), but this had no effect either upon the anticlerical Republicans or upon Catholic responses to Vatican desires for political unity.

During this entire period the Holy See's representative in Spain was Nuncio Federico Tedeschini, a moderate and an ally of Ángel Herrera Ória; he supported the progressive wing of the Church. Tedeschini had cordial relations with the moderate anticlerical Republicans. He made pro forma protests and believed that the best policy was one of conciliation. But the Holy See's policy was one of prudence, of which conciliation was only one face. For the other, the Pope appointed to the primacy of the Spanish Church as successor to the intransigent Cardinal Pedro Segura the equally intransigent but less temperamental Isidro Gomá. Ideologically alike, the two ecclesiastics represented that faction of the Church opposed to concessions to the Republicans: both hoped for a restoration of the monarchy. In a secret memorandum of a meeting Segura and Gomá had in France in 1934, both agreed that the Holy See's policy of conciliation was misguided, and Segura told Gomá that he found the Pope to be "a man without feeling, cold and calculating," an indication that Segura did not appeal to Pius' generally warm nature.[7]

This confidential statement from the two primates of Spain pointed to another problem the papacy had: the conflict between the

---

7. The memo was found among Gomá's papers in Toledo by Republicans during the fury and was later published, much to the embarrassment of Segura and Gomá; it is in Iturralde, I, 368–69. Garriga, p. 204, argues that the Pope appointed Gomá to the primacy so that he would have an intransigent opponent of the Republic in case the policy of conciliation supported by Tedeschini and Vidal should fail; Cárcel Ortí, p. 379, says that Gomá's appointment was indicative of Pius' true feelings toward the Republic and signified that the Holy See was going to take a harder line.

Vatican and national hierarchies. This was an age-old problem in the Church, for bishops had generally resented papal interference in their diocesan and national affairs. The problem had become less intense with the development of the ultramontane church of the late nineteenth century, but there were still bishops who felt Vatican officials and often the pope himself to be inadequately informed about affairs in the bishops' own countries. Generally, national hierarchies tended to adopt political (and hence short-range) stances to problems, while the papacy was more interested in social solutions (and hence long-range attitudes). It was not a problem that could be easily resolved, and the Spanish war certainly pointed out these differences.

After the Popular Front's electoral victory of February 1936 Tedeschini was recalled to Rome (a routine change, as Tedeschini had been made a cardinal in late 1935, and cardinals rarely serve as nuncios). Another moderate, the former nuncio to Argentina and Paraguay, Felipe Cortesi, was appointed to Madrid; and the Holy See accepted the anticlerical Luis de Zulueta this time as a replacement for Pita Romero. Presumably the situation in Spain had become so difficult and uncertain that moderate conciliation, at least on the surface, was the most prudent policy.[8]

When the war began in July 1936 and the anticlerical fury broke out, there was stunned silence in the Vatican at the violence of the attack. If the Pope and Pacelli listened to anyone at first, it was probably Cardinal Vidal, the first important churchman to escape the fury and get to Italy. From the beginning Vidal urged the Vatican to stay out of the conflict for fear of aggravating the problem.[9] He believed that any public statements would simply lead to increased persecution of Catholics in the Republican zone. Pacelli sent a formal protest to Ambassador Zulueta, who responded that he deplored the excesses, but the clergy were supporting the rebels in a wartime situation and they could not expect to be free from danger; he specifically cited Múgica's and Olaechea's August pastoral instruction.[10] On a private level the Vatican urged the French and Italian governments to aid in the evacuation of the clergy whose lives were in danger, and those two powers helped greatly.[11]

But the Vatican was not helping the Nationalists. The under secretary of state, Giuseppe Pizzardo, had supported the moderate

---

8. See my article "The Second Spanish Republic and the Holy See," *The Catholic Historical Review* 49 (April 1963), p. 67.

9. Muntanyola, pp. 395ff.

10. In Antonio Marquina Barrio, "El Vaticano contra la cruzada," *Historia 16* 22 (February 1978), pp. 41–42.

11. Raguer, "El Vaticano," p. 147.

Tedeschini's policy during the prewar period, and he urged the Pope and Pacelli to avoid a complete rupture with the Republic. Throughout the period of the fury the Vatican vacillated. At first the Pope was persuaded by Jesuit General Ledochowski that the fury was not simply a new and more violent expression of traditional Spanish anticlericalism but was in fact inspired by Soviet Russia as part of a plan to destroy religion everywhere; later, however, after the Nationalist executions of the Basque priests, the Pope came to feel that the Nationalists were as bad as the Republicans.[12]

The first public papal statement on the conflict came on September 14, 1936, when at his summer retreat at Castel Gandolfo Pius addressed a group of some 500 Spaniards, mainly clergy, including some emigré bishops, most of them ardently pro-Nationalist. Copies of the speech were distributed afterwards; it was not an extemporaneous statement and appeared to have been carefully thought out. In the speech the Pope emotionally sympathized with the persecuted clergy, calling their deaths "martyrdom in the full, sacred, and glorious meaning of the word." He lamented the outrage and cruelty and asked, "What is to be said when we are face-to-face with the stories of brothers killing brothers, which are daily being told?" He saw the persecution as a "satanic preparation" similar in kind to those in Russia, China, South America, and Mexico (an obvious reference to international communism), and he claimed that wherever in the world obstacles were placed in the way of Catholics, these aided the forces of subversion. After further analyzing the evils afflicting modern society in general, Pius bestowed his blessing upon "the defenders of God and religion" but warned that "it is only too easy for the very ardor and difficulty of defense to go to an excess. . . . Intentions less pure, selfish interests, and mere party feeling may easily enter into, cloud, and change the morality and responsibility for what is being done." After this warning against Nationalist attempts to use religion for partisan purposes, he ended his speech with an emotional plea for the persecutors:

> What is to be said of all these others who also are so near and never cease to be Our sons, in spite of the deeds and methods of persecution so odious and cruel against persons and things to Us so dear and sacred? . . . We cannot . . . doubt as to what is left for us to do—to love them and to love them with a special love born of mercy and compassion.[13]

12. Marquina Barrio, "El Vaticano," p. 40.

13. In L'Osservatore Romano, September 14–15, 1936, p. 1. There is an English translation in The Catholic Mind 34 (October 8, 1936), pp. 385–94.

Some of those attending this audience were so disturbed by the Pope's plea for forgiveness that they threw their copies to the floor as they left, and the Nationalist press never published the full text of the speech; instead it emphasized those portions referring to martyrdom and international subversion without mentioning the plea for forgiveness.[14]

This speech, a brief mention in the Pope's Christmas message of December 1936, and an oblique reference to Spain in his March 1937 encyclical *Divini Redemptoris* were the only public statements the Pope made on the Spanish war. In the meantime other representations were being made at the diplomatic level

Vatican recognition of the Nationalist regime, which came formally in May 1938, was preceded by informal recognition with the naming and sending of representatives. Meanwhile the Holy See did not formally break relations with the Republican government. It could be claimed that the Vatican thus kept its options open so that it would have representation with the victor, whoever won the war. More likely the Vatican was not as interested in standing in good stead with the victor as it was in having some form of representation with both parties so that it could work to protect the clergy and the Church's rights and possibly serve as mediator. But the fact is that in recognizing the Nationalists, a regime technically in rebellion against the Republican government, the Vatican lost the credibility of neutrality, and if its good offices were to be sought for mediation, it would be only a desperation move on the part of the Republicans. Pacelli knew this, but given the nature of the conflict and the possibility of problems with the Nationalists, the most prudent course was to work with the Republicans wherever able in order to alleviate the suffering of Catholics and at the same time to curry favor with the Nationalists so that the Church would not suffer persecution from them (as was happening to some German clergy and laity in Nazi Germany) and perhaps even to obtain a privileged position in the new regime. This policy became apparent only after 1937 when it appeared that the Nationalists would win the war, and as that likelihood increased, so did the strength of the Vatican's diplomatic representation to Burgos, the seat of the Nationalist government.[15]

---

14. Raguer, "El Vaticano," p. 152. In his citation of the document Montero Moreno, p. 741, reproduces only five paragraphs, and the *Espasa Calpe* encyclopedia article, pp. 1551–52, while citing longer portions, refers neither to the Pope's warning against the Nationalists nor to the plea for mercy.

15. The history of Nationalist-Vatican relations (with emphasis on negotiations for a concordat) is explained in detail in Marquina Barrio, *La diplomacia Vaticana.*

But this was not apparent at first. In 1936 the probable winner of the war could only be guessed at, so the Vatican played a passive diplomatic role. The Burgos government sent Antonio Magaz to Rome as its ambassador to the Holy See, but the Vatican did not accredit him or recognize the Burgos regime. Luis de Zulueta remained accredited as Spain's ambassador. However, the embassy employees, at Magaz' urging, refused to work for Zulueta, and he left Rome for Paris at the end of September 1936. Magaz occupied the embassy, but the Holy See refused to recognize him. In Republican Spain, at the nunciature in Madrid, Silverio Sericano was the chargé as the nuncio, Felipe Cortesi, had not arrived to take up his new post by the time the uprising began, and he was now delayed indefinitely (Cortesi was named nuncio to Warsaw in 1937).

Magaz wanted to obtain Vatican recognition of the Nationalist regime, but he failed, chiefly because the rebellion had not succeeded and the execution of the Basque priests by the Nationalists in October 1936 angered the Pope. Nor was Magaz' criticism of the Vatican's neutral policy welcome; it was clear by the end of 1936 that he had outstayed his effectiveness.[16]

A great deal of anti-Nationalist feeling still existed in Rome when Cardinal Gomá visited at the beginning of December 1936. He talked to émigrés and Vatican officials. He met with Pacelli and impressed upon him that the Vatican was not getting the correct news from Spain. He argued that all good Catholics were supporting the Nationalists, that the Burgos government offered the best hope for the Church, that most of its officials and supporters were practicing Catholics, and that someday soon the Holy See would find it useful and necessary to recognize it.[17] Four days later the Pope received Gomá from his sickbed and told him to convey his special blessing to General Franco. From there Gomá went to see Pacelli, who informed him that the Pope had named the Primate as "the Holy See's confidential and semiofficial representative to the Nationalist Government." At the same time Pacelli told Gomá to inform Franco that the General had all the Vatican's sympathies and desires for a quick victory.[18]

Gomá and Franco got along well. Gomá admired Franco, and it

---

16. Raguer, "El Vaticano," pp. 159–65.

17. Letter from Gomá to Pacelli, December 15, 1936, in Granados, pp. 94–96.

18. From Gomá's diary, December 19, 1936, in Granados, p. 97. If Pacelli had wished to keep the appointment confidential and secret, as implied in Gomá's new title, he had made a mistake, for immediately after Franco and Gomá met, the news was released to the press.

was to Franco's advantage to curry favor with the Church.[19] But there were points of disagreement: the Vatican was opposed to fascist, particularly Nazi, influence among the Nationalists, and it wanted the Republican anticlerical legislation abolished. At their first meeting in Gomá's new diplomatic capacity in late December 1936 Franco assured the Primate that he would not act unilaterally on church problems and that he could not abolish the anticlerical legislation immediately but would do so at the most opportune time.[20] A few months later, in March 1937, Franco expanded on this last point: he told Gomá that the anticlerical legislation was a dead letter, but he could not abolish all of it because he was still dependent on help from both Spaniards and foreigners who might oppose such a move; when he was able to act freely, he assured Gomá, the legislation would be abolished.[21]

Was Franco really fearful of losing the support of Nationalist anticlericals and German aid, or was he simply informing Gomá in couched language that he would support the Vatican's request in return for a concession—namely, full diplomatic recognition? It is difficult to say.[22] Gomá polled the bishops in Spain to ask them if they felt the Burgos regime should be recognized, and most responded affirmatively. He then presented a petition for such a move to the Holy See, but there was no favorable response.[23] The anticlerical laws were not abolished in 1937.

While Gomá and Franco parlayed over problems, the Pope issued three encyclical letters in March 1937. The first, *Mit Brennender Sorge,* was addressed to the German bishops: it denounced Hitler's violation of the 1933 concordat and condemned the Nazi doctrine of racial superiority. The second, *Divini Redemptoris,* on communism, was addressed to the whole world. In condemning communist doctrines the Pope devoted one paragraph (out of eighty-four) to Spain: he said the communist fury had destroyed churches and clergy, "above all those who have been devoting their lives to the working classes

---

19. Franco was a practicing Catholic, although not a fervent one; his court historian, Ricardo de la Cierva, *La historia se confiesa,* IV, 38, claims that he was greatly influenced on religious policy by his wife and her personal chaplain. Marquina Barrio, *La diplomacia Vaticana,* p. 60, says that Catholicism meant a great deal to Franco, but he had no intention of letting either the bishops or the Vatican influence his politico-religious policy.

20. Letter from Gomá to Pacelli, January 1, 1937, in Rodríguez Aisa, pp. 401–3.

21. From Gomá's observations of a meeting on March 3, 1937, in Granados, p. 107.

22. See Marquina Barrio, *La diplomacia Vaticana,* pp. 43ff.

23. Letter from Gomá to Pacelli, April 7, 1937, in Rodríguez Aisa, pp. 420–25.

and the poor," and that laymen "of all conditions and classes" have been slain for no other reason "than the fact that they are good Christians or at least opposed to Atheistic Communism."[24] The third encyclical, *Firmissimam Constantiam*, was addressed to the Mexican bishops, offering them counsel and direction in their struggle against the anticlerical Mexican government. After urging them to work for social justice and religious rights, the Pope said that if religious and civil liberties were attacked, then citizens had the right to defend themselves: with reservation and caution he stated that such defensive actions must not be intrinsically evil, that they must not do greater damage than the harm they seek to repair, and that the clergy must avoid any violence or lending themselves to political use.[25]

Although there was direct reference to Spain only in the second of these encyclicals, the German letter can be seen as a warning to Franco and the Nationalists about the pagan doctrines of their allies. It was not published in any of Spain's newspapers, apparently at Franco's and Gomá's wishes: Gomá told Pacelli that publication would hurt the Falange, "which has more or less Hitlerian tendencies," just when Franco was unifying the forces of the right, and this would have a detrimental effect upon the Nationalist military effort.[26] Only at the express wish of the Holy See was the German encyclical published in some diocesan papers and in the Spanish Jesuit monthly *Razón y Fe*.[27]

The Mexican encyclical is instructive: it contains theological justification for an uprising, and if the Pope had said the same thing about the Spanish war, it would have been sensational.[28] Even so the

---

24. In *The Church and the Reconstruction of the Modern World: The Social Encyclicals of Pope Pius XI*, ed. T.P. McLaughlin (New York, 1957), pp. 373–74.

25. Ibid., pp. 414–15. For an analysis of the Vatican and the Mexican struggle and comparisons with the Spanish war see Guenter Lewy, *Religion and Revolution* (New York, 1974), pp. 385–440.

26. Letter of April 24, 1937, in Rodríguez Aisa, pp. 432–33. Wilhelm Faupel, the German ambassador to Burgos, claimed that Franco told him that "he has recently instructed the Archbishop of Toledo that no mention should be made of the encyclical." Report of May 23, 1937, in *Documents on German Foreign Policy*. Series D. Vol. III. *Germany and the Spanish Civil War 1936–1939* (Washington, D.C., 1950), pp. 294–95.

27. Raguer, "El Vaticano," p. 174. The Vatican was most concerned with Nazi influence in Spain, a theme that runs through much of the diplomatic correspondence and letters. See Marquina Barrio, *La diplomacia Vaticana*, pp. 79–80.

28. Raguer, "El Vaticano," pp. 171–74, says that as far as the Spanish war was concerned, what was left unsaid was more important than what was said. The *Espasa Calpe* encyclopedia, p. 1552, does, however, use the Mexican letter as justification for the uprising.

letter is couched in such cautious terms that it is difficult to see how it could have been used to apply to the Spanish war, which had already been going on for nine months, and by any estimate the uprising had caused far more damage than the harm it sought to repair.

Meanwhile the Vatican was actively working with Cardinal Gomá to mediate peace in the Basque provinces. The Nationalist forces by the spring of 1937 were poised to invade Vizcaya, and it was obvious that the Basque autonomists, cut off from aid from Madrid and Barcelona, would be unable to hold out. If the Vatican could mediate peace, lives would be saved and a white terror might be avoided; otherwise the Basques might fight to the end. Gomá and Franco discussed a possible Vatican role, and as early as February 1937 Gomá wrote Pacelli that Franco was willing to negotiate to avoid a long and costly siege of Bilbao.[29] But these negotiations never took place. Early in May 1937 the Vatican sent Gomá a list of conditions as a basis for a possible peace. Gomá showed these to Franco and General Emilio Mola, the commander of the Nationalist armies in the north, and they were accepted. The conditions provided that there would be no terror in Vizcaya, that the defeated troops would be treated honorably, and that a social order based on papal teaching would be established there. Gomá tried to contact the Basque priest Alberto de Onaindía, who had handled earlier negotiations, but was unable to do so. The Vatican then sent the proposals to José Antonio de Aguirre, the Basque president in Bilbao, by way of the Republican government in Valencia. Aguirre never received them because the Republican premier, Francisco Largo Caballero, suppressed them (to avoid a separate Basque surrender), and the Vatican initiative fell through, although it was never fully explained why the Vatican sent these proposals uncoded through Republican hands.[30]

Immediately following the Basque defeat, the Pope decided to send a representative to the Burgos government with the specific charge of helping Basque prisoners of war in the newly conquered territory and arranging for the repatriation of some 20,000 Basque children who had been sent abroad for safety during the conflict in Vizcaya. He named Ildebrando Antoniutti as his apostolic delegate to Spain. Antoniutti arrived in late July 1937 after a delay at the frontier, where he was denied entry because his papers were not in order.[31] The prob-

---

29. February 4, 1937, in Granados, p. 156.

30. Accounts of the negotiations are in Iturralde, III, 203–9, Onaindía, pp. 196–228, and Gomá's role is in Granados, pp. 156–65.

31. Raguer, "El Vaticano," p. 175, claims that Franco ordered the delay so that

lem was soon resolved, and Antoniutti was shortly thereafter named chargé d'affaires from the Holy See to the Burgos government, a significant step toward full diplomatic recognition. He established an office in Bilbao to deal with the repatriation of the Basque children.[32] He also worked to help imprisoned Basques, including a number of clergy whom he was able to get released; but he was unable to save the life of Manuel Carrasco Formiguera, a Catalan Catholic activist and former seminarian who had studied under Gomá and who had escaped the fury in Barcelona only to be imprisoned and executed by the Nationalists for his autonomist views.[33]

The Pope himself also helped the exiled and imprisoned Basque clergy. Under pressure from the Burgos government to withdraw the ecclesiastical faculties of the Basque clergy (the right to dispense the sacraments) Pius not only refused this request but sent notices to papal nuncios abroad that they were to help the exiled clergy obtain faculties.[34]

Among other instances of humanitarian mediation Pacelli asked Franco early in 1937 to sign an agreement already negotiated with the Catalan Generalidad and the International Red Cross to allow noncombatants to leave Barcelona for foreign countries. Franco responded that anyone who wished to leave could simply cross over into Nationalist Spain but that he would sign no agreement with the Generalidad because he did not recognize its authority.[35]

While Antoniutti was chargé, the issue of nomination of bishops came up. Before 1931 the selection of bishops was governed by the 1851 concordat, which gave the Spanish Crown the right of nomination. The Republic had repudiated the concordat in 1931 and had allowed the Holy See to name bishops freely. After 1936 the Holy See continued to name whomever it wished, and Antoniutti informed the Nationalist government of the Holy See's choices simply as a matter of courtesy. The Burgos regime suggested an accord similar to the Lateran concordat with Italy (by which the Holy See asked the Italian government if it had objections to a nominee), but the Holy See did

---

the Pope's representative would have to come directly to him rather than through the Basque provinces. Antoniutti, in his memoirs, *Memoriae Autobiografiche* (Udine, 1975), p. 29, says that the delay was caused because his papers did not state that he was an official representative of the Holy See.

32. Onaindía, who was a member of the repatriation commission, describes its operation, pp. 278–91.

33. Cárcel Ortí, p. 380.

34. According to Onaindía as cited in Jiménez de Aberásturi, p. 201.

35. Raguer, "El Cardenal Gomá," p. 57.

not respond and continued to name bishops as it pleased. But Antoniutti's independence was compromised by a news photograph in which he was pictured giving a fascist salute in company with the German, Italian, and Portuguese ambassadors.[36]

By the spring of 1938 it was obvious that the Nationalists would win the war, but Franco was concerned about the poor image that his regime had abroad, particularly as news of reprisal atrocities was made public. He wanted the prestige that full diplomatic recognition by the Vatican would bring. The Pope, however, was concerned about Nationalist aerial bombing of Barcelona. He protested to Franco, asking that it be stopped. Antoniutti presented a note to Franco's foreign minister with similar protests. Franco responded that he would do everything possible to restrict the number of victims and alleviate the suffering and pain.[37]

Franco began to abolish some of the anticlerical legislation. Religious education in the state schools had been restored in October 1937; in March 1938 the Burgos government ordered that civil marriage be abolished, and in September 1938 annulled all civil marriages that had been contracted since the beginning of the war. Divorce petitions and proceedings were suspended, but the divorce law itself was not abolished until September 1939. In May 1938 the regime abolished the 1932 law which dissolved the Society of Jesus, and the Jesuits were once again recognized as having legal existence in Spain.[38] Apparently these acts prompted the Holy See to establish full diplomatic relations. In May 1938 the Holy See announced that it was sending Gaetano Cicognani to Burgos as its nuncio, and the Burgos government named José Yanguas Messía as its ambassador to the Holy See. Gomá had expressed his hopes to Pacelli that Antoniutti be elevated to the nunciature, but Cicognani was named, apparently because he was more experienced.[39]

The Nationalists had scored a diplomatic coup: it was the first recognition by a major power other than its allies of two years (Germany, Italy, and Portugal). But it did not solve all the regime's problems with the Vatican. Although relations between Cicognani and the Burgos officials were cordial, the problem of the nomination of

---

36. Reproduced in Jiménez de Aberásturi between pp. 111–12.
37. Raguer, "El Cardenal Gomá," pp. 77–79, describes the incident.
38. All of these orders are listed in Cárcel Ortí, pp. 386–87.
39. Marquina Barrio, *La diplomacia Vaticana*, p. 75, says that the Vatican appointed Cicognani because he was more familiar with Nazi ways (he had just lost his position as nuncio to Vienna because of the Anschluss) and would be able to counter them in Spain.

bishops came up again. The Burgos government argued that it was the moral heir of the monarchy and thus should exercise the rights expressed in the 1851 concordat. The Holy See would not accept this position and preliminary negotiations for a new accord were begun, and these culminated in a modus vivendi in 1940 and a concordat in 1953.[40] But the new ambassador to the Holy See complained in a confidential memo that the regime had thrown away bargaining cards by allowing the reestablishment of the Jesuits without a concession from the Holy See.[41] In Burgos' ministry of foreign affairs there were internal discussions on these issues and concern over the Holy See's relations with Catholic elements in Republican Barcelona.

The Franco regime still did not abolish all the anticlerical laws immediately after obtaining diplomatic recognition. The laws regulating the religious orders were not abolished until February 1939, and the clerical budget was not restored until November 1939, seven months after the war ended. But it would be difficult to see these as major issues in the regime's relations with the Holy See, for it had gone much further than even the pre-1931 monarchy in establishing a clerical state by giving the clergy control over education and the regulation of morals, rights of censorship, and even a law which limited the names of newly born children to those approved by the clergy.

By the time the Holy See recognized the Burgos regime in the spring of 1938 it was already involved with issues in Republican Spain, for a year earlier the Republican government had sought to normalize relations with the Holy See. This effort—ultimately unsuccessful—was probably doomed from the beginning by the fact of the anticlerical fury, and its failure dashed for decades to come the hopes of those who looked for a free and progressive church in Spain.

---

40. The discussions are detailed in Marquina Barrio, *La diplomacia Vaticana*, pp. 92ff.

41. May 18, 1938, in Raguer, "El Vaticano," p. 184.

CHAPTER 10

The Republican Government and the Church

When Cardinal Gomá was appointed the Holy See's representative to the Burgos regime in December 1936, the fury in Republican Spain was just ending. The Republican government was gaining control of the organs of power, and while it took until midsummer of 1937 to eradicate most of the power of the uncontrollables, it could plan with the realization that the fury and the terror were over. The government's overriding concern was military operations, but it had some domestic problems as well, and one of these was the Church. There was growing international disgust at the terror and the fury, the persecution had won support for the Nationalists both at home and abroad, and there was a flourishing clandestine church in Republican territory.

The issue was addressed by Manuel de Irujo, the only practicing Catholic in the Republican ministry. A Basque autonomist and minister without portfolio since September 1936, he had done what he could to alleviate the effects of the fury, but he had difficulty convincing his colleagues of the need to act on the problem, for international political reasons if for nothing else. On January 7, 1937, he presented a memorandum to the ministry.[1] After describing the destruction wrought by the fury, he said that the civilized world was repelled by the government's inaction, for it had placed no obstacles in the path of the destroyers. And while the fury had been blind and uncontrollable at first, the current systematic destruction of church buildings was no longer so. Irujo said that the civilized world saw the government either as impotent or as an accomplice because it was at that time transforming churches into factories, and there were

---

1. The memo is in Lizarra, pp. 200–4. The pseudonymous Lizarra is Andrés de Irujo, the minister's brother.

still innocent clergy in prison and priests continued to be executed.

He therefore called upon the government to take the following steps: to release from prison all clergy not charged with common crimes; to survey all church buildings to determine their condition and current use so that all not needed for military necessity be returned to religious use; to explicitly decree freedom of religious practice; and to prohibit police from entering private homes where religious services were privately practiced.

Irujo's motion was rejected, with himself the only vote in favor, although Foreign Minister Julio Álvarez del Vayo said that he supported it in principle but that the position of the Pope, "who has given himself over to fascism," would make it impossible to implement.[2]

What Irujo was proposing came to be called "normalization." What it signified was the hope that the Spanish Church would revert to its prewar status, namely, freedom of worship within the limits imposed by the Constitution of 1931, and that these freedoms and limited rights would be protected by the government.[3] As Irujo could not appeal to the normal ecclesiastical powers—the Spanish bishops—for they now supported the Nationalists, he had to go outside that channel. Two avenues were available: the Holy See and organized Catholics who supported the Republic. Such an approach would mean the elaboration and recognition of a two-Spains concept: that there was a Nationalist Spanish Church (with Vatican recognition), which most of the bishops and clergy supported, and that there would now come into existence a Republican Spanish Church, also with Vatican recognition, supported by those clergy and laity who supported the Republic.

There were two fundamental weaknesses from the beginning in this plan for normalization. One was that Irujo was the only ministry-level Republican official who cared enough about the plan to work for it. The other government officials saw the religious issue as distinctly secondary. Irujo never received more than lip service from his colleagues, most of whom showed great hostility to Catholics and considered them irretrievably in the enemy camp. The other weakness was the Vatican's lack of interest in the plan. While the Holy See wanted to protect Catholics in Republican Spain, Irujo's plan left no

2. In Lizarra, p. 205.

3. Actually, the only national legislation on the Church since the war began was the July 27, 1936, decree nationalizing that church property "which had a direct or indirect relation to the uprising" (Montero Moreno, p. 66). On the provincial and local levels there were decrees providing for the nationalization of all church buildings in most areas.

room for compromise. Its rejection by the ministry meant that if ever offered officially, it would probably be the Republic's maximum position (the government would not offer a return to the favored status of the Church in the pre-1931 monarchy), while for the Holy See, which had been protesting the Republican prewar anticlerical legislation for five years, the status of prewar 1936 would be a minimum position. It could hardly accept less. Thus, there was no room for compromise on the part of either, and from the beginning the proposal was doomed to failure, especially in view of the Nationalists' implied offer of meeting the Holy See's maximum position of favored status for the Church. Furthermore, as time went on, the inescapable fact that the Nationalists appeared each day more likely to win the war adversely affected any possible compromise.

In Irujo's favor, however, was the response of practicing Catholic Republicans who supported the government. The most important of these were members of two organized groups, the Basque Catholics who had moved to Barcelona after the fall of Vizcaya in mid-1937 and, more importantly, the Catalan demo-Christians, members of the *Unió Democràtica de Catalunya* (UDC).

The UDC had been founded in 1931 by a group of Catholics who supported the cause of Catalan autonomism but opposed the anticlericalism of the other autonomists. Its leaders had consistently opposed the Republican anticlerical legislation, and when the war broke out, they supported the Republic but opposed the anticlericals. Their position was analogous to that of the Basque autonomists. They had close ties to Cardinal Vidal i Barraquer (many were his personal friends), and they organized and operated a relief organization in Barcelona for persecuted priests.[4] They were horrified by the fury, but they opposed the Nationalists because, religious matters aside, they opposed fascism and the right-wing political ideology of the Nationalists and their component groups.

What Irujo's normalization plan offered them was the opportunity to construct a new and free church with a modern and progressive stance distinct from the traditionalist defensive church of the Catholic cultural ethic that dominated Nationalist Spain. Vidal was sympathetic to their aims. With the disappearance of the clergy during the fury the UDC had risen to dominate the Catalan Church. It was members of the UDC who ran the relief organizations, who hid priests from the uncontrollables, who arranged the countless details

---

4. Raguer, *La Unió Democràtica*, is a complete history of the organization; see especially pp. 464–511 for the war years.

of private masses in the homes of Barcelona. And they saw the fury not only as a persecution but as an opportunity for a renewal of the pristine evangelical element of a Christianity unfettered by the traditional ties that had developed over the centuries. This spiritual motivation was not without its political overtones, for they hoped that if the Republic won, their concept of the Church would predominate and that of the traditionalists supporting the Nationalists would be defeated. Even if the Republic lost, they could establish their church in Catalonia and work from there to convert other Spaniards to their view. As they saw it, and correctly so, the future course of the Spanish Church would be determined by the outcome of the war.

Thus, they wanted not only normalization but also some degree of Vatican recognition that would help them in their struggle against the traditionalist Catholics. But their plans ran afoul of the question of ecclesiastical authority, for the Vatican would hardly be willing to recognize a group of laymen as controlling the Church anywhere. Their titular metropolitan, Cardinal Vidal, was in exile in Italy, and the whereabouts of their bishop, Manuel Irurita Almandoz, was unknown.[5]

In any event, nothing could be done until the persecution was completely stopped and the situation became clarified. This did not come about until the midsummer of 1937, when three events provided the opportunity for an overture to the Vatican. These were the defeat of radical left-wing elements in Barcelona in May, the end of the fighting in the Basque provinces in July, and the publication of the bishops' collective letter in August.

In May 1937 Largo Caballero's government fell, and Juan Negrín, a moderate socialist, became the prime minister.[6] The events that led to this change also eliminated much of the uncontrollable anarchist influence and put the Republic on a more moderate course. One sign of this was Negrín's nomination of Irujo as minister of justice in his ministry. Irujo was now in a position to ensure that the courts administer justice equitably and to see that clergy not charged with common crimes be released from prison. Furthermore, as the official in charge of church affairs, he could, with the ministry's approval, decree legislation concerning religion. He announced in his first state-

---

5. Irurita had been killed in December 1936, one of the last episcopal victims of the fury, but the fact was not known until 1938 because he had not identified himself to his assassins, who took him to be a simple priest. See José Ricart Torrens, *Un obispo antes del concilio* (Madrid, 1973), pp. 181ff.

6. Negrín's only brother was a monk, but this fact is an indication of his origins rather than the reason for his moderation on the religious issue.

ment as minister of justice that freedom of religion existed in the Republic and that those who persecuted the clergy would be brought to justice.[7]

The second event which promised a new relationship was the defeat of the Basque autonomists in Vizcaya. A contingent of Basques escaped to Barcelona, where they established a chapel in the city and began a daily schedule of masses. Technically the Basque chapel was a private church and not open to the public; in fact, anyone who could get into the usually crowded chapel could hear mass daily.

Finally, the publication of the bishops' collective letter indicated a more formal alignment of the clergy outside of Catalonia and Vizcaya with the Nationalists: the fact that the bishops of Catalonia (Vidal of Tarragona) and Vizcaya (Múgica of Vitoria) did not sign the letter was taken as an indication that their perception of the Church's role in the war was different from that of the other bishops, and this led the Catalan and Basque Catholics to seek the two-Spains relationship with the Vatican.

Therefore, Irujo initiated a diplomatic offensive designed to obtain an exchange of diplomats between the Vatican and the Republic, which would in turn end the persecution of the clergy, for that would be the essential condition for any Vatican exchange.[8] Irujo tried to convince the ministry that decrees reestablishing the public practice of religion and establishing a government agency called the *Comisariado de Cultos* that would handle religious matters would lead to Vatican approval. The other ministers responded that as the Republic had not formally abolished the constitutional freedom of religion, there was no need to make a statement reestablishing it. At the same time, however, they believed it unwise to open the churches for the public practice of religion because they did not want to provoke anticlerical resentment against a clergy that elsewhere in Spain had formally allied itself with the enemy. Irujo was authorized to decree only that private chapels were allowed and could continue to hold services, and that persons who arrested or attacked priests without provocation would be punished. These decrees were promulgated on August 7, 1937.[9]

But this had no impact on the Vatican: what would impress the

---

7. In Raguer, *La espada*, p. 201.

8. Although relations between the Republic and the Holy See had not been formally broken, in fact there were no representatives of either in their respective embassies.

9. The decrees were believed by some Catholic Republicans to have counteracted some of the effects of the bishops' collective letter, which was published about the same time. See, on the whole topic, Vicente Palacio Atard, "Intentos del Gobierno Republi-

Holy See more than anything else would be the restoration of the freedom of public worship. The Basques in Barcelona could not understand why the Catalan Catholics simply did not open the churches to the public, as they had done in Vizcaya during the war there. Indalecio Prieto, the socialist minister of defense, proposed that the whole issue be solved by the celebration of a Te Deum mass in the Barcelona cathedral. The leaders of the UDC rejected this proposal because they believed that a public mass would be used as propaganda by the anticlerical Republicans, and furthermore, they said, a Te Deum mass was a celebration of thanksgiving, and there was nothing to be thankful for. Instead, the UDC suggested that the churches be opened in stages: first small chapels; and if there was no anticlerical reaction, then parish churches; and finally the cathedral, all of this to be done without publicity or propaganda exploitation. The UDC was most anxious to preserve the independence of their renewed Catalan Church.[10]

Irujo then encountered the most ironic situation of all: the anticlerical fury had forced the closing of the churches, but now the ecclesiastical authority to reopen them would not be granted. For it appeared that it was not easy to find a spokesman with authority for the Church. The UDC was specific and vociferous, but it did not speak with ecclesiastical authority. Their spokesman and secretary-general of the party was Josep Trías Peitx, who close to Irujo (and was his choice to head the Comisariado de Cultos if it should ever be established), but Trías was the first to agree that ecclesiastical authorization was necessary for the opening of any churches. And, in fact, there were two legitimate ecclesiastical authorities for the same jurisdiction. There was an authentic vicar-general for the diocese of Barcelona, Josep Torrent Llorens, who had been organizing the clandestine Church ever since Bishop Irurita had disappeared during the fury, and by the summer of 1937 he was administering the diocese with the full knowledge of the government; but Torrent denied at the time that he could act with authority for the bishop, whom he presumed was still alive. There was also a vicar-general for the archdiocese of Tarragona (Vidal's see and the metropolitan see of all Catalonia, and of which the diocese of Barcelona was a suffragan see): this was Salvador Rial i Llovera, who had been released from prison in June 1937 and then was named vicar-general by Vidal from his exile. But his authority over the Barcelona diocese was extremely limited, and in any event Rial was reluctant to act on his own without consulting Vidal.[11]

Who then spoke for the Church? The UDC deferred to ecclesiastical authority, Torrent said he had no authority and deferred to the Vatican, and Rial acted only after consulting Vidal, who agreed with the UDC's position that the opening of churches should not lend itself to political propaganda; furthermore, Vidal was disturbed by the fact that there were still priests imprisoned in Republican jails.

Irujo had begun to release imprisoned priests as soon as he took office, but he could not release those who had been convicted for aiding the rebellion, nor did he have so much power as to be able to release whomever he wished.[12] But he offered this action as a goodwill gesture and in August 1937 made a diplomatic overture to the Holy See. He sent his brother, Andrés, and Luis Nicolau d'Olwer, a highly respected Catalan economist and former minister of finance in the 1931 Republican government, to Paris as his personal representatives to open talks with Valerio Valeri, the nuncio to Paris. Cardinal Jean Verdier, archbishop of Paris, offered his services as well. For the Holy See Pacelli sent René Fontenelle to Paris. Verdier and Fontenelle consulted first, and they decided to send a mission to Republican Spain to report on conditions there. Verdier selected a priest sympathetic to the Republic, Josep Tarragó. Before leaving Paris, Tarragó wrote to Irujo, describing the Vatican's position as told to him by Fontenelle: he said the Vatican wanted to assure the Republicans of its impartiality and willingness to negotiate, but the government must release all imprisoned clergy as soon as possible and allow for the opening of churches for public worship.[13]

If this letter gave Irujo hope, events did not. Irujo's overture to the Holy See came under immediate attack from Premier Negrín because the day that Tarragó's mission was announced to the ministry, Cardinal Gomá published a response that Verdier had written to him praising the bishops' collective letter. This turned Negrín against Verdier and made him less willing to consider any concessions to the Vatican. Then Tarragó's report to Verdier was pessimistic: he said that the Republic could not win the war nor could it free itself from So-

---

11. On Rial see Hilari Raguer, "Le vicaire du cardinal: Mgr Salvador Rial Lloberas, vicaire général de Tarragone pendant la guerre civile espagnole," *Revue d'Histoire Ecclesiastique* 79 (April–June 1984), pp. 370–415.

12. Manuel de Irujo, *Memorias* vol. I: *Un vasco en el ministerio de justicia* (Buenos Aires, 1976), p. 14.

13. Letter of September 6, 1937, in Palacio Atard, "Intentos," pp. 96–97.

viet influence.[14] By the time this report was aired, Irujo's policy had foundered, as indeed it must have, given the lack of support from his own government and the unwillingness of the ecclesiastical authorities to commit themselves. Irujo had asked Torrent to authorize the reopening of the churches and said that he would guarantee their safety, but Torrent claimed that he lacked the authority to do so; the vicar-general then wrote Pacelli and said that, however good Irujo's intentions were, the government did not have the ability to offer guarantees. Pacelli accepted Torrent's judgment.[15]

By the end of 1937 Irujo's normalization plan appeared doomed. But he hoped to save it by the simple expedient of exchanging envoys with the Vatican. He believed that the Holy See had accepted the two-Spains concept *de jure* once it had named Gomá as its representative to the Burgos regime without making a formal break with the Republic. Hence, the exchange of envoys would confirm the existence of two Spanish churches. He began to formulate a new plan which would center on the actual exchange of representatives with the Vatican, along with the return of Cardinal Vidal to his see.[16] Before he could make any overtures, a new problem arose. Anselmo Polanco, the bishop of Teruel, was taken prisoner by Republican troops when they captured that city in January 1938. Polanco was a traditionalist, the author of a 1937 pastoral against the anticlericals, and he had signed the bishops' collective letter. He was taken to Barcelona and charged with treason on the grounds, as Defense Minister Prieto said, that the collective letter was an incitement to rebellion.[17] Three Basque priests, each of whom had lost a blood brother priest to execution by the Nationalists in the fall of 1936, signed a letter to Negrín asking for clemency and freedom for Polanco. Prieto wanted to free the bishop, but the cabinet would agree to this only if Polanco left Spain for the rest of the war. Irujo directed the secretary-general of the UDC, Trías, to make the arrangements, and he contacted Verdier and Vidal, both of whom urged the Vatican to act on the matter. But the Vatican made no response, although Verdier claimed that he was told that the Holy See could not prevent any bishop from returning to his diocese;[18] nor was Polanco willing to go into exile. So, Polanco

---

14. Letter of November 15, 1937, in Palacio Atard, "Intentos," p. 98.
15. Letter of December 29, 1937, in Raguer, "El Vaticano," pp. 196–97.
16. Palacio Atard, "Intentos," p. 103. Irujo had meanwhile resigned the Ministry of Justice in late 1937, but he remained as minister without portfolio.
17. In Onaindía, p. 345.
18. This point raises interesting comparisons with the case of Bishop Múgica of Vitoria. Raguer, "El Vaticano," p. 200, comments, "It is surprising that the Vatican

remained in prison for the rest of 1938 and into 1939, casting a further cloud over Vatican-Republican relations. In the last days of the war he was assassinated by a group of uncontrollables as he was being moved out of Barcelona.

Shortly after Polanco was arrested, Irujo's hopes were raised by Cardinal Verdier, who told him that the Vatican had accepted his proposal to exchange representatives and that Fontenelle had been proposed as the Vatican's emissary. Irujo immediately arranged for a *placet* (approval) for Fontenelle and nominated Alberto de Onaindía, the Basque priest, as the Republic's representative. But the matter ended there, for there was no further response from the Vatican.[19]

In April 1938 Negrín offered to negotiate peace with the Nationalists and published a thirteen-point peace plan. Point six stated, "The Spanish State will guarantee to its citizens . . . freedom of conscience and the free exercise of belief and religious worship."[20] The Nationalists rejected the plan.

Nor was Irujo successful in his overture to Vidal. In February 1938 Irujo wrote Vidal, inviting him to return to his archdiocese with a promise to guarantee his security and the respect for his position. Irujo wrote, "I am happy to make this offer as a minister of the Republic, as a Basque, and as a Catholic, in the hope that it will bring about better days for the Church, the Republic, and for Catalonia."[21] Vidal did not reply until the end of April (because the letter did not reach him until then), and his answer dashed Irujo's hopes. Vidal said that they could not return "with dignity" as long as there were any priests remaining in prison. Further, he said, the government had not made a single effort to apologize or to make any reparation for the damage wrought by the fury. Finally, Vidal asked why he had received no response to his proposal, made several times over the past year and a half, to return as a hostage in exchange for the freedom of all the imprisoned clergy.[22]

Irujo responded by begging Vidal to consider the enormous goodwill that would be generated by his return: "Think of how satisfying your first mass in the cathedral and at Montserrat would be. Think

---

never gave a response to Irujo's requests" about Polanco. See also Onaindía, pp. 351ff. Vidal's role is in Muntanyola, pp. 380–84.

19. See Onaindía, pp. 445ff.

20. In Lizarra, p. 209, who says that Irujo was the author of this point.

21. Letter of February 11, 1938, in Muntanyola, p. 344.

22. Letter of April 30, 1938, in Muntanyola, pp. 345–46; references to Vidal's earlier proposals are on pp. 338ff.

of how advantageous it would be for the Church and for peace." But Irujo denied any knowledge of Vidal's earlier offer.[23]

The matter ended there. Vidal had sent copies of his correspondence to the Vatican, saying that if the Pope wanted him to return, he would obey. But Pacelli saw no advantage to be gained now that the war was nearly over; nor had he supported Vidal's earlier proposal to offer himself as a hostage. Nevertheless, despite this refusal Vidal was sympathetic to the plight of Catholics in the Republican zone, and he instructed his vicar-general, Salvador Rial, to urge the clergy to at least a minimum amount of pastoral activity. Vidal also persuaded the Holy See to name Rial as apostolic administrator of the suffragan dioceses of Lérida and Tortosa, both of which were still in the Republican zone. Gomá objected to this and even more vehemently to Vidal's proposal that a bishop in southern France watch over the interests of Catalan Catholics. Gomá said that if the Vatican approved Vidal's proposal, any such person named would have to be acceptable to the Burgos regime.[24]

From Republican Tarragona Rial reported to Pacelli in August 1938 that the Republican government was sincere about normalizing relations and that the persecution had indeed ended and priests in his diocese were free to minister in private with full knowledge of government officials.[25] Vidal suggested to Pacelli that Rial be appointed to centralize and unify religious activities for all Catalans so as to take advantage of the situation.[26]

But this brought up the fact that there was already an ecclesiastical authority in Barcelona, the vicar-general Torrent, who was adamantly opposed to any concessions to the Republic. His sympathies were with the Nationalists, and he saw no reason to compromise with a regime that he believed would not last long and which, as time went on, began to show signs of weakness.[27] Torrent continued to refuse

---

23. Letter of May 23, 1938, in Muntanyola, pp. 347–48.

24. Raguer, "El Vaticano," pp. 200–2.

25. Letter of August 12, 1938, in Muntanyola, pp. 352–53.

26. Letter of August 14, 1938, in Muntanyola, p. 354. Rial was named president of the union of vicars-general of the dioceses of Catalonia, and the Republican press claimed that he was apostolic delegate to the Republic (which implied diplomatic recognition). Although the Republican claim was false, the Nationalists were angry because of the propaganda value, and the Nationalist minister of foreign affairs, Count Francisco Gómez Jordana, told the Spanish ambassador to the Vatican that it might be useful to threaten the Holy See with recall over the issue. See Marquina Barrio, *La diplomacia Vaticana*, p. 114.

27. Raguer, *La espada*, p. 212, claims that Torrent was also concerned that the

permission for the celebration of public masses despite repeated requests from Catalan Catholics and in fact threatened to suspend any priest who celebrated one.[28] Irujo again asked Torrent to open the churches and was again refused.[29]

But Torrent based his response to Irujo on more than speculation. He had been arrested in July 1938 when an informer revealed the workings of the underground network aiding priests. He was released in a few days, but this experience strengthened his conviction that priests were not safe in Republican Spain and that it was best to hold out for a Nationalist victory.

Meanwhile the Basque chapel in Barcelona remained open and flourished.[30] In October 1938 a Basque officer, Vicente de Eguía Sagarduy, was killed at the front, and his friends asked for a funeral mass and procession to the cemetery. Torrent counseled against such a public display, but he did not prohibit it. Thus a public funeral was held in Barcelona with a priest in robes leading the procession along the streets and with Julio Álvarez del Vayo as an official representative of Premier Negrín marching behind the coffin. Photographs were published and widely reproduced as proof of religious toleration in the Republic, but it was the only affair of its kind.

By the fall of 1938 the Republic's fate was truly sealed, and efforts by Vidal to get Rial appointed by the Holy See as apostolic visitor to all of Catalonia were unsuccessful. Vidal wrote Pacelli in November 1938 that the Church should reestablish herself in Catalonia without regard to the political or military situation, as early Christians had done during the violent persecutions of the Roman Empire.[31] But Pacelli did not respond to this. Irujo had resigned his ministry in September 1938, and there was pressure from Gomá and the Nationalists for the Holy See to take no action concerning the Republic.

The Catalan Catholics themselves tried to normalize the situation in a frenzied, last-minute attempt to get a Vatican exchange before the Nationalist army, poised on the frontiers of Catalonia, invaded. The leaders of the UDC proposed to Negrín that he decree religious freedom and establish the *Comisariado de Cultos*. Both were done

---

Catalan clergy not be accused of any sort of collaboration with the Republicans and thus suffer a white terror as the Basque clergy had.

28. Palacio Atard, "Intentos," p. 111.

29. In Raguer, *la espada*, p. 234.

30. One Republican official commented, "these Basques have re-proclaimed the Edict of Nantes!" In Lizarra, p. 228.

31. Letter of November 7, 1938, in Muntanyola, p. 354.

on December 8, 1938. Jesús Bellido y Golferichs, a physician and practicing Catholic, was named to head the *Comisariado*. He ordered that a chapel in the cathedral of Tarragona be opened to the public. Rial, the vicar-general, agreed, but he had to get Vidal's approval, and by the time Vidal was consulted, Tarragona had been captured by the Nationalist troops.[32] Franco rejected on the grounds of military urgency a papal appeal for a Christmas truce and launched his assault on Catalonia on December 23, 1938. Barcelona fell by the end of January 1939, and Torrent celebrated the first public mass in Barcelona in the Plaza de Catalunya with the Nationalist army in attendance.

Vidal had tried to lessen the impact of the coming white terror. He asked Pacelli to plead with Franco for moderation, and Pacelli directed the nuncio to do so. But when Tarragona was captured, Rial was arrested by the Nationalists and held for a week before he was released. Vidal began making plans to return to Spain, but he was told by an intermediary from the Spanish embassy in Rome that he would be allowed to return only if he resigned his see; the reason, he was told, was his refusal to sign the bishops' collective letter, his support of Rial's activities, and his contacts with the Republican government.[33] Vidal went to Rome to see Pacelli and the Pope and to protest to the Spanish ambassador. But the ambassador would not see him, and before the Holy See could take any action, Pope Pius XI died on February 10, 1939.[34]

At the conclave that met to elect a successor to Pius XI, the three Spanish cardinals Vidal, Segura, and Gomá met. Vidal and Gomá treated each other most cordially, and Vidal later said that Gomá told him that Vidal was being treated unjustly in not being allowed to return to his see.[35] Apparently Gomá was beginning to have misgivings about his role in supporting the Nationalists, and he later com-

---

32. Raguer, "El Vaticano," pp. 206–7.
33. All of the documents are in Muntanyola, pp. 397ff. See also Marquina Barrio, *La diplomacia Vaticana*, pp. 442–45, for the letter from Yanguas Messía to Jordana, February 9, 1939; for the rough draft of a letter Vidal showed Pacelli in which he congratulated Franco for the "pacification" of Tarragona and asked to be allowed to return to his see, p. 136; and for Marquina Barrio's claim that if Vidal had returned to Spain without permission, the Nationalist government would have tried him for treason, p. 138.
34. Muntanyola, p. 409, recounts the rumor that the Pope had planned to announce publicly that Vidal was returning to his see and thus present Franco with a fait accompli. Marquina Barrio, *La diplomacia Vaticana*, pp. 138–39, says that while such an action by Pius XI was possible, it was most unlikely that the Vatican's position would have changed so quickly.
35. Letter from Vidal to Pacelli, June 3, 1939, in Muntanyola, p. 412.

mented that Vidal had been right in not signing the collective letter.[36]

Cardinal Pacelli was elected pope in the conclave on March 2, 1939. A month later, on April 1, the Nationalist army entered Madrid, and Franco announced that the war was over. On April 16 the new Pope, Pius XII, broadcast a speech to the Spanish people: "It is with great pleasure that we address you," he said, "to express our paternal congratulations for the gift of peace and for the victory with which God has deigned to crown the Christian heroism shown in so many generous sufferings." The Spanish people "rose in defense of the ideals of faith and Christian civilization" and were able to resist "the pressure of those who were deceived into believing in a humanitarian ideal that exalted the poor, but who were actually fighting to benefit the forces of atheism." He exhorted the clergy and government officials to show these deceived folk that individual and social justice must be based on Christ's gospel and Church doctrine, and the Pope did not doubt that Franco would do this, having already given proof of his "Christian sentiments" by protecting religious interests in conformity with the teachings of the papacy.

Pius recalled the sacred memory of the many clergy who gave their lives for the faith and recognized the heroic sacrifices of those who died for God and religion on the field of battle. He hoped that the innocent children sent abroad (the Basque children) would be returned to their parents. And before ending with a blessing on the faithful and all those who fought for the faith, he urged Spaniards to follow the principles taught by the Church and "so nobly proclaimed by the Generalissimo: justice for all criminals and benevolent generosity toward the mistaken."[37]

---

36. Gomá said, "the only one who could see clearly in this matter was Vidal." From the testimony of Ramón Timoneda, in Muntanyola, p. 413.

37. *L'Osservatore Romano*, April 17–18, 1939, p. 1. The message is also in Montero Moreno, pp. 744–46. Payne, *Spanish Catholicism*, p. 180, says that the last part of the broadcast, urging generosity, was cut off the air by the regime. Marquina Barrio, *La diplomacia Vaticana*, pp. 158–60, says that the message did much to soothe Nationalist officials who were not pleased with Pacelli's elevation because they believed that he lacked confidence in Franco; there were also unfounded fears that the new Pope would appoint Cardinal Tedeschini, the former nuncio to Madrid, as his secretary of state.

CHAPTER 11

The Debate on
the Theology of War

The most striking characteristic of the Spanish Civil War and the feature for which it will be remembered above all else is the passionate ideological commitment it engendered both in Spain and abroad. Spaniards had been passionate about their politics since the beginning of the nineteenth century, but none of the liberal-Carlist struggles had the ideological impact of the 1936 conflict. In the Western democracies the Spanish issues were debated with a degree of intensity unheard of over a conflict in a foreign country since perhaps the 1848 revolutions. Of all the ideological issues the political was shortly given the lie by revelations of communist influence, opportunism, and hypocritical propaganda, and it is the theological, moral, and religious issues that stand out as generating the most intensity, and they remain today as the lasting legacy of the conflict, revealing the importance of the war as a religious experience.

These issues centered on the perception of the war as a just and moral conflict and raised questions about the theology of war for the first time in centuries; in no other prenuclear conflict in modern times was the question of a just war raised to such a degree. Indeed the question went beyond justice, for the Nationalist partisans claimed that the uprising was more than just, that it was in fact a holy war, a crusade. The passions generated by these issues did not subside easily; three decades after the end of the conflict historians who called the Spanish conflict a civil war were being criticized by others for not calling it a crusade.[1]

---

1. See J. Díaz de Villegas, "Nuestra cruzada no fue jamás una guerra civil," Guión 266 (1964), pp. 25–29, and in general, Vicente Marrero Suárez, La guerra civil española y el trust de cerebros (Madrid, 1961), pp. 147–81. Juan Rey, S.J., ¿Por qué lucho un millón de muertos? (Santander, 1962), calls for forgiveness, but not oblivescence, as does Ángel García, pp. 167ff.

One reason for this controversy is that the conflict was indeed a religious war, a fact that has been consistently downplayed in the West, perhaps because the fury and the scandal are embarrassments to partisan historians. But there can be no doubt that the anticlerical fury, the destruction, the assassinations, and the iconoclastic violence clearly made the war, in large part, a religious conflict. Priests were killed because they were priests, and anticlericals were killed because they were anticlericals. Religion was an issue.

Hence the need for a justification of the morality of the uprising. Christianity is a religion of peace. Even allowing for varying interpretations, there can be no gainsaying the fact that Christ preached a religion of love and forgiveness of one's enemies. This is not to deny that some of Christ's other words can be interpreted as support for those who would defend Christ's church with arms, but the central thrust in Christianity is peace and love, humility, suffering, and forgiveness. And at the same time Christians have fought—and have always done so—with the blessings of the clergy. Their swords and tanks and airplanes and ships have been blessed, military masses have been celebrated, and the heroes of the pantheon have often been canonized. This apparent contradiction is often explained by resorting to the concept of a just war, a concept that does not always satisfy because it is a philosophical solution to a moral and theological problem.

The Spanish war thus generated a debate on the justice of the uprising, and this in turn forced attention upon some of the deeper issues of the war. And if the writings on the part of clerical-Nationalist supporters appear strident and bitter, it is because of the anticlerical fury. Unlike many modern wars where the clergy are deferred from military service or where war does not directly affect them, in the Spanish war the clergy were themselves the object of the most violent attacks of the entire war. Those in Nationalist Spain had relatives (for clerical vocations frequently run in families), seminary classmates, and friends who had been killed, and usually not for any culpability on their part, but simply for being clerics. One can imagine the deep hatred they felt for the persecutors who had killed their friends and brothers and sisters and who had burned their churches and mocked their holy ceremonies, who had destroyed all that they held dear. It would have been unrealistic to expect these clerics to view the war dispassionately and to try to pacify both sides with comforting words of wisdom and peace. Their bitterness and hatred could be assuaged only by taking part in the conflict, and the only way they could justify their feelings and actions in the light of Christian teaching was by constructing a theology of war.

A theology of war existed, both a general theology and a specifically Spanish one. But it was not a well-developed theology, especially in view of the detailed expositions of other moral problems, and there is a comparative paucity in theologians' writings on the problems of war. Four names stand out among the theologians of war: Saint Augustine of Hippo (fl. 400), Saint Thomas Aquinas (fl. 1270), and two sixteenth-century Spaniards, Francisco de Vitoria and Francisco Suárez. There is no fundamental disagreement among them on what constitutes a just war. The sixteenth-century theologians' views are more developed, but they are based on Thomistic and Augustinian principles.

Vitoria and Suárez state that a defensive war requires no special moral justification: armed response to an armed attack upon a peaceful people is always justified. On the other hand, an offensive or aggressive war—armed response to an injurious action—is different. It can be justified only under six conditions, all of which must be present: 1) the war must be declared by a legitimate authority; 2) it must be fought for a just cause; 3) it can be fought only as a last resort, after all attempts to solve problems have been exhausted; 4) it must be fought with the right intentions, that is, not for personal gain but to solve the issues at hand; 5) it must be fought in a proper manner, following the generally accepted rules of war; 6) the rule of proportion must be observed, that is, that the war cause no more damage than would have occurred had the original injurious action been allowed to continue unchallenged.[2]

Consideration of these principles, however, tends to obscure the fact that there were not two independent nations fighting in Spain, but rather one group of Spaniards against another. Technically the Spanish war was a rebellion, a revolt against the government. A theology of rebellion was necessary.

Church teaching generally emphasized obedience to legally constituted authorities as a general principle. However, medieval theologians, including Thomas Aquinas, argued that rebellion against a tyrant was justified as long as the principle of proportion was observed. John of Salisbury in 1159 said that if a king acted arbitrarily or against the common good, he thereby broke the implied contract with his subjects, and rebellion (or tyrannicide) was justified. Suárez argued

---

2. See Bernice Hamilton, *Political Thought in Sixteenth-Century Spain: A Study of the Political Ideas of Vitoria, DeSoto, Suárez and Molina* (Oxford, 1963), pp. 135–57; and R.A. McCormick, "Morality of War," *The New Catholic Encyclopedia* (New York, 1967), XIV, 802–7. Some theologians maintain that holy wars are not bound by these rules because they are fought in the name of God, who is not obliged to observe conventional rules of morality.

that the norms of a just war should apply to rebellion as well but warned that only a nation and not an individual had the right to rise against a tyrant. The sixteenth-century Jesuit Juan de Mariana argued that an individual had such a right, and as a result, Jesuits in seventeenth- and eighteenth-century Europe were considered advocates of tyrannicide. By the eighteenth century theologians had developed theories of legitimate resistance, and most moralists had come to accept John Locke's contractual theory of government, which stated John of Salisbury's argument in more modern terms: rebellion was justified if the ruler broke his contract with the ruled.

The French Revolution initiated the nineteenth-century era of left-wing, often anticlerical revolts, and these attacks upon the clergy changed theologians' views of rebellion. Pope Gregory XVI in 1832 condemned all rebellion and sedition and said that obedience to all constituted powers, no matter what their makeup, must be observed. In the same year he refused to support Polish Catholics in their attempts to overthrow their Russian overlords. Pius IX condemned rebellion against legitimate authorities in the *Syllabus of Errors* in 1864. Even the more moderate Leo XIII in 1881 agreed only to the justification of passive resistance.[3]

But the Spanish rebellion was a right-wing uprising that supported traditional values and the Church against a legally constituted government that condoned or at least could not prevent the anticlerical fury and terror. Hence the problem: given the theological traditions that had been developed, each side could claim justification for its views. But it does seem that the weight of the greatest and most respected theologians—Aquinas and the sixteenth-century Spaniards —support the idea that rebellion under certain conditions was legitimate, a view that the reigning pope, Pius XI, came to accept in his encyclical letter to the Mexican bishops in 1937.

To these traditional theologies one must add the theology of war developed in nineteenth-century Spain. As a nation Spain, at any time since the sixteenth century, probably had more theologians per capita than any other Christian country, and they were willing to pronounce on any and all matters. Indeed, the clericalism so prevalent among the Carlists and other conservative elements was in large part a willingness to be directed by clerics and theologians on matters that other Western people no longer considered the province of moral theologians. This concern with war theology first began in the war against

---

3. For all of these views on rebellion see M. A. Gallin, "Revolution," *The New Catholic Encyclopedia*, XII, 450–51.

Napoleon and the French in 1808. The clergy were authentic popular leaders in the struggle against the foreigners whom they pictured as agents of atheism in the guise of anticlerical ideas and legislation. Their defense of the Church's privileges coincided with Spain's national interest against French domination, and the clergy reaped a great deal of popular acclaim for this role. The French reacted with violence, burning churches and conventos or using them as barracks. Some priests responded by bearing arms in defense of Spain and the Church.[4]

The theologians of 1808 viewed the war and its effects as punishment for sins (especially freethinking) and therefore as a cleansing process; as a just war because of French attacks on property, liberty, and religion, and as a defense of national honor; and as part of a divine plan, a continuation of the wars of Israel, the medieval crusades, and the reconquest of Spain from the Moslems.[5]

This sort of clerical response to war and crisis continued throughout the nineteenth century in all of the wars, upheavals, and uprisings of the period. In the two Carlist wars priests bore arms; the most famous of the priest-warriors was Manuel Santacruz (Cura Santacruz), the pastor of Hernialde, who led Carlist troops against the Liberal forces in 1872.[6] Church leaders did not hesitate to condemn anticlerical policies or to call the faithful to action, although there were no invasions from abroad throughout the rest of the century to 1936. There was thus ample precedent for the clergy's pastoral letters and open support for the Nationalists in 1936. Spanish priests and bishops had not downplayed their political roles before, and there was no need for them to do so in 1936. They were an intensely political clergy—probably the most political in the Western Church—and with reason, for they were defending more than a religion; they were defending a cultural ethic. Spain could become a modern nation only at the expense of that ethic, and it is not surprising that the clergy reacted.

Even before the war began, the clerical writer Aniceto de Castro Albarrán published in 1934 a work that argued the legitimacy of rebellion against the Republic, largely because of the anticlerical legis-

---

4. This also was a tradition. See Henry Kamen, "Clerical Violence in a Catholic Society: The Hispanic World, 1450–1720," *The Church and War*, ed. W.J. Sheils (London, 1983), pp. 201–6.

5. Revuelta González, V, 11–14.

6. "Although assiduous in the daily reading of his breviary, Santa Cruz felt no scruples at having twenty prisoners shot without benefit of confession." Callahan, *Church, Politics and Society*, p. 267.

lation.[7] Within a month after the uprising there were official clerical pronouncements supporting the Nationalists. One of the earliest was the lengthy pastoral of Enrique Pla y Deniel, bishop of Salamanca, and by 1937 nearly every bishop in Spain had made some pronouncement of support.[8] By this time moral theologians were beginning to write more substantial works, justifying the war by working within the Thomistic framework.[9] Most of these works follow common lines of reasoning on the justice of the war. A good example of one of the more cogently argued is that of the Jesuit Juan de la Martínez in ¿Cruzada o rebelión? published in Saragossa in 1938.

Martínez explained the traditional theology of war and rebellion, arguing that it was legitimate for a people to rise up against an illegitimate and tyrannical power: "Given the case of an obviously intolerable tyranny against which all peaceful means of active and passive resistance have failed, it is licit for the nation to rise up in arms against that tyranny, provided that victory can be anticipated so that the evils of war can be compensated for by subsequent prosperity."[10] This argument, incidentally, changed the traditional rule of proportionality; it had to be this way, for the Spanish war was too violent and destructive to meet the rule that the damage caused by the war be no worse than the evils the rebellion set out to eliminate. Even the bishops' collective letter skirted this issue in arguing that the war was just, listing only three conditions, proportionality not among them.

Martínez further cited Pius XI's letter to the Mexican bishops as justifying rebellion, but as this was written in March 1937, nearly nine months after the uprising in Spain, the argument does not convince. Pius had said that citizens had the right to defend themselves "against those who make use of public power to bring it to ruin"; but that such solutions (rebellions) had to be "licit actions and not intrinsically evil"; that the law of proportionality apply; and that the clergy and church organizations not be involved.[11]

As regards the Spanish war specifically, Martínez justified it by

---

7. Aniceto de Castro Albarrán, *El derecho de la rebeldía* (Madrid, 1934). Some Catholics tried unsuccessfully to get the book condemned by the Vatican. See Robinson, p. 168. Castro Albarrán's book was expanded and published in 1941 as *El derecho al alzamiento* (Salamanca).

8. Most are listed in Arbeloa, "Anticlericalismo," pp. 162ff.

9. Bernardino M. Hernando, *Delirios de cruzada* (Madrid, 1977), pp. 153ff., lists the more important works in chronological order.

10. Juan de la Martínez, ¿*Crusada o rebelión?* (Saragossa, 1938), p. 44.

11. In *Church and Reconstruction*, ed. McLaughlin, pp. 414–15.

arguing both the illegitimacy of the Republic and the consequent legitimacy of the Nationalists. The Republican government was illegitimate, he said, because it was based on corrupt elections in 1931 and 1936 and because the ministries formed under its laws did not reflect the party strength in the Cortes; it was tyrannical because it planned the sovietization of Spain, as the government had planned a coup that would have transformed both Spain and Portugal into Iberian Soviet republics.[12] The Republic was an incurable tyranny, so that there was no recourse other than war. The Nationalists, he said, entered the war with the solid probability of victory because they had a preponderance of the goods of war—material supplies, moral justification, and international support—and the army was well disciplined and imbued with patriotism and religious enthusiasm and because they represented the Catholics, who were a majority in Spain. Further, the Nationalists waged war in a just and charitable manner: they gave a clear ultimatum to the Republican forces at the time of the uprising, and they followed all the rules of war. If, Martínez confessed, there had been "excesses," these were individual cases and not part of a systematic policy.[13]

Martínez's book and other works justifying the uprising found this last point—the Nationalist reprisals—difficult to fit into their scheme, but in general they argued that such individual reprisals did not invalidate the justice of the rebellion in the first place. They all also emphasized the communist nature of the Republic and maintained that the uprising was in effect a preemptive first strike (to use nuclear terminology) because the communists were planning a coup to overthrow the government of the Republic at the same time.[14] Most of the works also cited the violent anticlericalism under the Popular Front from February to July 1936 as evidence of a secret Soviet master plot to destroy the Spanish Church. Some cited cryptic masonic instructions to prove a similar intention.

What is important about this emphasis upon communism is that it helped to justify the uprising and war. According to traditional theology it was more difficult to justify an internal rebellion than it was a war against a foreign power. Thus, communism could be seen as an international force and therefore a foreign power. The Spanish

---

12. As proof, Martínez cited the Socialist premier Francisco Largo Caballero's statements about revolution, along with various newspaper articles and General Franco's statements.

13. Martínez, pp. 97ff., 171ff., 189ff.

14. There was in fact such a scare in May and June of 1936, and although later proved false, it was widely believed by many at the time. See Thomas, p. 180.

proletarians were lumped together as communists and as such were categorized as Russian pawns. The Nationálists could then be justified as leading a national rising against a subversive but foreign power. Indeed, every justification, including the bishops' collective letter, emphasized the machinations of the communists as being Russian-directed and anti-Spanish.

The most difficult problem faced by the justifiers was the rule of proportionality. It is difficult to see how anything the Popular Front government did before the war could justify the hundreds of thousands of deaths caused by the war, including the anticlerical fury itself. Luigi Sturzo, the antifascist Italian priest and opponent of the Spanish clergy's stance, argued that under any circumstance it was difficult to judge if a revolt would cause more damage than that incurred by allowing a tyrannical government to exist. As an example he cited that Irish independence was won at a relatively small cost, and certainly the Spanish generals thought that their revolt would be immediately successful. Neither the generals nor the government wanted the destructive war that followed, but the risk of a prolonged conflict had to have been considered. Given all aspects of the horror of war and the inability to determine proportionate means, Sturzo said that it would have been better for Spanish Catholics to have followed the example of the early Christians and not offer armed resistance.[15]

Martínez answered Sturzo's last point by arguing that early Christians were in a minority and they had no chance of "protecting a religious unity that did not exist."[16] But by this time another issue was commanding attention, an issue that had been raised very early in the war and which eclipsed the argument about the justice of the uprising. This was the contention that the uprising was not only just but that it was a holy war, a crusade.

The use of the term crusade (cruzada) generated as much controversy as any other aspect of the religious experience of the war. It gave foreign and domestic opponents of the Nationalists a concept that was easier to refute than the justice of the uprising. Practically everything about the term created controversy: how it was used, who used it first, what purpose it served, even whether it should still be used to refer to the war.

Generally most clergy and Catholics accepted the term. After

---

15. Luigi Sturzo, *Politics and Morality*, trans. B. B. Carter (London, 1938), pp. 209–12.
16. Martínez, pp. 97ff.

all, it was not a unique term in a country whose modern nationality had been forged in a centuries-long crusade against the Moslems. The discovery and conquest of the New World and the extension and preservation of Spanish hegemony over Europe in the sixteenth century were frequently seen in religious context. Spaniards were reputed to have a crusading mentality; even the proletarians of 1936 were convinced that their struggle was a sort of crusade to bring the workers' utopia to Spain. As recently as 1921, a scant fifteen years before the civil war, the Spanish clergy called the war in Morocco a crusade in a pastoral letter.[17] King Alfonso XIII, in a 1923 speech at the Vatican, had offered Spain's services to lead a new crusade if the pope should declare one.[18] In the first days of the uprising the Navarrese constantly referred to the war as a crusade, confessing and communing and going off to battle singing hymns, so much so that one of their chaplains was utterly convinced the war was a religious crusade in popular opinion.[19]

The first clerical writer to use the term was Bishop Pla y Deniel in a pastoral letter, "Las dos ciudades," published in late September 1936, an overly long polemic that touched on practically all the issues raised by the war and claimed that the Nationalists were leading the defense of Western civilization.[20] Cardinal Gomá used the term in his pastoral letter "El caso de España" in November 1936.[21] Most of the other bishops used it in the pastorals they wrote in the fall of 1936 and the spring of 1937.

The most publicized defense of the conflict as a crusade argued in more rational terms and with deliberation was the work of a Dominican priest, Ignacio G. Menéndez-Reigada. In an article in the Dominican review *La Ciencia Tomista*[22] he analyzed the war and its

---

17. Cited in José Manuel Cuenca Toribio, "El catolicismo español en la restauración," in Cárcel Ortí, ed., *Historia de la iglesia en España*, V, 328. Nor were priests reluctant to counsel Spaniards to kill for their faith. In 1902 a Jesuit argued in a Bilbao periodical that Christians should prefer to die a martyr's death, but if they could not be martyrs, they could a least kill for their faith and country. In Lannon, "Modern Spain," p. 584.

18. Ben-Ami, p. 103.

19. Urra Lusarreta, pp. 14ff. A Carlist soldier said, "we firmly believed that if we died at the front we would be martyrs to God and country—and that we would be assured eternal happiness." In García Escudero, p. 1448.

20. The pastoral is in Montero Moreno, pp. 688–708.

21. Gomá, *Por Dios*, pp. 17–39.

22. Ignacio G. Menéndez-Reigada, "La guerra nacional ante la moral y el derecho," *La Ciencia Tomista* 56 (1937), pp. 40–57; 57 (1937), pp. 177–95.

attendant moral problems, stating that the Spaniard was naturally Christian—nowhere else in the world were people naturally so—and even those Spaniards who attacked the Church had an ember of Christian faith; as proof he claimed that most of these adversaries confessed their sins when faced with death.

The Spanish uprising was licit, Menéndez-Reigada argued, because the Popular Front government was tyrannical, corrupt, and unjust; it had attacked the most sacred institutions of the nation. The Nationalist government was legitimate because it rose up against an illegitimate government, and it was composed of parties and groups that were Catholic. Then Menéndez-Reigada took the most extreme stand of any defender of the uprising: Catholics, he said, must support the uprising because it was not only a holy war and a crusade, but it was the holiest war in all of history. In all earlier crusades, he said, Christians were at least fighting those who believed in God (e.g., the Moslems), but now they were fighting militant atheists, the anti-God forces. Hence this was the holiest war in all history. Even putting Christianity aside, he said, this was a war in defense of all humanity because the other side was dominated by communism, the great menace to society and civilization.

Menéndez-Reigada's arguments, along with those of other defenders, found a response in Republican Spain from one of the few priests who supported the Republic. José Manuel Gallegos Rocafull, a canon of the Córdoba cathedral, wrote a justification of Republican Catholics. In a pamphlet published by the Republican embassy in London[23] he argued that while the anticlerical fury was terrible, the proper response was not to kill the anticlericals but to preach to them and "awaken their consciences" so that they would recognize the sincere Christianity they were looking for. The fury, he said, was the last act of the apostasy of the masses, and the response should be charity and love, not more bloodshed. He rejected the notion that the communists dominated the Republic, but he said that if they did come to power, it would be because the revolt itself had stimulated the development of communism within the Republic.

But Menéndez-Reigada's contention that the Spanish conflict was the holiest war in history drew blood. It focused the ire of one of the most intellectually powerful Catholic thinkers of the twentieth century upon the clergy's support of the Nationalists. It also carried the debate on the war outside of Spain. A few weeks after Menéndez-Reigada's article appeared, the foremost Thomistic philosopher in the

---

23. José Manuel Gallegos Rocafull, *Crusade or Class War* (London, 1937).

world, Jacques Maritain, responded with an article in *La Nouvelle Revue Française.*[24]

Maritain did not condone the Republicans' anticlerical violence and in fact saw the two contending sides as offering Spaniards a choice between two horrible alternatives. But he pointed out the historic resentment of the people against the clergy in Spain, and he said that this was so because religion had become so confused with clerical power that the clergy became obsessed with the external show of spiritual authority. The clergy thus sought the support of the wealthy, and this led to a "moral chasm" between the people and the Church.

The uprising could not be justified he said. It was easy to find arguments to support it, but it was difficult to justify it on the rule of proportionality because the uprising caused greater loss of life and destruction than "years of civic strife even under the worst conditions." The leaders of the uprising did not exhaust all means of resisting injustice before they rose; they precipitated war without the excuse of a legitimate defense.

Maritain saved his strongest attack for Menéndez-Reigada's argument that the existence of religion was at stake in Spain. "One may doubt," he said, "that Providence has no other means of saving these primordial bases of human life than by the military triumph of the Nationalists and their allies." As for the holy war argument, Maritain contended that there was no such thing as a holy war; if sacred values are at stake, war and violence secularize these values. Wars may be just, he said, but not holy.

He addressed the reprisals and the white terror and said that they were worse than the red terror because they operated under the sign of religion, and in an impassioned outburst said, "It is a horrible sacrilege to massacre priests—be they 'fascists' they are still ministers of Christ—out of hatred for religion; and it is another sacrilege, horrible also, to massacre poor people—be they 'Marxists', they are still the people of Christ—in the name of religion."

Menéndez-Reigada replied to Maritain that the bishops' collective letter had answered the French philosopher's criticism. He said that since God was all holiness, then his Church and its representatives were holy also; hence destroying them was antiholy, and defending them made the war a holy war. He chided Maritain for calling for a peace without victors or vanquished as a disservice to the thou-

---

24. Jacques Maritain, "De la guerre sainte," (July 1, 1937), pp. 21–37. There is an English translation in Alfredo Mendizábal, *The Martyrdom of Spain: Origins of a Civil War,* trans. C.H. Lumley (New York, 1938), pp. 1–48.

sands of martyrs who had shed their blood for an ideal. Finally, the Dominican said that he believed that the Spanish conflict would begin a new era in which Christianity would flourish throughout the world, initiating a new epoch of faith.[25]

Menéndez-Reigada's arguments failed, of course, to convince Maritain, and the debate on the war was carried outside of Spain to those countries where a free press allowed the controversy to be fully aired. In such a way did the Spanish war come to influence the moral consciousness of Western Christians.

---

25. Ignacio G. Menéndez-Reigada, "Acerca de la 'guerra santa', contestación a M.J. Maritain," *La Ciencia Tomista* 58 (1937), pp. 356–74.

CHAPTER 12

French Catholics and the War

N o event of political or social significance since the beginning
of the nineteenth century engendered such heated religious
debate among Christians worldwide as did the Spanish Civil War. The
conflict found Christians more concerned and more knowledgeable
than ever before about society and politics, and it became the first
great crisis of social Catholicism, just as the French Revolution of 1789
had been the first great crisis of political Catholicism. Pope Leo XIII
and some of the bishops of the late nineteenth century had addressed
the problems of oppressed workers, but their counsels were largely
ignored by Catholic employers and workers alike. The Spanish war
raised these problems again with a more intense immediacy: downtrodden workers in a Catholic nation, alienated from their Church,
were demanding justice. Most Catholics outside of Spain responded
emotionally to the anticlerical fury and to their own bishops' appeals
to back the Nationalists. They accepted the communist conspiracy
explanation of Spanish events. But ranged against this majority, a vocal
minority of Catholics in most Western countries argued that the social implications of the war called instead for aid to the Republicans
or, more often, for an above-the-struggle neutrality.

The strength and volume of this minority depended upon the
number of Catholics in each country and also upon the other factors
that had conditioned the history of Catholicism in that country. In
France, a majority Catholic nation with a strong tradition of anticlericalism and a powerful intellectual community, there was a loud and
prestigious anti-Nationalist group. In Great Britain, where there was
a smaller Catholic community and a tradition of persecution with
which the English could identify, there were practically no anti-
Nationalist intellectual leaders, but there were journals and readers
who took up the anti-Nationalist cause. The Irish were caught up in
their own struggles, but they sent troops to fight for the Nationalists,
almost exclusively for religious reasons. Catholics in the United States,

although their number and percentage were large, tended to be anti-intellectual and submissive to the traditions of an authoritarian immigrant church.[1] In Belgium a group of demochristians who edited *Avant-Garde* claimed that the uprising was unjustified, as did some like-minded Swiss in their journal *Popolo e liberta*. In Germany and Italy Catholics were not free to support the Republic, at least not without significant political pressures. Cardinal Ildefonso Schuster of Milan, like most Italian Catholics, praised the Italian troops in Spain as modern crusaders.[2] In Latin America there were too many internal problems or indigenous struggles against secularism for Catholics to become involved in the Spanish war to an appreciable degree.[3]

In all of the literature on the war there is one great unstated fact: if it had not been for the religious issues, working-class Catholics in other countries would have supported the Republicans. In England this would have made little difference. In France and particularly in the United States where Catholics made up the bulk of the trade unions, the policies of both countries might have been changed from nonintervention and neutrality to at least some degree of active support and sympathy for the Republic.

Of course, the mass of practicing Catholics everywhere did not concern themselves about the issues of a foreign civil war. It was easier and simpler to believe what they were told from the pulpit. Questions concerning the morality and the theology of war were probably beyond their interest. Effective preachers stressed the anticlerical fury, and their own bishops' statements were not unlike the Spanish bishops' letters, only less heated. The support asked for was monetary (aid for Spanish Nationalist relief), political (opposition to intervention on the side of the Republic), and moral and religious (prayers for the victims of the fury). Atheistic communism was everywhere emphasized as the cause of the Spanish war, and the existence of a communist plot that the Nationalists had risen to forestall was almost universally accepted as truth. There is no evidence that the Catholic masses anywhere objected to this interpretation or voiced it if they did. Traditions of authority, reverence, and obedience to the clergy were strong, particularly in Anglo-Saxon countries.

---

1. See Herbert Southworth, *El mito de la cruzada de Franco* (Paris, 1963), p. 100.

2. In Aldo Albonico, "Los católicos italianos y la guerra de España," *Hispania* 139 (1978), p. 382. See also on Italy, Giorgio Rumi, "Mondo cattolico e guerra civile spagnola: l'opinione Ambrosiana," *Rivista di Storia della Chiesa in Italia* 36 (1982), pp. 35–48.

3. On Latin America see Mark Falcoff and Fredrick B. Pike, eds., *The Spanish Civil War, 1936–39: American Hemispheric Perspectives* (Lincoln, Nebraska, 1982).

The opposition to the quest for support for the Nationalists came from publicists who, by their nature, tended to be extremists. It is certainly unlikely that the average working-class Catholic read their journals or indeed even knew about them. Publicists were a distinct minority in every country, even in France.

Furthermore, the questions they raised and the issues of the war as they perceived them must be understood in the setting of the 1930s with all the currents of that troubled decade. Western Christian civilization was barely surviving the shock of World War I. Liberal capitalism was being buried under the upheaval of the Great Depression. Values were being questioned. The Spanish war came to be a focus of these questions, and the religious issues were set in the context of the conflict with communism. Some Western observers perceived that the Marxist experiment appeared to be the last hope for a shattered Western civilization. These favorable observations about communism struck terror into the hearts of traditionalists and especially clerics: they saw the struggle against secularism that had begun in the nineteenth century suddenly become doubly fearful as militant socialism allied with hostile rationalism against traditional values.

The historian Keith Watkins grasps one of the great effects of the Spanish war in its worldwide impact. It was, he says, "a mirror into which men gazed and cast back at them not a picture of reality but the image of the hopes and fears of their generation."[4] It was also a mirror that reflected the issues that divided their own nations, as foreigners came to superimpose their own religious tensions and relations upon the Spanish war. It was easier for Protestants in Anglo-Saxon countries and anticlericals everywhere to support the Republicans because—aside from the political and social issues—the Republicans were anti-Catholic or anticlerical. Catholics came to support the Nationalists, not because they favored the Nationalists' authoritarian political views, but because the Nationalists supported the Church, an institution under attack in their own countries.

The war thus became for Catholics a point of conflict both against anti-Catholic and secular opinion and, within the Catholic community, between clericals and anticlericals or between those who accepted their bishops' stance and those who did not.

The Spanish war touched France more closely than any other country. Republican refugees were unwelcome in Portugal, and the

---

4. Keith Watkins, *Britain Divided: The Effect of the Spanish Civil War on British Political Opinion* (London, 1963), p. 13.

Nationalists came to control the frontier early in the war, so refugees from both factions gravitated to the border into France. The French people living along the frontier were the first to hear of the anticlerical fury as well as of the Nationalist repressions. Their impulse was to sympathize with the faction with which they identified. For most French Catholics (and there was a greater proportion of practicing Catholics in southern France) the war was a source of fear. The similarities with France's past were too strong to ignore: they also had had a history of tense church-state relations, and anticlericalism was endemic in France as well. In fact, however, there had been little violent anticlericalism since the Paris Commune of 1871, and actually little before that since the Revolution of 1789. French church-state relations had reached a more or less stable solution by the 1930s. But the fear was still there. Most French Catholics believed that if Spanish priests and nuns were being killed as part of a Soviet plan to wipe out Christ's Church, then it was obvious that France would be the next target of the communist attack.

The fear was also part of a general paralysis that had gripped the French conservative classes. For two decades they had feared bolshevism, and now the revolution was at their borders.[5] The anticlerical fury was the most evident part of the terror; certainly it was the easiest for rightist propagandists to exploit. For if the clergy were innocent victims of the revolution, and if the demonstrably innocent were being killed, what terrors lay in store for those who were guilty of practicing capitalism?

Thus France, the only power with sufficient strength to effectively aid the Spanish Republic in the early days of the war, did not do so. The French government was beset with enormous social, economic, and political problems that stemmed from its representation of exclusively one faction in the polarized French situation, and the Spanish fury and terror were important factors in its decision to stay out of the war. Even though French premier Léon Blum's government was a popular front with strong sympathies for the Spanish Popular Front, and Blum wanted to answer their appeal for aid, after a few hesitant days he followed Britain's lead and decided to pursue a policy of nonintervention. The terror had created such fear that it had deepened the divisions between clericals and anticlericals, between liberals and conservatives, between the middle class and the workers, so

---

5. "In the very heart of the Latin world," according to Arnold Toynbee, *Survey of International Affairs, 1937,* vol. II: *The International Repercussions of the War in Spain (1936–7)* (Oxford, 1938), p. 151.

that the French government could not support either side in Spain without alienating a large part of the French populace.[6]

For most French Catholics the Spanish war was only one of a number of crises that had affected the French Church since the Revolution of 1789. As in Spain, so also the French Church had experienced the dechristianization of the working classes in the nineteenth century. Unlike the Spanish Church, the French Church had formally been separated from the state since the turn of the century, and most French Catholics had begun to adjust to the fact. For those who could not, there was a conservative ultranationalist, antihumanistic, and antisecularist reaction that centered around the Action Française movement and expressed its desire for—and prophetic expectation of —a restoration of the monarchy and the revival of the traditional church-state union. These Catholics were largely antisemitic and opposed to the French Third Republic as a matter of form. But the Action Française movement had been weakened by the World War, in which religious and political vendettas were put aside in the interests of unity against the foreign invader, and by the intervention of the papacy into the French struggle. In 1926 Pope Pius XI condemned the Action Française movement and forbade Catholics to read its daily newspaper L'Action Française.[7]

The beginning demise of Action Française coincided with the rise of another movement, one which emphasized progressive acceptance of separation as a blessing in disguise and that called for a policy and practice of social awareness, especially toward the creation of a social Catholicism to revive the French Church and bring the working classes back into the fold. This movement had been gaining strength since the death of Pope Pius X in 1914, and by 1936 had clearly captured the intellectual momentum within the French Church. Pius XI supported it, largely through the appointment of socially aware moderates to important bishoprics.[8]

These conservative and progressive factions clashed with predictable reactions to the issues of the 1920s and 1930s: the condem-

---

6. See J. Bowyer Bell, "French Reaction to the Spanish Civil War, July–September, 1936," *Power, Public Opinion, and Diplomacy*, ed. L.P. Wallace and W.C. Askew (Durham, 1959), pp. 269ff.

7. The reason given was that the movement "set party above religion," (i.e., used Catholicism for political purposes). See Eugen Weber, *Action Française: Royalism and Reaction in Twentieth-Century France* (Stanford, 1962), pp. 230ff.

8. Thus the nominations of Jean Verdier to Paris and Achille Liènart to Lille. See Adrien Dansette, *Religious History of Modern France*, vol. II: *Under the Third Republic*, trans. J. Dingle (New York, 1961), pp. 356ff.

nation of Action Française, the rise of communism, the Italian invasion of Ethiopia in 1935, and early in 1936 over the Popular Front elections in France.[9] The Spanish Civil War further polarized them. But not at first. The shock of the anticlerical fury produced a unanimous condemnation from all French Catholics. They united against those who wanted to send arms to support the Spanish Republic. After this initial reaction French Catholics fought out the issues of the Spanish war largely among themselves. There was no large Protestant anti-Catholic faction. There were traditional anticlericals in France, but the social implications of the fury and the terror were too frightening to encourage sympathy for the Republicans solely because they were anticlerical, as was the case in other countries.

An excellent record of this reaction exists in the French Catholic press, certainly the largest and most varied press of any country in Christendom. In addition to the provincial Catholic dailies there were three Catholic-oriented dailies published in Paris: La Croix, a moderate, semiofficial paper; the proscribed L'Action Française; and the demochristian L'Aube (none of which could match the circulation of the secular newspapers or L'Humanité, the Communist daily).[10] There were three Catholic weeklies, the largest being Sept, edited by French Dominicans with the express approval of Pius XI as a popular edition of their more intellectually oriented biweekly La Vie Intellectuelle. Among others there was the Jesuit Etudes, a biweekly, and the most vigorous and progressive monthly was Emmanuel Mounier's Esprit.[11]

The first person to break the united Catholic front against the Republic was François Mauriac, who was rapidly becoming the premier French Catholic novelist. Mauriac wrote occasional articles for

---

9. See René Rémond, Les Catholiques, le communisme et les crises, 1929–1939 (Paris, 1960) for a good documentary sense of these conflicts.

10. David Wingeate Pike, Conjecture, Propaganda, and Deceit and the Spanish Civil War: The International Crisis over Spain, 1936–1939, as Seen in the French Press (Stanford, 1968), pp. 3ff., has statistics. Pike's later work, Les Français et la guerre d'Espagne (Paris, 1975), is a slightly expanded edition of his earlier one.

11. Lucio Pala, I cattolici e la guerra di Spagna (Urbino, 1974), pp. 136–379, has an especially fine annotated and almost complete bibliography of all articles published by all Catholic periodicals in France on the religious issues of the Spanish war. There is a good discussion of the issues in Maryse Bertrand de Muñoz, La guerre civile espagnole et la litterature française (Ottawa, 1972), pp. 93–116. See also, on L'Aube, Françoise Mayeur, L'Aube. Etude d'un journal d'opinion, 1932–1940 (Paris, 1966); on Sept, Aline Coutrot, Un courant de la pensée Catholique. L'Hebdomadaire "Sept" (Mars 1934–Août 1937) (Paris, 1961); and on Esprit, John Hellman, Emmanuel Mounier and the New Catholic Left, 1930–1950 (Toronto, 1981).

the conservative-oriented *Le Figaro*, and shortly after the war began he registered his opposition to Blum's proposed intervention on the side of the Republic.[12] But by the middle of August Mauriac had come out against the Nationalists. The massacre of Republicans in the bull-ring at Badajoz on the sacred feast day of the Assumption—August 15 —had roused his anger: the Nationalists, he wrote, "should not have spilled on the Blessed Mother's feast day one drop of blood more than was demanded by the atrocious law of war."[13] A small but intellec-tually powerful group rallied to Mauriac's position, which, he always pointed out, did not condone the anticlerical fury but rather con-demned both sides for the atrocities each committed; however, as the Nationalists had the support of most of the clergy and claimed that their uprising was a crusade, they deserved the burden of criticism from Catholics who were aware of the facts. War, he argued in the same article, was terrible, but to bless this horror and make it a holy war was hypocrisy and sacrilege.

The moderate Catholic daily *L'Aube* and the weekly *Sept* both picked up on this theme. *Sept* had taken a neutral stance early: on August 7 its editor said, "I deplore that these insurgents have had to confide the cause of national order to rebel generals and mobilize colo-nial troops against their own flesh and blood. And I deplore the loy-alty of those Republicans who defend a blood-guilty government which is powerless to restore the order it has allowed to be destroyed."[14] By late August *Sept* had condemned the Nationalist atrocities, repudi-ated the idea of a crusade, and argued against the legitimacy of the revolt. It rejected the extremist views of both sides: the Nationalists, it said, were not "exterminating angels" nor were the Republicans the "beasts of the apocalypse."[15]

L'Aube's chief writer on Spain, Georges Bidault, also rejected the idea of a holy war.[16] Its editor, Francisque Gay, published articles de-scribing eyewitness accounts of the anticlerical fury and later wrote one of the first books on the fury, a work that engaged him in a po-lemic with Parisian left-wing newspapers who criticized him for say-ing nothing about Nationalist atrocities.[17]

---

12. *Le Figaro*, July 25, 1936, p. 1.
13. *Le Figaro*, August 18, 1936, p. 1.
14. *Sept*, August 7, 1936, p. 1.
15. *Sept*, August 21, 1936, pp. 6, 7; August 28, 1936, pp. 1, 13.
16. *L'Aube*, August 21, 1936, p. 1. Bidault later founded the demochristian MRP and was a premier in the Fourth Republic.
17. Francisque Gay, *Dans les flammes et dans le sang* (Paris, 1936). Gay later condemned the Nationalist reprisals. See Mayeur, p. 132.

L'Aube also published the first important article on the morality of the war. In early September 1936 Luigi Sturzo, the exiled priest and leader of the Italian demochristian Partito Popolare, a most respected Catholic politician (and professional sociologist) who had been living in London since he was forced out of Italy in the mid-1920s, wrote an article, "'Politique d'abord' ou 'morale d'abord." Sturzo denied moral approval to either side, and particularly refused to allow the Nationalist cause the nature of a crusade: "We should not give the insurgents a religious character which they do not and can not possess."[18]

La Croix, the Catholic daily with the largest circulation, was more official than the other periodicals, and although it called for neutrality at first, it printed the Spanish bishops' pastorals and gradually became more favorable to the Nationalists, but not to the extreme of *L'Action Française*, which supported the Nationalists from the first day of the war. On the far left, *Esprit* published articles written by the Spanish Catholic Republican José María Semprún Gurrea.[19]

The controversy died down in the late fall of 1936 but began anew in the early months of 1937 when the Basque war heated up. The proximity to France, the closeness of the two Basque peoples— French and Spanish—the strength of the Basque Catholics, and the revelation of Nationalist atrocities, all highlighted the religious issues of the war again. The International League of Basque Friends was formed, and among its active officers was Clement Mathieu, the bishop of Dax. Its honorary committee included Cardinal Jean Verdier of Paris, the primate of France, and Maurice Feltin, archbishop of Bordeaux. Much of the League's concern came to be focused on the refugee problem, particularly that of the 5,000 Basque children sent to France for safety.[20]

It was the bombing of Guernica that crystallized French Catholic opposition to the Nationalists. In May 1937 a number of prestigious intellectuals signed a manifesto of protest, arguing that "it behooves Catholics, irrespective of party, to be the first to raise their voices to spare the world the pitiless massacre of a Christian people."[21] The manifesto was signed by Jacques Maritain, Francois Mauriac, Ga-

---

18. *L'Aube*, September 6–7, 1936, p. 1. In response to criticism Sturzo later cited the Vatican's *L'Osservatore Romano* of September 18, 1936, which called the uprising primarily military, and hence, Sturzo wrote, "the war is not a crusade, not a holy war." *L'Aube*, October 3, 1936, p. 1.

19. See especially *Esprit*, November 1, 1936, pp. 291–319.

20. See Legarreta, pp. 71–73, on the Basque children in France.

21. *Sept*, May 14, 1937, p. 6. See also Herbert Rutledge Southworth, *Guernica! Guernica!: A Study of Journalism, Diplomacy, Propaganda and History* (Berkeley, 1977).

briel Marcel, Maurice Merleau-Ponty, Luigi Sturzo, and Emmanuel Mounier, among others. Later that month Mauriac wrote that he had signed only after careful and agonized reflection, aware of the criticism that would be made that the signers had not protested the anticlerical fury of 1936; however, the Basques, he said, should not be "able to claim that only the mortal enemies of the Church helped them. . . . A Christian people is lying in the ditch, covered with wounds. In the face of their misery it is not playing into Marxist hands to show the world the profound unity of all Catholics."[22]

The French press debated the Basque issue with predictability, the right criticizing the autonomists for making common cause with the communists and disobeying their bishops' pastoral instruction, and the left portraying them as an ideal Christian community.[23] The Basque controversy came to an abrupt end with the fall of Bilbao in the summer of 1937, and the religious significance of the war took on added dimensions with the publication first of Maritain's article on the morality of the war and then with the Spanish bishops' collective letter. Maritain had, by 1936, become the leading French Catholic thinker and perhaps the leading Catholic philosopher in the world. While he had been active in the campaign to help the Basques, he had previously written nothing on the war aside from signing the Basque manifesto and a protest against the bombing of Madrid in February 1937. His article on the morality of war, published on July 1, 1937, in *La Nouvelle Revue Française*, was directed against the notion that the Spanish uprising was a holy war (see the development of this in chapter 11). He argued that true conservatives were lacking in Spain because they closed their ears to the Church's teaching and to the cry of the poor. He did not spare the Republicans, criticizing them for tolerating crimes against the clergy, noting that the government "neither disowned them nor condemned them officially"; but

---

22. *Sept*, May 28, 1937, p. 20. The manifesto was not the only action taken to help the Basques. Both Mauriac and Maritain worked to get the Holy See's intervention to arrange a surrender and occupation that would be free of repression. See Southworth, *El mito*, p. 104.

23. Spanish Dominicans, in *La Ciencia Tomista* 57 (1937), p. 277, responded to the French Catholic left by telling them that they did "not ask, nor want, nor need lessons in humanitarianism," nor would they tolerate "pharisiacal intercessions." Mauriac appealed for justice again in the preface to a work on the Basques by the Republican Catalan priest Josep Tarragó, who wrote under the pseudonym of Victor Montserrat, *Le drame d'un peuple incompris* (Paris, 1937), (and who had been selected as Cardinal Verdier's informant on Spain. See chapter 10). See also Paul Vignaux, "Cattolici francesi de fronte ai fascismi e alla guerra de Spagna," *Cristianesimo nella storia* 3 (October 1982), p. 395.

he said that just as it was wrong for anarchists to burn churches, so also it was wrong to parcel out detentes to Moslems to kill in the name of Christ. He addressed remarks to those who criticized French Catholics who did not support the Nationalists, and observed that Spain was threatened by two dangers: antireligion on one side and enslaving religion on the other.

Maritain's article appeared at the same time as the Spanish bishops' letter, and although he had not written in response to it, he included a postscript in later editions of his article in which he criticized them for not dealing completely with the barbarities of the Nationalists and the responsibilities of those who started the war.[24]

Maritain's article was reprinted in other French journals and was roundly criticized by L'Action Française, which argued that the Spanish war was indeed holy and that support for the Nationalists was not only permissible but obligatory. Maritain was told that one could not be neutral in a war of values — with Christian civilization at stake one could not legitimately stand outside the conflict and criticize both sides — and that the Spanish bishops certainly knew more about what was going on in their own country than he did, and their word was preferable to his.[25]

By 1937 the French right had rallied to the support of the Nationalists, and some apparently felt that the Pope's implied condemnation of the Republicans as expressed in his encyclical on communism, Divini Redemptoris, had brought the Pope and the French right back together again, as they had been before the papal condemnation of the Action Française movement. Certainly it appeared to them that the Vatican should have learned its lesson in tolerating leftist regimes. An attempt was made to send aid to the Nationalists to help counter the aid given the Republicans, and a French unit, the Jeanne d'Arc bandera, comprising some 200 Frenchmen, went off to fight for Franco.[26] It appeared that even Cardinal Verdier was coming to support the Nationalists: he sent a letter to Cardinal Gomá in response to the Spanish bishops' collective letter in which he acknowledged that the Span-

---

24. Maritain cautioned other readers that the Spanish bishops' intention was not to impose a choice in conscience upon Catholics throughout the world. His postscript was signed in August 1937 and is included in Mendizábal, pp. 46–47. See also Bernard E. Doering, Jacques Maritain and the French Catholic Intellectuals (Notre Dame, 1983), pp. 85–125, for an analysis of Maritain's position.

25. L'Action Française, October 28, 1937, p. 2. See also the same argument in Vice-Admiral H. Joubert, La Guerre d'Espagne et le catholicisme (Paris, 1937).

26. David Wingeate Pike, "France," Historical Dictionary of the Spanish Civil War, ed. Cortada, pp. 216–18. There were some 9,000 French international brigadiers fighting for the Republicans.

ish war was a struggle "between Christian civilization and the so-called civilization of Soviet atheism" and that "what is at stake in this contest is the Catholic Church and the civilization which she had founded." Later in the letter he called for the "forgiveness of the Church's torturers and the union of all her children in obedience and charity, with a social order restored in the light of the papal encyclicals."[27]

The French Catholic right had its own outstanding intellectual. If the left could summon Maritain and Mauriac, the right had Paul Claudel, one of France's most prestigious dramatists and poets (and a statesman as well, for he had just finished terms as ambassador to Japan and the United States). Claudel wrote an impassioned poem, "To the Spanish Martyrs," an emotional paean to the clergy killed in the anticlerical fury. He placed them within the tradition of all the martyrs in Catholicism and rejoiced in their steadfastness and rejection of compromise, their facing the challenge head-on:

> Look you, here's the challenge, sudden change and martyrdom,
> Heaven in one hand, hell in the other; forty seconds to choose
> in; come!
> Forty seconds is too much; Sister Spain, holy Spain, thy choice
> is made!
> Eleven bishops, sixteen thousand priests butchered, and not one
> renegade!

Claudel characterized the anticlerical murderers as "unclean beasts" and ironically urged them on:

> Kill, Comrade, kill, wreck and get boozed and make love.
> There's solidarity of man!
> All those priests alive or dead looking on at us, they provoked
> us, deny it who can?
> People doing us good without pay, when all's said and done you
> can't stand that!
> . . . .
> Bring petrol! Set fire to God! A splendid riddance that!

Finally (and many of the Nationalists' supporters ignored this) he called for mercy:

---

27. The letter was lauded in *L'Action Francaise*, October 14, 1937, p. 2.; it was published in *La Documentation Catholique*, October 20, 1937, pp. 535–40. None of the left or moderate Catholic papers printed it. The letter was considered so laudatory of the Nationalists that Verdier's ability to play a role in peace negotiations was compromised. See chapter 10.

The time of the ploughing is over, the time of the sowing is now;
The tree is done with its pruning, the reprisal season is in.
The idea that budded in ground, holy Spain, in thy heart all
    around
The endless reprisals of love.[28]

The controversy between the two French factions became important in causing the suppression of *Sept*, the Dominican weekly. It was the only French periodical under official religious auspices that supported the anti-Nationalist position on the war. From the beginning it had argued for neutrality, seeing both sides as equally repugnant. In January 1937 it editorialized that it could not favor the Nationalists because they were supported by Fascists and Nazis, while at the same time good Catholics such as the Basques supported the Republic. if Catholics supported Franco for political considerations, that was one thing, but, *Sept* said, one could not "identify the cause of Catholicism with the Nationalists."[29]

There were complaints. Although *Sept* published Claudel's poem and the Spanish bishops' letter, it did not change its moderate editorial position. The French ambassador to the Vatican reported maneuverings by pro-Nationalists to suppress the weekly.[30] *Sept* was also taking positions on non-Spanish affairs that angered rightists: it published an interview with Socialist Premier Léon Blum that lent a favorable view to his remark that Catholics and communists could collaborate in solving social problems. In August 1937 *Sept* was suspended on orders from the Dominican superior in Rome. When asked about the suspension, the superior said that it was disciplinary, not doctrinal, and that the disciplinary problems stemmed from divisions within the order over *Sept*'s attitude toward Spanish affairs, in particular *Sept*'s criticism of Cardinal Gomá's pastoral; this criticism, he said, was insensitive to the anticlerical fury, in which over a hundred Spanish Dominicans had been killed.[31]

---

28. Published in *Sept*, June 4, 1937, and as a preface to Estelrich, pp. 7–13. There is a good English translation by John O'Connor in *The Colosseum*, September 1937, pp. 108–17. Mauriac, in *Le Figaro*, June 17, 1937, p. 1, challenged Claudel to add a stanza or "a single line of poetry" in honor of the thousands of Christians killed by the Nationalists in the name of a holy war and crusade.

29. *Sept*, January 8, 1937, p. 1. The editors concluded that "while we must pray for Spain's deliverance from Red domination and all it implies, it still is not easy to share enthusiasm for the lesser evil which seems to be its unavoidable concomitant."

30. François Charles-Roux, *Huit ans au Vatican* (Paris, 1947), p. 181.

31. In Coutrot, pp. 290–91, which has the best analysis of the suspension, pp. 272ff.

The suspension of *Sept* was cushioned by the appearance of a new weekly, *Temps Présent*, with the same list of subscribers, the same reporters and writers, but now under lay control. *Temps Présent* continued the original editorial position of *Sept*, now with renewed vigor. François Mauriac became one of its chief writers on Spanish affairs. But the point had been made.

Maritain was on the editorial board of the new weekly. Along with others he helped organize the French Committee for Civil and Religious Peace in Spain with the aim of ending the war as soon as possible.[32] The committee performed humanitarian work, particularly with refugees. It protested the Nationalist bombing of civilian populations in Barcelona in the spring of 1938. Mauriac wrote an article in October 1937 protesting papal silence on Nationalist atrocities.[33] In response to criticism of Maritain by the Spanish Nationalist minister of interior, Ramón Serrano Suñer, who called Maritain a "converted Jew" (Maritain's wife was a Jewish convert to Catholicism), Mauriac defended Maritain and went on to denounce the Nationalist repression done in the name of Christ as a worse crime than any other.[34] And early in 1938 André Malraux's romantic novel *L'Espoir* appeared with its criticism of the Spanish Church and its vision of a deinstitutionalized religion, to the praise of anticlerical reviewers.

In the midst of this ideological conflict Cardinal Verdier was interviewed about the French hierarchy's attitude toward the views that divided French Catholics on Spain. Verdier answered that "the Hierarchy withholds any pronouncement of opinion on the subject. It remains content with trying to mitigate sufferings."[35]

It was no wonder that Verdier was asked this question, for another controversy had just erupted with the publication in the spring of 1938 of Georges Bernanos' *Les Grands cimitières sous la lune*.[36] Where Maritian had written with logic, Bernanos wrote with indignation and fire, a match for Claudel. Bernanos wrote of his experiences in Mallorca, where he had gone to live in 1935 after having established a reputation as one of France's leading writers with his sensitive study of a rural priest, *Journal d'un curé de campagne*. He had been a mem-

---

32. A British group with similar aims was also organized. See Raguer, *La Unio Democratica*, pp. 443ff.

33. *Le Figaro*, October 13, 1937, p. 1.

34. *Le Figaro*, June 30, 1938, p. 1. The entire controversy with Serrano Suñer is narrated in Southworth, *El mito*, pp. 109–12.

35. In *The Tablet*, July 23, 1938, p. 106.

36. The English translation by Pamela Morris is titled *A Diary of My Times* (London, 1938).

ber of Action Française and was clearly a conservative, a man of the right. Indeed, when the Spanish war began, he expressed admiration for the Nationalists and approved of his son's joining the Falange. As a correspondent for *Sept* he wrote reports on the war from Mallorca which lauded the aims of the Nationalists.[37] But when the Nationalist reprisals began, he turned against them and the clergy who approved them. He was horrified at the spectacle of priests lending support to a repressive regime and to acts of reprisal: "I clearly state that the Nationalist Reign of Terror in Spain would long since have burned itself out, were it not that the more or less open, more or less conscious endorsement of priests and church-goers had finally succeeded in endowing it with a religious aspect."[38]

Bernanos took on the archbishop of Mallorca, José Miralles y Sbert, as an accomplice of the repression, and in fulminating against the Spanish bishops' collective letter he said of Miralles, "I only hope the pen shook in his senile hand."[39]

Bernanos' book fed the controversy. It is claimed that the Pope read it and forbade its condemnation.[40] Simone Weil, in Spain supporting the anarchists, wrote him a letter of praise and described her experiences of witnessing anarchist atrocities: from opposite sides both had come to a similar horror of war.[41] And it was significant that through it all Bernanos remained a convinced royalist; the charge that he was a communist dupe could not be made against him.[42]

Over all of this controversy, which drew to a close in 1939 as the French began to face the threat of war themselves, there was continuing concern with the refugees. As early as September 1936 Cardinal Verdier had made a national appeal for help for the victims of war. Bishop Gerlier of Lourdes had helped Republican wounded who had crossed into France. By 1939 the numbers of refugees had increased greatly as the Nationalist forces swept into Catalonia, threatening the last escape routes to France. Many Frenchmen were hostile to this

---

37. *Sept*, July 31, 1936, p. 10; October 16, 1936, p. 9; November 27, 1936, p. 9.

38. George Bernanos, *Diary*, p. 94.

39. Ibid., p. 113. Raguer, *La espada*, pp. 175–76, claims that the criticism of Miralles was unjust, as the Archbishop was one of only two Spanish bishops who voluntarily published in their diocesan bulletins Pius XI's anti-Nazi encyclical *Mit Brenender Sorge*.

40. Thomas Molnar, *Bernanos, His Political Thought and Prophecy* (New York, 1960), pp. 160–61.

41. Weil's letter is in Sperber, pp. 258–63.

42. François Maret wrote a counterpolemic, *Les Grands chantiers au soleil* (Paris, 1938), and the Dominican Mario Cordovani wrote a critical article in *L'Osservatore Romano*, January 2–3, 1939, p. 1.

large influx of desperate humanity. Cardinal Verdier took the lead in organizing French Catholics to appeal to the French government for humanitarian aid to these unfortunates.[43]

When the Spanish war ended in 1939, the division among French Catholics was more apparent than ever before. But a new solidarity had been forged among those who opposed the Spanish Nationalists. Men of such disparate temperament and ideology as Mauriac, Maritain, Bernanos, and Mounier had drawn together in a common cause that stood them well in facing the onslaught of Nazi barbarism the next year.

---

43. Louis Stein, *Beyond Death and Exile: The Spanish Republicans in France, 1939–1955* (Cambridge: Mass., 1979), p. 49.

CHAPTER 13

British Catholics and the War

The religious issues of the Spanish war meant little to most Britons. The anticlerical fury had little effect upon English non-Catholics, although the terror certainly inspired fear among the upper classes. But most Britons saw the war in the context of political issues: fascism, communism, democracy, law and order.[1] This was partly because there were so few Catholics in Britain, only 7 percent of the entire population. But for these Catholics the religious issue was more important than any other. Their concern had no political effect, for they supported the British government's policy of nonintervention, and they were numerically unimportant anyway.[2]

They were anxious, however, to defend their religion, and by implication that of Spanish Catholics, against criticism, especially from the established Anglican Church. From the beginning of the conflict English Catholics found themselves in a defensive position, forced to support a Spanish Church that many of them did not approve of, for English Catholicism was certainly more socially forward looking. But to demonstrate the conviction of their own Catholicism they felt they had to support the other members of the Universal Church. And they had to explain it as well.

One way of explaining the Spanish Church was to romanticize it. Spaniards were depicted as picturesque, somewhat backward Europeans with quaint ways and violent tempers, folk who never did things halfway. They lacked moderation and the spirit of compromise: this enabled them to produce great saints as well as great sinners. One could not expect the same behavior from Spaniards as from other, more

---

1. For British government policy see Jill Edwards, *The British Government and the Spanish Civil War, 1936–1939* (London, 1979).

2. There is a brief discussion of British Catholic attitudes on the Spanish war in Thomas Moloney, *Westminster, Whitehall and the Vatican: The Role of Cardinal Hinsley, 1935–43* (Turnbridge Wells, 1985), pp. 63–73.

civilized Europeans.[3] If the Spanish clergy were guilty of burning heretics and persecuting liberals in the past, these were simply excesses of devotion. And such views helped to explain violent anticlericalism as well.

This patronizing attitude was probably bolstered by the fact that English Catholics themselves came out of a tradition of persecution; not that of a sudden and intense anticlerical fury, but rather that of long centuries of hiding priests and suffering civil disabilities. While this gave them some sense of identification with suffering Spanish Catholics (albeit generations removed, and if looked at closely, English Catholic tradition had more in common with long-suffering Spanish Protestants), it also led to a superior attitude on the part of English Catholics: they had endured centuries of persecution as the price of maintaining the Faith, and now it was the turn of Spaniards.

If the British Catholic population was relatively small, it contained a vociferous and articulate minority of writers and publicists, all of whom came to support the Nationalists. There were no Catholic intellectuals of the prestige and caliber of the French; indeed, Britain's leading Catholic thinkers, such as Douglas Jerrold and Arnold Lunn (both Nationalist supporters) were distinctly second rate.[4] The only significant English poet to support the Nationalists was Roy Campbell. All the other important British poets and writers either supported the Republicans or claimed neutrality, and few except for Campbell referred to the religious issue.[5]

Although Britain lacked first-rate Catholic intellectuals, it had first-rate journalists, and the English Catholic press was strong and flourishing. The Tablet was arguably the best-written, most informative, and most tasteful Catholic weekly in the world. Among the better monthly journals there were the Dominican New Blackfriars, the Jesuit The Month, and the quarterly The Colosseum, edited by Catholic laymen. There was also the scholarly Studies, published in

---

3. See Michael Alpert, "Humanitarianism and Politics in the British Response to the Spanish Civil War, 1936–9," European History Quarterly 14 (1984), p. 432.

4. G.K. Chesterton had died in June 1936, on the eve of the Spanish war, and the only other significant Catholic thinker was Hilaire Belloc, whose concerns were so caught up with the sophistry of his anti-industrial and rural "distributive state" that he can be dismissed as a crank. See Jay P. Corbin, G.K. Chesterton and Hilaire Belloc: The Battle Against Modernity (Athens, Ohio, 1981). Luigi Sturzo, the Italian priest who had founded the Partito Popolare, lived in London exile and supported neutrality, but most of his work was published first in French journals.

5. See Valentine Cunningham, ed., The Penguin Book of Spanish Civil War Verse (Harmondsworth, 1980), for a good representative sampling.

Dublin. An Englishman who read these publications was probably better informed than any other Catholic in the world. In addition the English reader could sample the large output of books written in English on the Spanish war.[6]

For the masses and the more casual reader there was the daily non-Catholic but pro-Nationalist press; among these Lord Rothmere's publications stand out, particularly *The Daily Mail*. During the anticlerical fury this press accepted and published all atrocity stories, frequently without attempting to verify them. Lurid detail was invented, although the truth was bad enough. Many of these atrocity stories found their way into Catholic publications, especially those of a more pious nature.

There were also the pamphlets published in the propaganda war between the two factions. Both sides published admittedly biased books and pamphlets to try to convince the English populace of the justice of their respective causes. Invariably the Spanish Church was portrayed by the pro-Republicans as abettors of the uprising and therefore guilty of armed rebellion and treason, while the pro-Nationalist faction saw the clergy as the innocent victims of a communist plot.[7]

Although Catholics and Protestants were at odds over the religious issue in Spain, most Catholic periodicals at first refused to accept the facile explanation of a communist plot as the cause of the anticlerical fury and instead looked for deeper motivations. The lay-run *Colosseum*, even before the war began, examined the anticlerical incendiarism of the prewar months and concluded that church-burning in Spain was not part of a communist plot but rather stemmed from the Church's loss of the working classes.[8] Six months later, however, after the fury had run its course, it urged support for Franco, claiming that if the army had not risen, the masses would have followed Moscow.[9] The Jesuit *Month*, although it urged support for the Nationalists in the fall of 1936, cited favorably in January 1937 comments that the Spanish Church had lost the working classes because of poverty and injustice and that "the Church did nothing to rebuke or correct" those "friends of the Church who exploited them."[10]

---

6. See the bibliography in Thomas R. Greene, "The English Catholic Press and the Second Spanish Republic, 1931–1936," *Church History* 45 (1976), pp. 70–84.

7. As examples see the pro-Republican H.R.G. Greaves and David Thomson, *The Truth About Spain* (London, 1938) and the pro-Nationalist William Foss and Cecil Gerahty, *The Spanish Arena* (London, 1938).

8. Viator, "Thoughts on May Day," *The Colosseum* 3 (June 1936), pp. 116–19.

9. Ibid. 3 (December 1936), p. 247.

10. *The Month* 169 (January 1937), p. 5.

The Dominican monthly *New Blackfriars* took the most consistently neutral stand throughout the war and refused to accept the explanation of a communist plot. In September 1936 its editors asked why there was such intense hatred not only of the Spanish clergy but of the symbols of the Church as well: "The answer is to be found in the rottenness of conventional bourgeois religion which crushes the spirit of man."[11]

The Tablet, the most widely read Catholic periodical in Britain, from the beginning of the war saw the Church as a victim in a situation from which she could not possibly profit.[12] But whatever considerations the editors of *The Tablet* might have felt about agreeing with the neutrality of *New Blackfriars*, it was to them that the task fell of defending the Spanish Church against the attacks of English Protestants. As early as August 1936 *The Tablet* was criticizing English Catholics for not coming to the defense of the Church.[13] The Protestant attack against the Spanish Church took two forms, both reflecting the smug feeling that the Spanish clergy deserved what they got. The cruder of the two was the argument that the clergy had brought the fury on themselves by lending their sacristies for arsenals and their churches for fortresses and had themselves joined in the uprising to fire on the Republicans. They deserved death as either combatants or traitors.[14]

The other form of attack was the argument that the Spanish clergy had brought the attack upon themselves by their intolerance, oppression, and domination of Spain for centuries. This argument appeared with some frequency in the official paper of the Church of England, *The Church Times*. It was echoed by Josiah Wedgwood, MP, in a letter to *The Times:* he argued that churches were burned in Spain because of "fourteen hundred years" of theocracy and that the fear of the fires of the inquisition led to the torching of churches: "We are indignant that they burn down splendid churches, but they see other

---

11. *New Blackfriars* 17 (September 1936), pp. 704–12. It further cited an article in the *Catholic Herald* that said the destruction of the Spanish Church "was often only the destruction of a shell whose kernel had already decayed." Later it mentioned an article from the *Catholic World* which argued that the apostasy of the masses was caused by the Church's refusal to support the poor (October 1936, p. 783).

12. *The Tablet*, August 1, 1936, p. 134.

13. Ibid., August 29, 1936, p. 264.

14. As late as 1938 this was the argument of the Duchess of Atholl, who visited Republican Spain and claimed that arms were found in the "overwhelming majority" of churches attacked and that "most of the priests killed had met their deaths in the firing line." *Searchlight on Spain* (Harmondsworth, 1938), pp. 64, 97.

fires in Spain."[15] *The Tablet* answered that Wedgwood ignored the killing of priests and nuns and said that "no failings or omissions" in the
past could justify the present fury and opined that "the Church is hated
not so much for standing with the conservative order as for deeper
grounds, because its doctrine of the nature of man cuts right across
secularist ideals; and the fury rages because the doctrines live."[16]

By October 1936 *The Tablet* was attacking "Anglican dignitaries"
who "sit in the comfort and security of episcopal palaces and dean-
eries" and "withhold the name of Christian from the brave men who
have borne the peril and heat of the conflict in Spain."[17] As the fury
came to an end, *The Church Times* contended that the Spanish Church
was responsible for the anticlericalism of the Republicans and that
it was "associated with privilege and wealth" and was the "greatest land-
owner in Spain" and was "interested in banking and commerce." The
Anglican paper concluded, "unhappy is the church that waxes fat when
the people are pitifully lean."[18] *The Tablet* scored a telling response
by pointing out that the Spanish Church had lost its landed property
in 1835, that the salary of the archbishop of Toledo was one-tenth that
of the archbishop of Westminster, and it cited many of the charitable
works done by the religious orders in Spain and said that many of the
clergy were devoted to the principles of social justice. It compared the
Anglican Church in England to the Spanish Church and noted that
many of the same charges could be levied equally against the Church
of England, especially in its control of national wealth in England,
"where the bulk of the population live lives of great poverty and in-
security and care little for the Church."[19]

Further hostility between the two churches arose over two trips
made by Anglican clerics to Republican Spain in the winter and spring
of 1937. The first was made in late January by the Anglican deans of
Chichester and Rochester and four other clerics after consultation with
the archbishop of York. It found "no evidence of organized Godless
propaganda" but noted that all churches were closed or secularized.
The group reported that clergy had been killed either after a trial
"which proved them involved in the rebellion" or by mob violence,
and unless the particular priest "was actively unpopular, he was not
killed by his own people." The regular clergy were objects of great

15. *The Times* (London), August 12, 1936, p. 11.
16. *The Tablet*, August 15, 1936, p. 200.
17. Ibid., October 24, 1936, p. 548.
18. As cited in *The Tablet*, January 16, 1937, p. 76.
19. Ibid., January 16, 1937, pp. 76–79.

hatred, and the discovery of large stores of money in "clerical and con-
ventual houses exacerbated the passions of the mob." The report went
on to record what the Anglican clergy said were passed on to them
as the causes of this anticlericalism: the lack of a Protestant reformation, neglect of the social gospel, close political connections between
the clergy and landowners, a large amount of "ill-developed" land owned
by the Church, and, finally, the failure of the Church authorities to
understand the people's needs.[20]

The second trip was made by the dean of Canterbury and eight
other persons including two Catholics in April 1937. The aim of the
trip was to "enquire into the religious and social situation" in Republican Spain. Most of the thirty-two-page report they issued was taken
up with economic and political matters and very little with religious
concerns. A visit to Bilbao convinced them that they "had never been
in a country anywhere in Europe in which religion was more real and
more alive as a social force," and they concluded their report by noting that "probably no less than ninety per cent of the clergy were im-
plicated in the rebellion" and that "the Church cannot be acquitted
of responsibility for the hostility which she evidently inspired."[21]

The Tablet did not respond to this specific report. Instead it ran
a series of articles by Arnold Lunn on his trips to Nationalist Spain.[22]
It did take note of the dean of Canterbury's remarks upon his return
to England from Spain to the effect that the Spanish Republicans
were religious men who believed in social brotherhood. The Catholic
weekly attacked the dean for his "readiness to swallow and report
what his hosts chose to tell him about the Church in Spain."[23] The
Catholic archbishop of Westminster implicitly criticized these visitors and said that "all who are not wilfully blind see the battle raging
between Christian civilization and the worst form of paganism that
has ever darkened the Earth."[24]

---

20. The report was published on February 16, 1937, and is in Henry Brinton,
Christianity in Spain (London, n.d.), pp. 70–81. The Tablet, February 20, 1937, pp. 255–
57, responded with detailed criticism of the report and concluded that the Anglican
clerics appeared "more anxious to make the best of any vague deism or cultivated Atheism of the enemies of the Church than to enter into the point of view of those whose
sacred beliefs they share."

21. Dean of Canterbury, et al., Report of a Religious Delegation to Spain, April
1937 (London, 1937), pp. 9, 31, 32. The report was published on April 26, 1937.

22. These were collected and published as Spanish Rehearsal (London, n.d.).

23. The Tablet, April 24, 1937, p. 576.

24. In Toynbee, p. 160. The archbishop's pastoral letter, from which this quote
is taken, was not published in The Tablet, nor was his letter to Cardinal Gomá in support of the Spanish bishops' collective letter.

By late 1937 this controversy with non-Catholics began to fade. When the English literary establishment signed a manifesto of support for the Republic, *The Tablet* criticized them as "wittingly or unwittingly committing a great betrayal."[25] Later, in April 1938, it took on the bishop of Chelmsford, who claimed in a rally that there was no religious persecution in Spain.[26] *The Tablet* praised a group of Protestant clergymen who formed a group called the United Christian Front to express its solidarity with Catholics and its sympathy with Catholics suffering persecution.[27]

Besides expressing their indignation at Protestant clerics, Catholics also sought to do something practical to support Spanish Catholics. Almost from the beginning of the war some form of aid was collected and sent to Nationalist Spain. The Bishops' Committee for the Relief of Spanish Distress collected funds for medical aid and relief, emphasizing that none of the aid was to be used for military purposes. They ran a weekly column in *The Tablet* noting the amount collected and describing what it was used for, most often ambulances or medical supplies.[28] Some Catholics wanted to go to Spain to fight.[29] Others found it easier to support the only significant group of foreign volunteers from a free Western country to fight for the Nationalists. This was the Irish Brigade, led by General Eoin O'Duffy, a leader of the protofascist Irish Blue Shirts. He was suggested to Spanish Carlists by the cardinal-primate of Ireland, Joseph MacRory, as the person who might best lead a military contingent. Some 1,000 men volunteered for action, and 700 were involved in a brief skirmish early in 1937. They clearly identified religion as their chief motivation, and they carried papal flags and wore Sacred Heart badges contributed by Irish nuns. O'Duffy claimed that the brigade was not fighting for any Irish political party but for "Christ the King against Communism," and for this reason his contract with the Nationalists spelled out a refusal to serve against the Basque autonomists "for reasons of religion and traditional ties between the Basques and the Irish."[30]

25. *The Tablet*, December 11, 1937, pp. 796–97.

26. Ibid., April 30, 1938, p. 560.

27. Ibid., September 25, 1937, p. 404.

28. Organizers of Catholic financial support stressed the large number of small contributors. See Alpert, pp. 429–30.

29. One of the few who went to fight for the Nationalists (some 2,000 Britons volunteered for the international brigades to fight for the Republic) was Peter Kemp, inspired by Christian ideals to fight against "atheistic communism." See his memoir, *Mine Were of Trouble* (London, 1957).

30. Eoin O'Duffy, *Crusade in Spain* (London, 1938), pp. 117, 195. See also Francis McCullagh, *In Franco's Spain* (London, 1937) by a correspondent who traveled with the Irish Brigade.

No Englishmen are recorded as having joined O'Duffy's brigade. Indeed, there was division in Ireland itself over the brigade and Ireland's role in the Spanish war. The IRA opposed any action in Spain on either side as a diversion from the struggle in Ireland against the British. And although the Irish Catholic bishops wholeheartedly supported the Nationalist cause with money and prayers, there were some militant Catholics who publicly supported the Republicans.[31]

The major crisis that pointed to a division among English Catholics was the same one that divided French Catholics: the morality of the war. There was little division among the English at first, and many of their arguments were directed more against the French supporters of the Republicans than against English neutralists. Controversy began when the war in the Basque provinces intensified. It was highlighted by the traditional ties between Basque and English Catholics; for years upper-class Basques had sent their children to English schools, and commercial ties strengthened the bonds between the two. *The Tablet* published the Basque bishops' pastoral instruction shortly after it was written in August 1936, but little else was said until Cardinal Gomá and Basque President Aguirre began their public debate early in 1937. *The Tablet* published a pro-Basque article explaining the autonomist position, but in the same issue it editorially criticized the Basques for subordinating the cause of religion to the aims of nationalism.[32]

Two specifically Basque problems came up in 1937: the bombing of Guernica and the repatriation of Basque refugee children. Most Catholic periodicals accepted the Nationalist interpretation of the destruction of Guernica—that the town had been destroyed by retreating Basque troops rather than by Nationalist-German aerial bombardment. As for the Basque children sent abroad for safety, *The Tablet* published a letter from Bishop Múgica of Vitoria to the archbishop of Westminster begging that the children be raised as Catholics.[33] A discordant note was sounded by the Jesuit *The Month*, which found the Basque children in England not what they expected: the children,

---

31. The government of the Irish Republic continued to maintain diplomatic relations with the Spanish Republic in the face of clerical criticism. See J. Bowyer Bell, "Ireland and the Spanish Civil War, 1936–1939," *Studia Hibernica* 9 (1969), pp. 137–163.

32. *The Tablet*, February 27, 1937, pp. 292–94. An English priest, H. T. Johnson, answered the editorial in a letter, March 27, 1937, p. 454, claiming that if the Basques were to be accused of putting politics before religion, then Franco was doing the same thing: if Franco wanted the restoration of Catholicism, he should make peace with the Basques and allow religion to flourish.

33. Ibid., May 8, 1937, p. 682.

"so far from being Catholic, seem to be, as far as their years allow, militant communists, as undisciplined and ungrateful as such upbringing might suggest."[34]

Over 3,000 of these children had been sent to England, accompanied by 60 Catholic teachers and 15 priests to safeguard their religious welfare. After Bilbao fell, the question of repatriation was raised. A Basque Children's Committee was founded, with representation of Archbishop Arthur Hinsley of Westminster. But the committee was predominantly pro-Republican, and Hinsley's representative, Canon Craven, resigned when the committee refused to send any child back without a specific request from the child's parents. The committee was not satisfied that the Vatican's representative in Bilbao, Ildebrando Antoniutti and his representative, a Father Gabana, accurately represented the wishes of the children's parents.[35] In late October 1937 an agreement was reached whereby nearly 800 children's parents' wishes were authenticated.[36]

By the summer of 1937 the Basque issue had become absorbed in the larger issue of the morality of the war, stimulated largely by the questions raised by Jacques Maritain (see chapter 11). *New Blackfriars* took a consistently anti-Nationalist stand and approvingly quoted articles from its French counterpart, *Sept*. The Dominican Gerald Vann argued that there was no such thing as a just war, and *New Blackfriars* cited the Dutch Catholic press which likened the stance of Spanish Republican Catholics to that of sixteenth-century Dutch Catholics who rejected and fought Philip II's appointees.[37]

The Tablet in fairness printed letters that condemned the uprising on the basis of just-war theory, but it also published two highly critical responses to Maritain: an editorial that disputed his contention that a Nationalist victory would be a misfortune for the Church, called Maritain a rash prophet, and criticized Bernanos' equation of Republican persecution of the clergy with Nationalist persecution of the poor; and an article by Reginald J. Dingle heatedly claiming that the Spanish clergy knew more about the issues than did a handful of Frenchmen. Dingle characterized Bernanos and Mauriac as "out-

34. *The Month* 170 (July 1937), p. 2. See also Alpert, pp. 431–35, and Legarreta, pp. 119ff., on the Basque children.

35. Gabana was refused entry into England by the foreign secretary on the grounds that the priest was engaged in propaganda activities and that the government's policy of nonintervention did not allow this. See *The Tablet*, June 5, 1937, p. 825.

36. Alberto de Onaindía, p. 291, who negotiated the agreement, claims that some parents' signatures were forged "by Jesuits."

37. *New Blackfriars* 17 (December 1936), pp. 900–6; 18 (April 1937), p. 298.

side the main line of Catholic thought" and Maritain as ignorant of the facts.[38]

Immediately with the controversy over Maritain's article there appeared the Spanish bishops' collective letter, which the English bishops supported. And although the Spanish hierarchy in their letter did not call the war a crusade, some English publicists did. Arnold Lunn argued that the uprising was a crusade and said that "a crusade is not un-Christian because few crusaders are Christ-like."[39] *The Month* opined that the Spanish struggle was "ultimately but one phase of the organized rising of Antichrist against Christ which marks these latter days" and claimed that the war was holy and "in accordance with the divine will."[40]

Another issue in which the morality of war was cited concerned the ethics of bombing civilians. This was occasioned by the bombardment of Barcelona in 1938. It raised a protest by the British Committee for Civil and Religious Peace in Spain, an anti-Nationalist group that had a French counterpart. *The Month* claimed that their criticism of Nationalist bombing was unfair and said, "it is surely significant that the outcry against bombing has arisen only when the Christian forces appear likely to win."[41] The committee defended itself by noting that it had been seeking a ban on bombing for some time.[42]

While criticism of the idea that the uprising was morally or theologically justified was one thing, support for the Nationalists was quite another. Maritain himself had argued that his criticism of the Nationalists implied, not support for the Republicans, but rather a desire to end the war by not supporting either side. Many Catholics argued that this view was nonsense: the best way to end the war was to support the Nationalists, who by 1937 had a preponderance of military support and were on the offensive. As for stories of atrocities committed by the Nationalists, these were explained away as either communist lies or else the Nationalists were depicted as hearty fellows who had been carried away by the fury and therefore were justifiably angry.[43] General O'Duffy's *Crusade in Spain* described the anticlerical fury with a vividness more lurid than that of any Spanish

---

38. *The Tablet*, August 7, 1937, p. 181; August 21, 1937, pp. 248–49. Dingle later said in *The Month* 172 (August 1938), pp. 129–36, that Maritain was "too long a sojourner in the realm of pure ideas."

39. *The Tablet*, July 31, 1937, pp. 153–54.

40. *The Month* 170 (July 1937), p. 1; 170 (December 1937), p. 488.

41. *The Month* 171 (March 1938), pp. 263–65.

42. *The Tablet*, March 12, 1938, p. 341.

43. *The Month*, 169 (May 1937), pp. 433–39, and 170 (August 1937), pp. 135–41,

eyewitness. *The Tablet* printed frequent articles by visitors to Nationalist Spain who found no evidence of reprisal atrocities but rather order, discipline, and respect for the clergy.[44]

There was also the poetry of Roy Campbell, the only notable poet who supported the Nationalists, although among pro-Republican artists W.H. Auden said that he was disturbed "about the treatment of priests," and later he credited his experiences of seeing Spanish churches closed as leading to his return to Christianity.[45] Campbell's poems appeared frequently in *The Tablet*, and his most important collection, *Flowering Rifle*, was published in 1939. He used vigorous imagery to defend the Spanish clergy and the Nationalist cause. Campbell typified that bully attitude toward war so beloved of the British middle class: the notion that force would solve all problems and that if the Nationalists knocked a few proletarian heads together, it was good form.[46]

Despite the general support given the Nationalists by the Catholic press in Britain, it should be noted that the other side had a voice. Indeed, when the uprising began, there was little support for the Nationalists other than as the lesser of two evils. From the beginning the letters column in *The Tablet* printed correspondence condemning support for Franco, praising the Basques, questioning the morality of the uprising, and criticizing Nationalist atrocities. Interestingly, of all the issues of the war the one that generated the most reader response was an article by a physician, Dr. D. J. Collier, who described a trip to Republican Barcelona in mid-1938. She reported that she had attended mass in Barcelona, had talked to priests, and generally described the new religious freedom of the changing conditions of later 1938.[47] Her report occasioned a flurry of letters, many denying that she was telling the truth, and some questioning her faith. It appears

published two short fictional stories by T.W.C. Curd, both set in Britain of the future with a British Catholic clergy under anticlerical attack similar to Spain's.

44. These included articles by Sir Walter Maxwell Scott, March 20, 1937, pp. 401–2; Arnold Lunn in a weekly series that began on April 10, 1937, pp. 505–6ff.; G.S. Burns, S.J., September 4, 1937, pp. 314–15; and Denzil Batchelor, February 19, 1938, pp. 231–32. There was also an interview with General Franco, August 28, 1937, pp. 281–83.

45. In Cunningham, p. 72.

46. In his autobiography, *Light on a Dark Horse* (Chicago, 1952), p. 304, Campbell talks of threatening his new bride with a "real spanking" to keep her from the danger of provoking anticlericals by wearing a mantilla to mass in Toledo before the 1936 uprising. See the analysis of Campbell in Katherine Bail Hoskins, *Today the Struggle: Literature and Politics in England During the Spanish Civil War* (Austin, 1969), pp. 40ff.

47. *The Tablet*, October 15, 1938, pp. 485–86.

that many of her critics were unaware of the changing conditions as the war came to an end.

By late 1938 concern over the Spanish war began to fade as Britons faced the possibility of their own war against Nazi Germany. *The Tablet's* articles on Spain began to deal with problems of the future. The controversy over the war had changed the outlook of some journals completely. *The Colosseum,* which had begun as a moderate quarterly, ended with articles praising Franco and did not hesitate to offer its readers the lurid journalism of the Austrian publicist Erik von Kuhnelt-Leddihn, who claimed that the display of a ripped-up nun's body hung like a side of beef in a Barcelona bookstore in 1936 was a "common sight."[48] Only *New Blackfriars* maintained its neutrality. On the occasion of Franco's victory it offered what might be considered the epitaph on foreign Catholic reaction to the war: it noted that the end of the war would mean the end of a "conflict of conscience" for millions of Catholics throughout the world. The journal hoped that Spanish Catholics would try to understand the position of Catholics abroad who could not support Franco because for foreign Catholics the religious issue was not the totality of the war, nor was it the only issue.[49] And if British Catholics were mostly united in their opposition to the Spanish Republic before 1939, the revelation of Nationalist reprisals after the Spanish war ended caused a division within the Christian community. Some Catholics left the Church over the issue, and for others it poisoned relations with Protestants to the extent that ecumenical relations were set back for decades.[50]

---

48. *The Colosseum* 5 (October 1938), pp. 178–88.

49. *New Blackfriars* 20 (April 1939), pp. 299–301.

50. See Stuart Mews, "The Sword of the Spirit: A Catholic Cultural Crusade of 1940," *The Church and War,* ed. W. J. Sheils (Oxford, 1983), pp. 409–30.

CHAPTER 14

American Catholics and the War

The United States was far removed from the Spanish war. It should have had little impact on Americans. There were important economic ties between the two countries, but they were hardly crucial for either. Americans could have ignored the Spanish war with little peril to themselves, certainly more so than the British and French could. Yet the war had a significant influence upon American life and thought, and the religious issue was debated more heatedly between Catholics and non-Catholics in the United States than elsewhere. It was the mirror of generations of tensions between American Catholics and Protestants.

American Protestants feared above all that the Catholic Church in the United States aspired to the same position of power and control that the Spanish Church had before the overthrow of the monarchy. American Catholics did little to disabuse them of this notion. They were confused, uneducated in modern theological thinking, and their leaders and educators were stubbornly wedded to outmoded nineteenth-century politico-religious concepts that their English and French coreligionists had long since given up or simply ignored.

They were also probably the most docile group of Catholics in the Western world. They supported their bishops with their hearts and purses, although not with their minds, which were concerned with secular affairs. And their bishops, drawn from the same immigrant community that made up the American Church, reflected their upbringing.[1] The more important ones had been educated in Rome. They were obsessed with things Roman; indeed, the bishops were frequently more papal than the pope. They defended papal pronouncements with

---

1. James Hennesey, *American Catholics: A History of the Roman Catholic Community in the United States* (New York, 1981), p. 235, says that in the 1920s the Catholic community "remained prey to institutional narcissism which drained energies into narrowly focused crusades for what were deemed church interests."

a vigor not found elsewhere. It is no wonder that American Protestants reacted to such behavior so as to become aggressively anti-Catholic.

Anti-Catholicism had been, for years, much of the reason for the popularity of American Protestantism. Catholicism had been viewed not only as a threat to Protestant religious beliefs but to the American system of religious freedom as well. Other factors were bound up with this feeling: there was resentment and fear of recent Catholic immigrants, particularly from Italy, and concern with Irish Catholic political and social aggressiveness. Secular agnostics—especially professors in state and Ivy League universities, and publicists in *The Nation* and *The New Republic*—shared these Protestant fears, so much so that there was no appreciable difference between Protestants and secular agnostics in their responses to the Spanish war. Catholics, in turn, reacted with what George Shuster, the leading American Catholic liberal of the 1930s, called "minorityitis"—an emotional response to the anti-Catholicism of the Protestant and agnostic community.[2]

Both Catholics and Protestants were arrogant and ignorant. Each faction was absolutely certain that it alone possessed the truth. Catholics could always find some clerical pronouncement that could be applied to all problems, and for Protestants opposition to the Catholic position, whatever the merits of the issue, was an automatic response. Nor was either humble. Each side knew little about the Spanish issues they were willing to pontificate on.[3]

By the mid-1930s American Catholics were on the verge of acceptability in American political society. They had weathered the attacks of the Ku Klux Klan in the 1920s, and they had survived the anti-Catholicism of the 1928 presidential election, the first in which a Catholic, Al Smith, was nominated by a major political party. They were 17 percent of the population, 20 million strong, the largest single religious group (although less than all Protestants united). They wielded an influence greater than their numbers because it was believed that they could be persuaded to vote as a bloc. They were considered a necessary part of the great coalition forged by Franklin Roosevelt in his presidential victories of 1932 and 1936. They formed

---

2. George Shuster, "A Catholic Defends His Church," *The New Republic*, January 4, 1939, pp. 246–48.

3. The literature of the war reveals that anti-Catholics were probably more ignorant than Catholics: no Catholic spokesman could match the uninformed views of the Protestant cleric John A. MacKay, the president of Princeton Theological Seminary, who said that there had been no antireligious feeling or anticlericalism in Spain before 1931. (In *The New York Times*, March 6, 1937, p. 6.)

powerful voting units and pressure groups in such large cities as New York, Boston, Philadelphia, Chicago, and St. Louis. There were also Catholic politicians who were eager and willing to defend the Church and clergy against all attacks. Congressman John McCormack of Boston worked closely with Boston Cardinal William O'Connell to prevent any support or aid for Republican Spain.[4] Senator Pat McCarran of Nevada was the father of two nuns and an avid Nationalist supporter. In neither France nor England were there such influential politicians who could be specifically identified with Catholic interests.

Whether or not Catholics could be marshalled to vote for or against Spanish issues is, however, debatable. According to public opinion polls after two and a half years of war, by December 1938, only 58 percent of American Catholics sympathized with the Nationalists; 42 percent sympathized with the Republicans, a remarkable statistic in view of the overwhelming efforts made to promote support for the Nationalists by the clergy and by Catholic publications in general.[5] But Catholic politicians could claim to muster the votes of the faithful, and the threat or promise was sufficient to influence the government.

Catholics had a formidable press and radio network: every diocese had a weekly newspaper or distributed one from a larger diocese. While there was no national Catholic daily as in France, the National Catholic Welfare Conference provided a common news source for all these publications, and the effect was that of a national Catholic newspaper. There were also mass-circulation weeklies and monthlies. *The Catholic Digest* monthly condensed and reprinted articles of interest to Catholics. The most important of the weeklies were *America*, published and edited by the American and Canadian Jesuits, and *The Commonweal*, a lay-edited review. Various religious orders had monthlies: the most independent was the Paulist *The Catholic World*, and there was the proletarian-oriented *The Catholic Worker*. There were no intellectual periodicals, nothing on the level of *New Blackfriars* or *La Vie Intellectuelle; Thought*, the only journal with intellectual pretensions, was edited by the Jesuits who published *America*, and its articles on Spain were reprints from *America*. Actually there were no outstanding Catholic intellectuals in the United States. This fact, in itself, was the reason for much of the emotional reaction to the war and for much of the simplistic response.

---

    4. Donald F. Crosby, "Boston's Catholics and the Spanish Civil War: 1936–1939," *New England Quarterly* 44 (March 1971), pp. 82–100.
    5. Hadley Cantril and Mildred Strunk, eds., *Public Opinion 1935–1946* (Princeton, 1951), pp. 807–9.

Reporting in the press on Spanish affairs before the uprising was sparse. The chief foreign issue of Catholic concern in the 1920s and 1930s was Mexico, where the anticlerical Mexican government had instituted stringent control and limitations upon the Mexican clergy. There had been some violence (infinitesimal compared to the Spanish anticlerical fury), but American Protestants and Catholics did not react strongly to Mexican affairs. As for Spain there seemed to be a general feeling that Spaniards should solve their own problems. Both the secular press and Catholic periodicals agreed that Spaniards had to cope with immense social problems, and while Catholics criticized wealthy Spaniards for ignoring papal social teaching, *The New Republic*'s Louis Fisher reported from Spain in the spring of 1936 that the Spanish people were not religious and that they hated the Church because it was the agent of their oppressors.[6]

As in other countries there was shock when the full extent of the anticlerical fury became known. The Catholic press gave it full coverage, as did the Hearst chain of newspapers. The *New York Times* reported fully and generally with objectivity on the killing of priests and the burning of churches. It would have been difficult for any literate American to have argued that he was ignorant of the fury. But some secular publications mocked the clerical assassinations by satirically commenting on the lurid headlines of the pro-Nationalist press (which headlines were actually correct).[7] This tasteless jibing, along with such reports from the opposite camp as those of Jane Anderson de Cienfuegos, who falsely claimed to have actually seen a crucified seminarian,[8] was a fairly common occurrence on both sides. Novelist Theodore Dreiser believed as late as 1939 the uprising to have been the result of a strange Catholic-masonic conspiracy.[9] Until the end lurid atrocity tales from the pro-Nationalist camp vied with pro-Republican denials of any extensive fury or a simple lack of reporting the facts.[10]

---

6. Louis Fisher, "Spain Tries to Avoid Revolution," *The New Republic*, May 20, 1936, pp. 38–40.

7. For a good example see "Faking the Spanish News," *The Nation*, September 19, 1936, p. 322.

8. "And then I saw. In the small interior of the chapel an immense cross rose above the broken altar. And on the cross there hung the body of a lad in his teens, his loins girded with the crimson banner of the Communists. His arms were bound with thongs. Nails were driven through the palms of his hands and between the bones of his feet. Heavy drops of blood glinted as they fell from the lacerated flesh." "Horror in Spain," *The Catholic Digest*, August 1937, p. 69, as condensed from *The New York American*, May 16, 1937.

9. Stanley Weintraub, *The Last Great Cause: The Intellectuals and the Spanish Civil War* (New York, 1968), pp. 297ff.

10. As late as February 4, 1939, *The Catholic News* (New York) reported that

Catholic periodicals exaggerated the numbers of clergy killed, but there was no reaction from the secular press to the first statement from the Vatican early in 1937 that 13,400 priests—nearly half of the entire Spanish diocesan clergy—had been killed.[11] But *America* protested as early as September 1936 the lack of "righteous indignation" in the non-Catholic press concerning the clerical assassinations; *America* had already come out in favor of the Nationalists, but it qualified its support by disclaiming any sympathy with fascism.[12] In November 1936 it said that both sides were guilty of atrocities, "but those of the Communists have been more inhuman" and "less blood will be shed by the Right than by the Left."[13] In January 1937 it saw Franco as a republican who would restore the Republic and disclaimed that the Nationalists were crusaders, saying that Catholics had supported and died for the Republic, but that "Catholic Spain has given its allegiance to Franco."[14] *America's* editor, Jesuit Francis X. Talbot, argued (correctly) that Franco was not a fascist, although he said that Catholics would choose fascism in preference to communism, but only as the lesser of two evils, and later he claimed that a Catholic could collaborate with fascism but not with communism.[15]

With the significant exceptions of *The Commonweal, The Catholic Worker* (which argued for Christian pacifism in Spain and opposed any use of force),[16] and *The Catholic World,* most of the other Catholic periodicals followed *America's* lead in urging support for the Nationalists. Of the diocesan papers, only *New World,* Chicago Cardinal George Mundelein's paper, maintained a neutral stance. Most of the others reflected the view of Bishop Daniel J. Gercke of Tucson, who said that Franco would save Spain, observing that the Nationalist leader "received Holy Communion several times a week."[17] Support for Franco had become so strong in Catholic periodicals by mid-1937 that he was idealized almost beyond recognition. In fact, as early as October 1936 Jesuit Robert I. Gannon, president of Ford-

---

three priests had been "crucified and burned alive" by members of the international brigades during the evacuation of Barcelona. (This was months after the brigades left Spain; furthermore, Montero Moreno, p. 63, says he could find no evidence of any crucifixions during the war. See chapter 3.)

11. *The New York Times,* February 2, 1937, p. 11.
12. *America,* September 19, 1936, pp. 554–55; August 8, 1936, p. 420.
13. Ibid., November 21, 1936, pp. 156–57.
14. Ibid., January 23, 1937, pp. 362–63; January 30, 1937, pp. 397–98.
15. February 15, 1937, p. 445; May 1, 1937, pp. 76–77.
16. *The Catholic Worker,* November 1936, p. 4.
17. In a letter to *Commonweal,* April 2, 1937, p. 640.

ham University, praised the Spanish Nationalists as rebels, "glorious outlaws like George Washington and the Irish saints."[18] Picturing Franco as a liberal democrat in the tradition of the American rebels of 1776 was one way for American Catholics to rationalize their support of the Spanish uprising.[19] *America* saw the uprising as "not fascist but democratically Christian."[20] Jesuit poet Leonard Feeney penned a verse, "The Spanish 'Loyalists,'" on the anticlerical fury:

> There are so many noses broken
> Of Our Sweet Lady's image—she whose spoken
> Message as a maid, made a Magnificat—
> Would we not fail her to forgive them that?
> Her ruined spires, her steeples bend towards Hell,
> The battered belfry and the broken bell
> Issue no more the clarion note of Peace,
> Redemption, Revelation, and Release.
>
> Their killing of priests I mind not much:—
> But oh, the things they touched they should not touch!
> O God! O Christ! O Franco! Anyone!
> Avenge us, please, for some things they have done![21]

But how could Americans comprehend the anticlerical fury? There was no tradition of anticlericalism within the American Church. American Catholics were an obedient lot. How could the Spaniards—idealized for years as the quintessentially religious beings—burn churches and kill priests? The solution to this puzzling question could be found in the same simplistic answer given by the Spanish clericals: communism. The fury was seen as a communist conspiracy to destroy the Church, the first point of attack in the international communist revolution. This answer needed no intellectual explanation; all it required was an emotional response.[22]

---

18. *The New York Times*, October 14, 1936, p. 27.

19. See Allen Guttmann, *The Wound in the Heart: America and the Spanish Civil War* (New York, 1962), p. 30, and Richard P. Traina, *American Diplomacy and the Spanish Civil War* (Bloomington, 1968), p. 143.

20. August 8, 1936, p. 420. Harvard historian Bernard Fay reported after a trip to Nationalist Spain that Franco went to mass daily, that he was a "thorough Christian," and that "generally you can see him at church at the close of the day." *America*, December 11, 1937, p. 221.

21. *America*, November 27, 1937, p. 188.

22. See George Q. Flynn, *Roosevelt and Romanism: Catholics and American Diplomacy, 1937–1945* (Westport, Conn., 1976), pp. 35ff.

This obsession with communism was not solely an American phenomenon, but most English and French responses were tempered by the awareness that there were other issues involved and that communism grew in countries where social problems were great. In the United States most Catholic publicists were not that knowledgeable. *America* was one of the most active proponents of the communist issue, not infrequently tying it in with a masonic conspiracy. The letters columns of Catholic periodicals showed a grass-roots concern with communism inculcated by the clergy.[23]

Two important Catholic periodicals opposed this line. *The Catholic World*, edited by Paulist priests, from the beginning was skeptical about communist penetration and argued that the lack of social justice was of greater importance as a cause of the anticlerical fury.[24] *The Commonweal*, the lay-edited weekly, argued that although there were communists in Spain, the anticlerical fury was caused by the Spanish clergy's alliance with those who had been responsible for social injustice; communist-trained agitators had seized upon the issue, and all churchmen had suffered. *The Commonweal* criticized clerical support for the Nationalists, and although it published articles by those who argued the communist conspiracy theory, it was the only Catholic weekly to give favorable reviews to the French Catholic opponents of the Nationalists.[25] But its editors were divided on policy. The founder and chief editor, Michael Williams, had become a partisan of the Nationalists, and he was disturbed by the secular press' inattention to the anticlerical fury. The managing editor, George Shuster, and the journal's board of directors had different views. Shuster was upset by Talbot, *America*'s editor, who, when the war began, invited Shuster and other editors of Catholic journals to a meeting to discuss a common editorial position for the Catholic press. Shuster urged that they obtain information before making a decision and was under the impression that Talbot agreed with him, but within a month after the meeting *America* came out in support of the Nationalists.[26]

---

23. The popular preacher Fulton J. Sheen preached the communist cause of the Spanish war in apocalyptic tones. *The New York Times*, August 24, 1937, p. 19.

24. *The Catholic World* 147 (March 1937), pp. 648–49. Its editor, James Gillis, practically alone among Catholic publicists (and secular ones as well) confessed his puzzlement at the entire Spanish situation.

25. *The Commonweal*, August 28, 1936, pp. 413–14; October 16, 1936, pp. 569–70; March 5, 1937, pp. 516–17.

26. See J. David Valaik, "American Catholic Dissenters and the Spanish Civil War," *The Catholic Historical Review* 53 (January 1968), p. 538, and Rodger Van Allen, *The Commonweal and American Catholicism* (Philadelphia, 1974), p. 61.

Shuster responded with an article that described as simplistic those rightist views that praised Franco, and he scored American leftists as well, whom he said were as blind to the excesses of the Republicans as Catholics were blind to Franco's brutality. It was foolish to believe that Franco would inaugurate a "beneficent and progressive social order," he said, and one could not call all of the international brigadiers bolsheviks, for there were honest humanitarians among them.[27] Editor Williams had dissociated himself from Shuster's view in a preface to the article, arguing that he was convinced that there was a communist conspiracy that could not be overlooked. *America's* Talbot responded by claiming that Shuster was ignorant of Spanish affairs and denied that Franco was a fascist: "It is true that Fascists have submitted to his leadership as a component part of his army, but so have Monarchists, and so have Republicans, and so have Centrists."[28]

The barrage of criticism of Shuster's article and the corresponding support for Williams and Talbot were reflected in letters columns in both periodicals. Archbishop John T. McNichols of Cincinnati forbade the sale of *The Commonweal* in the churches of his archdiocese. Williams further responded by publishing articles by less critical pro-Nationalists Owen McGuire, Nena Belmonte, and Aileen O'Brien, but he could not ignore the criticism of his board of directors. They were ready to force him out, and what probably convinced them to act was Williams' organization of a rally for Spanish relief funds in May 1937 at Madison Square Garden in New York City. The rally was under the patronage of Cardinal Patrick J. Hayes of New York, and it included a processional hymn composed by Williams, along with pro-Nationalist speakers, including one of the more extreme, the priest Edward Lodge Curran.[29]

Associating *The Commonweal* with this group distressed the board of directors, and they forced Williams out the following year, although they allowed him to continue to write a weekly column.[30]

One of Williams' chief arguments was that the secular press was not paying attention to the anticlerical fury and that it was unfair in its presentation of news from Spain.[31] He singled out *The Nation* and *The New Republic* as examples. He was certainly on target: one of *The Nation's* first comments on the war was an editorial claiming

27. *The Commonweal*, April 2, 1937, pp. 625–27.
28. *America*, April 10, 1937, pp. 9–10.
29. See the accounts in *The New York Times*, May 20, 1937, p. 8, and Van Allen, pp. 67–69.
30. *The Commonweal*, June 24, 1938, pp. 229–30 and 241–42.
31. *The Commonweal*, May 7, 1937, pp. 33–37.

that most of the money behind the uprising came from the Jesuits.[32] *The New Republic* was unabashedly pro-Republican and matched the pro-Nationalist Catholic press in its vehemence. As early as September 1936 *The New Republic* published an article arguing that the Spanish clergy were killed because they were involved as conspirators in the uprising and were "virtual combatants" and that it was the "unconfirmed belief" of most Spaniards that the Church "has largely financed the rebellion."[33] Ralph Bates, a novelist living in Lérida, described a church-burning in an article, telling how he had helped the incendiaries determine the artistic value of the sacked sacred objects, aiding consignment of those whose taste offended him to the flames.[34] *The New Republic* ran other provocative anti-Catholic articles,[35] but it also published George Shuster's response: he examined his fellow Catholics' position on Spain and said that the anticlerical fury was a "golden opportunity" for them to respond with "pent-up, smoldering resentment" at the anti-Catholics in the United States.[36]

Shuster's criticism of anti-Catholics was mild considering the response they made to the Spanish war. Pro-Republicans formed committees for Spanish relief and organized tours of Republicans to traverse the United States to beg for funds and support. Two priests appeared with the entourages: Luis Sarasola, a Spaniard, and Michael O'Flanagan, an Irishman suspended by his bishop for engaging in Feinian activities. The appearance of these priests on lecture platforms claiming that the Spanish clergy were not being persecuted to the extent reported and that they deserved what they got naturally angered Catholics more than anything else. In St. Louis a Jewish bacteriologist who had taught at Jesuit Saint Louis University Medical School for twenty-three years was dismissed for lending his name to the list of sponsors of the organization that invited O'Flanagan to speak in the city, a dismissal that was pressured by Archbishop John J. Glennon.[37] These traveling Republicans included prominent Spaniards as well, and their grasp of the facts was often not much better than that of

---

32. *The Nation*, August 1, 1936, p. 116.

33. Robert Neville, "Spain: Church Against Republic," *The New Republic*, September 16, 1936, pp. 145–47.

34. Bates described the anarchist incendiaries in such idealistic terms as to be unrecognizable: "Note with what courtesy the churches have been burnt!" *The New Republic*, October 14, 1936, pp. 274–76.

35. Ibid., November 16, 1938, pp. 34–36; November 8, 1938, pp. 6–9.

36. George Shuster, "A Catholic Defends His Church," *The New Republic*, January 4, 1939, pp. 246–48.

37. *St. Louis Post-Dispatch*, January 26, 1939, p. 1.

their antagonists. José Bergamín, a prominent Catholic journalist and editor of the moderate Catholic Spanish review *Cruz y Raya* claimed in New York that Cardinal Vidal was in Rome "not as a refugee but as a director of Loyalist Catholics."[38] Jesuit Talbot responded that Vidal had not signed the Spanish bishops collective letter because he was "in a sanitarium for nervous disorders."[39]

The organization of lecture tours to raise funds, and more importantly to marshall opinion to support intervention in Spain, quickly became a sectarian affair. The Protestant clergy were divided into two camps: pacifists and supporters of the Republic. They viewed the war as a class conflict and believed that Spanish Protestants had been systematically killed in Nationalist Spain.[40]

In September 1936 Robert L. Paddock, a retired Anglican bishop, formed the pro-Republican Friends of Spanish Democracy. Prominent (chiefly Anglican and Methodist) clergy became active in the organization.[41] The event that completely separated the Protestant and Catholic communities was the publication of the Spanish bishops' collective letter in September 1937. Within a week after the letter appeared in *The New York Times* Professor James T. Shotwell of Columbia University, a leading professional historian, wrote a response, because, he said, the issues the Spanish bishops raised were of concern to all Christians. He accused the bishops of being unwilling to accept a compromise before the war began and of giving Thomistic philosophy on revolution a reactionary meaning. He charged them with excusing Nationalist atrocities, but not Republican ones, and finally asked why, if the uprising was, as they said, a national plebiscite, were foreign troops—Moors, Italians, and Germans—being used by the Nationalists?[42] Shotwell's letter raised a stream of charges on both sides; the chief Catholic response was that the Spanish bishops were in a better position than any American to assess the situation, and their word should be accepted unless otherwise proved wrong.[43]

But the strongest response to the Spanish bishops came in the

---

38. *The New York Times*, April 12, 1938, p. 4.
39. *The New York Times*, April 16, 1938, p. 12.
40. Traina, pp. 179ff. Guttmann, p. 69, says: "The arguments of Protestants often betray a deep-seated dislike of Romanism and a barely-concealed delight in the sufferings of the Spanish Church."
41. *The New York Times*, September 26, 1936, p. 10. The Rabbinical Assembly of America also went on record in support of the Republicans. Ibid., June 8, 1937, p. 13.
42. *The New York Times*, September 7, 1937, p. 20.
43. See the letter from Jesuit John LaFarge in *The New York Times*, September 11, 1937, p. 16.

form of an open letter by 150 American Protestant clergymen, educators, and laymen on October 4, 1937. The Protestants said that it
was hard for them to believe that the Spanish bishops' letter had been
written in the twentieth century. They charged that the Spanish bishops condoned rebellion against their own views of 1931 and against
papal teaching as well and that the Spanish Church had always sided
against the people and therefore could not represent the anticlerical
fury as a foreign import. The Protestants further charged the Spanish
clergy with ignoring social and economic abuses and of falsifying recent history in their interpretations of the 1936 elections and the necessity of the uprising. The Protestants did not deny the excesses of
the fury but claimed that they were the work of irresponsible elements
and that the Republican government had made every effort to punish
the guilty and was now anxious to protect religious liberty. They
charged the bishops with concern over Republican atrocities while
saying nothing about "the murder of priests and nuns in Rebel territory" or the execution of Protestant ministers by the Nationalists. They
cited Maritain (incorrectly: they meant Mauriac) on the Badajoz reprisals and claimed that the Nationalists' violence was deliberate, not
mob violence, and that "Franco allows religious liberty only to Catholics sympathetic to Fascism." The Protestants said that it was regret-
table that religion was an issue in Spain when it was clear that the
Spanish war was a struggle between the forces of progress and democracy against special privilege. They were loath to believe that the
Spanish bishops' letter expressed the position of the Catholic Church,
and they pointedly asked if the collective letter represented the views
of the Vatican, and if so, if it applied to the United States as well. The
Protestants' letter was signed by a number of clerics and educators
from throughout the United States.[44]

Within two days Michael J. Ready, the general secretary of the
National Catholic Welfare Conference, answered with a statement addressing the specific charges and claiming that the Protestants were
acting in bad faith, for the Spanish bishops were obviously speaking
for themselves, and the collective letter did not apply to the United
States.[45] But a stronger response came ten days later when 175 Catho-

---

44. The letter is in *The New York Times*, October 4, 1937, p. 12. Among the
signers was Adam Clayton Powell of the Abyssinian Baptist Church, Professor John
Dewey of Columbia University, and Reinhold Niebuhr of Union Theological Seminary (who commented later that month, "it never seems to have occurred to these ignorant bishops to explain why the poor people of Spain hate the Church so much."
In Ralph Lord Roy, *Communism and the Churches* [New York, 1960], p. 119).
45. *The New York Times*, October 6, 1937, p. 6.

lic clergy and laity published an open letter answering the Protestant letter. The Catholics denied the necessity for anyone to support the Nationalists, but they said it was necessary to condemn actions against religious liberty perpetrated by the Republicans. Spanish Catholics, they said, were faced with no alternatives between "liberty and life," just as Americans had been in 1776. The Spanish Church was faced with a destructive attack by a communist-inspired and directed "conscious and fanatical minority which with cold intelligence made use of the passions of the mob"; the agitators took advantage of the social abuses, but the fury was not caused by "deep popular resentment created by social abuses." The Catholics defended Franco: they said that if an election were held immediately, Franco would get an overwhelming majority, but they said that the Church was not committed to fascism. In answer to the Protestant charges they called for the withdrawal of all foreign troops and pointed out that the Republican record on atrocities was worse than the Nationalist one: admitting that there were reprisals at Badajoz, they said that this did not justify the killing of "14,000" clerics. They asked if American Protestants supported a regime that had carried on a ruthless persecution of Christians, and closed by stating that the Spanish bishops' cause was that of "all men who believe in social and international peace and the moral law." The signers included the editors of all Catholic newspapers and journals, the presidents of all Catholic colleges, and assorted prominent laypersons and educators.[46]

Bishop Robert Paddock, one of the authors of the Protestant letter, wrote a conciliatory response assuring Catholics that there was no intention of maligning the Spanish bishops and called for brotherly love and devotion to truth.[47] But the exchange of open letters served only to heighten the controversy. Franco was lauded by Catholics even more. Joseph F. Thorning, a priest and historian at Mount St. Mary's College in Emmitsburg, Maryland, made the Spanish war a personal crusade; he wrote letters to *The New York Times* defending the Nationalists whenever religious issues were raised. The American Catholic bishops at their annual meeting gave unanimous support to the Spanish bishops' letter.[48]

The Spanish bishops were addressed again in an open letter from 61 Protestant bishops in March 1938, asking them to use their influence with Franco to stop the Nationalist bombings of Madrid and

---

46. The letter is in *The New York Times*, October 14, 1937, p. 20.
47. *The New York Times*, October 15, 1937, p. 22.
48. *The New York Times*, November 21, 1937, p. 33.

Barcelona. Thorning replied, asking the Protestants why they did not criticize the Republican government for the anticlerical fury.[49] When sixty congressmen sent what appeared to be perfunctory New Year's greetings to the Spanish Republican Cortes at the beginning of 1938, Catholics responded with anger, and several congressmen retracted their signatures and others admitted ignorance of the meaning of their action. The Catholic Knights of Columbus protested the showing of the pro-Republican film *Blockade* and prevented it from being shown in several cities. A Jesuit wrote to *America* suggesting a boycott of D.C. Heath textbooks because they had published a grammar textbook by a Columbia University professor who was organizing Spanish teachers in favor of the Republic (the suggestion was withdrawn when the professor denied that he was partisan to either side). Bishop John Mark Gannon of Erie, Pennsylvania, went on a fact-finding trip to Spain and returned to describe the effects of the fury, claiming that 11,000 priests had been killed. Catholic groups threatened to boycott *The St. Louis Post-Dispatch* and *The Philadelphia Record* for their pro-Republican stands.[50]

There had been little intellectual debate on the justification for the war. Although *The Commonweal* and *The Catholic Worker* published Maritain's critical articles, letters columns in diocesan papers and reviews such as *America* revealed no more than emotional responses, largely based on anticommunist reactions. Nor were secular liberals any more intellectual in their reading of Maritain or of understanding Catholic teaching on the theology of war. Statements were taken out of context on both sides. Neither bothered to define the other's position. Catholics could correctly point out that not all Nationalists were fascists, but they could not see that all Republicans were not communists; and secularists and Protestants could define the myriad groups supporting the Republic, but to them all Nationalists were fascists.

There were few prominent American Catholic laymen who supported the neutralist position or who were not publicly pro-Nationalist. Some, such as Professor Carlton J. Hayes of Columbia University (Roosevelt's World War II ambassador to Spain), worked quietly behind the scenes to curb pro-Nationalist excesses in *The Commonweal* con-

---

49. *The New York Times*, March 21, 1938, p. 4; March 28, 1938, p. 4.

50. *The New York Times*, January 31, 1938, p. 1; February 1, 1938, p. 4; September 13, 1938, p. 12; *America*, April 24, 1937, p. 66; May 29, 1937, p. 185; see also F. Jay Taylor, *The United States and the Spanish Civil War* (New York, 1956), pp. 150–51.

troversy.[51] Among the higher clergy Cardinal Mundelein of Chicago appeared less pro-Nationalist than his colleagues.[52]

The religious controversy affected humanitarian concerns. When Basque refugee children were being sent abroad in 1937, American Catholics urged the State Department to refuse them visas. *America* said they should be helped but claimed that they were being exploited for political purposes; Franco had offered to take them back under his protection, and in any event there was no need to send them as far abroad as the United States.[53] John McCormack, congressman from Boston, was particularly influential in preventing their entry, and the State Department gave in and refused them visas.[54]

By late 1938 another humanitarian concern arose. The International Red Cross had been sending relief aid to Republican Spain, but it had run out of funds; it was proposed that the American government step in and send surplus wheat to both sides: to prevent starvation in Republican Spain and to equalize the treatment so as not to offend Nationalist supporters. President Roosevelt appointed a committee to carry out the task and appointed a Catholic as chairman to forestall criticism, but Catholics criticized anyway, pointing out that such aid would simply prolong the war, which was all but won by the Nationalists by late 1938; and pro-Republicans criticized the shipments to Nationalist Spain, which had a wheat surplus, arguing that Franco would use the wheat to purchase arms from Nazi Germany. Cardinal Mundelein supported the shipments, and Roosevelt relied upon the Chicago Archbishop's interpretation of Catholic feeling, but there was too much pressure and the plan fell through.[55]

The proposal to send wheat to Spain coincided with the last great conflict of the war in the United States: the embargo controversy. An attempt by some congressmen and the President to end the arms embargo to both sides, which would enable the Republicans to purchase much-needed weapons, failed partly because of organized Catholic pressure. Catholics held rallies and organized a national petition-signing campaign against changing the Embargo Act. Students in Catholic colleges were most active, and Cardinal Dennis Daugherty of Philadelphia directed all Catholics in his archdiocese to

51. Van Allen, pp. 70–71, and Valaik, "Dissenters," p. 554.

52. Mundelein and Bishop Edwin V. O'Hara of Kansas City supported *The Commonweal's* neutralist position. See Valaik, "Dissenters," p. 551.

53. *America*, January 15, 1938, pp. 343–44.

54. Traina, pp. 194–96.

55. See Traina, pp. 196–201, 212, for an account of the entire affair.

sign. The President gave in, and Catholics felt new political muscle.[56]

By the beginning of 1939 the Republicans were desperate. The Spanish ambassador to the United States, Fernando de los Ríos, claimed that there was freedom of worship in Republican Spain and invited Catholics to investigate. Fulton Sheen responded by saying that he would accept if the bishops of Madrid and Barcelona would ask their pastoral clergy to send invitations, but he knew that was impossible, he said, because they had all been assassinated.[57]

The Spanish war ended on this strident note. A week after Madrid fell and Franco proclaimed the war over, 450 Protestant clergy and laymen sent a message to the Pope. They pointed out that he had "invoked divine assistance" on Franco after his victory and that he should now voice his disapproval of Franco's "unchristian reprisals" including numerous violations of human rights, and they asked his help in the humane evacuation of prisoners. Later in the month the Protestant petitioners asked Roosevelt to use his influence against Nationalist reprisals.[58]

In a letter to *America* early in 1937 a reader said that Catholics were making an error by idealizing Franco as a crusader, just as their opponents were making an error by thinking that the Republicans were simply "fighting another battle for democracy against fascism and Catholicism."[59] This was one of the few voices of sanity in the flood of ink on Spain. In the end the Spanish war intensified centuries-long hatreds between Catholics and Protestants, confirming each group in its myopic view of the other.

---

56. See J. David Valaik, "Catholics, Neutrality, and the Spanish Embargo, 1937–1939," *The Journal of American History* 54 (1967–68), pp. 73–85. Flynn, pp. 47–49, and Traina, pp. 204ff., agree that Catholic pressure was only one reason, and not the decisive one.

57. *The New York Times*, January 9, 1939, p. 8; January 10, 1939, p. 1.

58. *The New York Times*, April 7, 1939, p. 10; April 28, 1939, p. 10.

59. J. J. Burns, in a letter to *America*, February 27, 1937, p. 497. Flynn, p. 38, has perceptively pointed out that in the United States "too much was made of communist persecution in Spain. But perhaps too little was made of clerical persecutions."

CHAPTER 15

Conclusion:
The Fury and the Scandal

The Spanish Civil War afforded Spanish Catholics both their finest and their worst moments. Nearly seven thousand clerics and untold thousands of laypersons were killed, for the most part simply because they were Catholics. They sacrificed their lives for their faith, and for most of them the thrust of that faith was based on the concept of brotherly love. No other group of clergy or laity in Christian history gave its members' lives in such abundance over so short a period.

It was their worst moment as well. The anticlerical fury was a visible indictment of Catholic attempts to channel the essence of Christianity into narrow parochial ends. And worse, those Catholics who were not sacrificed to the fury condoned by their silence unchristian, inhuman reprisals against victims of circumstance, and they publicly lauded and supported a regime built in large part on oppression and special privilege. They became the clergy and laity of the church of vengeance, and they lost the opportunity to form the truly Christian church of reconciliation.[1]

It is difficult to condemn an institution caught up in the cruel paradox of Christianity. To preach salvation effectively, the Church has had to institutionalize itself; and the most basic law of survival is that institutions must compromise their ideals in order to endure. At the same time Christianity teaches that the principles of Christ must not be compromised, that the faithful must hold true to their taught ideals. Under attack from their mortal enemies the clergy were,

---

1. Raymond Carr, *The Spanish Tragedy: The Civil War in Perspective* (London, 1977), p. 261. Vicente Cárcel Ortí, p. 381, himself a priest, says that the logic of war is terrible and that the clergy's conservative instincts won out: their choice was "a very human, but not a very Christian one."

by their own teaching, obliged to respond with love and forgiveness, the very antithesis of their human reaction to persecution. Many clerics failed to do so, just as ideologues of all kinds—including anarchists, communists, socialists, liberals, traditionalists, fascists, and monarchists—failed to live up to the nobler sentiments implicit in their own doctrines. It was a very nearly impossible position.[2]

Christianity is one of the great social myths that people live by. Like all religions it is ultimately incapable of rational explanation. It offers a means of transcendence and helps to answer the ultimate questions of life, death, suffering, and purpose. When people feel that the Church's answers become compromised or useless—as many Spaniards felt after the mid-nineteenth century—the institution itself becomes superfluous to the people's needs, and it becomes a drain on the national social and psychological effort. A useless church becomes a problem that demands a solution. One solution is to destroy the Church—the violent anticlerical approach; another is to renew the Church through constructive anticlericalism and a more meaningful expression of the faith. The violent anticlerical solution failed in Spain, partly because it helped create the exact circumstances of death and suffering that the Church is so good at coping with and offering solace for. But the clergy's initial reaction was, in many cases, to support the repression of its enemies, a reaction which, however human, went against the grain of Christianity.

Some clerics perceived the problem. One was Cardinal Gomá, who, although he had used his influence to support the Nationalists during the war, was not pleased with the reprisals and repressions that characterized Franco's Spain after the victory of 1939. Even before the war ended, the Primate in 1937 wrote Cardinal Pacelli of his fear that a Nationalist victory might bode ill for religious feeling: "We may win the war but lose the peace," he said.[3] He was also growing fearful of Nazi German influence in Spain, a fear shared by the Vatican,[4] and both were concerned over the regime's insistence upon assuming the defunct monarchy's right of presentation in the appoint-

---

2. There were exceptional clerics who did live up to their ideals, but they are seldom recorded in history. José María Gironella's fictional but verisimilar priest, Mosén Francisco, could easily represent them all when he says in the midst of the fury: "It is a privilege that we can exercise our vocation in a spot of earth where the people admonish the priests by saying: 'Be perfect, for if you are not you will feel our anger!'" *One Million Dead*, trans. J. Maclean (Garden City, 1963), p. 103.

3. Letter of June 26, 1937, in Marquina Barrio, *La diplomacia Vaticana*, p. 63.

4. Both worked successfully to prevent it. See ibid., pp. 142–53; 181–223.

ments of bishops.[5] More importantly, Gomá spoke out against the reprisals, although not as forcefully as he could or should have. In his first pastoral letter after the war he called for the pardon of all the enemies of the Church, and he counseled all Spaniards against the spirit of vengeance; but it was a mild statement, tucked away in a long letter.[6] Even so his complaints against the growing powers of the state and its totalitarian tendencies led to prohibitions against the publication of the pastoral outside of diocesan bulletins. The Primate wept bitterly at this turn of events and also at the condition of Spain's three cardinals: he lamented to his secretary that Cardinal Vidal remained in forced exile, Cardinal Segura in Seville was in open conflict with the regime over the Falange, and he himself was mortally ill and unable to devote his full energies to Church affairs.[7] Gomá was dead within a year, and Enrique Pla y Deniel, the bishop of Salamanca and one of the Nationalists' most fervent supporters, was elevated to the primacy and the see of Toledo, a position he occupied for the next twenty-seven years.

The hierarchy's unwillingness to publicly and forcefully condemn the reprisals became a public scandal. They fought the regime's encroachment on clerical freedom but not its violation of human rights. Hundreds of thousands of Spaniards were in prison for the sole crime of having supported the Republic or having served in its armies. Thousands more had been killed, executed in the reprisals and retaliations. As in the red terror, the innocent suffered along with the guilty. What would it have cost the clergy to condemn these acts of injustice? It is not a charge that can be lightly dismissed: for if it can be argued

---

5. See the letters from Gomá to Cardinal Maglione (the papal secretary of state), September 2, 1939, and to Pius XII, February 2, 1940, both in Rodríguez Aisa, pp. 511–19. The Concordat of 1851, which the Nationalist government insisted was still in force because it had never been repudiated by the Holy See (although the Spanish Republic had unilaterally abrogated it in 1931), provided the Spanish government with the right of presentation—the nomination of clerics for appointment to most of the bishoprics and other key ecclesiastical positions. The Republic had not used the power, and the Holy See had freely appointed bishops from 1931 to 1936. After the Vatican recognized the Franco regime in 1938, it informed the regime of its appointees but did not ask for approval nor grant the right of presentation.

6. Isidro Gomá, "The Lessons of War and the Obligations of Peace" (August 1939), in Granados, pp. 390–429.

7. Granados, p. 257. Segura threatened to excommunicate government officials and publicly criticized Franco over their support of the Falange's fascist tendencies; only with restraint was the regime dissuaded from exiling Segura. See Marquina Barrio, *La diplomacia Vaticana*, pp. 243–67.

that during the war many priests were unaware of the reprisals—and it is conceivable that many did not know about them or else ascribed them to Republican propaganda—such a defense could not be made after the victory of 1939.

Were the clergy so fearful of another fury that they were willing to close their eyes to the white terror? Cardinal Vidal, still in Italy and vainly trying to return to his Catalan see, wrote to the Pope about the reprisals and was able to intercede to prevent some deaths. But Vidal died in exile in 1943, to the end exhorting the Vatican and the Spanish clergy to stay out of partisan politics.[8]

But to no avail. The clergy came to support the Franco regime to a degree unprecedented in modern Spanish history. They were given more educational and social power than at any time in the previous century and a half. They lauded the dictator at home and abroad. It was national Catholicism at its worst. The clergy's ties with the regime were both heady and humiliating. No imprisoned Republican could be freed without a certificate signed by a priest.[9] In an accord signed in 1941 with the Holy See and confirmed in a concordat in 1953, the state was given the right of presentation of bishops to vacant sees.[10] Despite this concession the political importance of the accord was probably less than the symbolic impact of a church compromised by a vengeful state.

It need not have been. The Church was the one quasi-autonomous institution in Spain, and the regime was, in fact, as dependent on the Church as the clergy believed they were dependent on the state.[11] Throughout the 1940s and 1950s it appeared that the clerical decision to support the Franco regime would result in another anticlerical fury when the inevitable change of regime should come. As late as 1960 there were rumors that when Franco died, the rebuilt statue of the Sacred Heart on the Cerro de los Angeles would be blown up before the dictator's body could be buried.

---

8. Muntanyola, pp. 418–45. Vidal had asked the Pope to intercede with Franco to allow him to return, and Pius XII did so on at least three occasions. He was met with adamant refusal. The issue was a continuing problem in the regime's negotiations with the Vatican for a new concordat. The government argued that the Vatican's acceptance of Segura's exile in 1931 by the Republican government constituted a precedent for Vidal. See Marquina Barrio, La diplomacia Vaticana, p. 132.

9. Garriga, p. 269.

10. The state's rights were less than those in the Concordat of 1851. There is a good discussion of the Church in Franco's Spain in Payne, Spanish Catholicism, pp. 171–212. See also Joaquín L. Ortega, "La iglesia española desde 1939 hasta 1976," Historia de la iglesia en España, ed. Cárcel Ortí, pp. 665–714.

11. Carr, Spanish Tragedy, p. 261.

Memories die hard, but they do die. By the early 1960s a change had come over the clergy.[12] Although the bishops were men who had been priests during the war, the younger clergy had no personal memories of the fury. But they knew the scandal. They began to support oppressed workers, and they became champions of Basque and Catalan cultural nationalism. The clergy could no longer be counted upon as a bulwark of the regime and in fact were becoming its chief opponents. Priests were imprisoned for their antiregime activities. Part of this change came from the reforms of the Second Vatican Council and general opposition everywhere to the traditional church-state ties.[13] As part of the process of clerical reform, a representative assembly of Spanish bishops and priests met in Madrid in 1971 and called for a rejection of the clergy's favored position in the national Catholic regime. A majority supported a resolution on the clergy's actions during the Civil War: "We humbly recognize and ask forgiveness for the fact that we failed to act at the opportune time as true ministers of reconciliation among our people who were divided by a war between brothers."[14] By the time Franco died in 1975, the clergy, including many of the bishops, had shifted their stand so that the Church could no longer be portrayed as the church of the rich and for the most part had now come to be the church of the oppressed.[15] In the first few years following Franco's death the new monarch, Juan Carlos, voluntarily renounced the right of presentation, and the government negotiated a new accord with the Vatican that ended the traditional ties, all with the approval and even the urging of the clergy.

There were, of course, external factors involved in this astounding change. The onset of the industrial revolution in Spain and the general growth of secularism throughout the world, as revealed in a decline in the personal religiosity of the laity (as measured by traditional methods), contributed to the transformation.[16] Yet there were

---

12. See *Analisis sociológico del catolicismo español* (Barcelona, 1967), and *Cambio social y religión en España* (Barcelona, 1975), pp. 19ff., for observations on these changes.

13. And perhaps from the desire to disengage themselves from a rapidly dying regime. See the discussions in Ruíz Rico, pp. 182–271; Guy Hermet, *Les Catholiques dans l'Espagne Franquiste* (Paris, 1980); Linz, p. 258; and in Norman Cooper, "The Church: From Crusade to Christianity," in Paul Preston, ed., *Spain in Crisis* (Hassocks, 1976), pp. 48–81.

14. See the discussion in Cooper, p. 74. The vote on this resolution was 137 to 78 in favor, with 29 abstentions; not sufficient for the two-thirds necessary for adoption in the final report.

15. See the comments of Gil Robles in Gironella, *Cien españoles*, p. 268.

16. González Anleo, p. 440.

many clergy and laity who rejected this role and who stimulated a new anticlericalism of the right, who called the attempts at reconciliation defaming to the memory of the martyrs of the fury.[17] But the power of historic left anticlericalism in Spain had come to an end. It was a spent force. The blood bath of 1936, the exhausting climax of the fury, was a large part of the resolution of the religious conflict.

Hugh Thomas perceptively notes about the Spanish war that "all the problems at stake . . . were essentially present twenty years before it broke out as a major conflict. Some might say that the Civil War simply represents that time when the Spanish conflicts, by an unhappy juxtaposition of international accidents, were rendered international in character."[18] This insight can be applied to the religious struggle as well, for the Spanish conflict was also an international religious war.

It affected the prestige of the papacy at a time when that institution's fortunes were on the rise after the disasters of the nineteenth century. Gregory XVI's condemnation of the Poles for rising up against their Russian masters, and Pius IX's 1864 strictures in the *Syllabus of Errors* against most of the moral advances of Western civilization, including religious freedom, had led to a loss of popular support among the growing literate and professional classes that no amount of pious propaganda could cover up. With Leo XIII and Benedict XV and their more tolerant attitudes and humanitarian activities the papacy began to recover prestige among both Catholics and non-Catholics. Pius XI, despite the Lateran Pact with Mussolini and the Reich Concordat with Hitler, was widely respected, especially for his social encyclicals and his condemnations of Italian Fascism and German Nazism. But Pius XII's statement congratulating Franco on his victory at the same time that thousands of Republicans were suffering reprisals resurrected many antipapal feelings. Pius XII said nothing about the reprisals, and only the rescue of the papacy's good reputation through its humanitarian activities during World War II preserved Pius XII's public esteem until the discovery of a greater scandal—the silence of the Pope on the destruction of the European Jews—eclipsed the Spanish shame.

The Spanish war intensified Catholic-Protestant antagonisms in the United States and England, and it divided Frenchmen.[19] There

17. José Jiménez Lozcano comments on the anticlericalism of the right in Gironella, *Cien españoles*, p. 295.

18. In Philip Toynbee, ed., *The Distant Drum: Reflections on the Spanish Civil War* (London, 1976), p. 30.

19. Arnold Lunn, "The Catholics of Great Britain," *Atlantic Monthly* 174 (Oc-

were few Catholics abroad who were able to grasp the significance of the scandal and fewer yet who could relate the scandal to the fury. They were not as aware of the scandal as were Catholics in Spain; certainly they continued to talk as if the Republicans of 1938 and 1939 were the same group of terrorists who dominated the Republic of 1936. And, simply put, the conflict between Catholics and non-Catholics abroad broke down into the fact that Catholics emphasized the fury, while non-Catholics emphasized the scandal.

Indeed, the war was so shrouded in propaganda that it is difficult to determine what people knew and what they believed. The dilemma for Catholics of goodwill was that their instincts told them to help and support the Republicans as the party of the oppressed and downtrodden, while their Church told them to support the Nationalists, the traditional oppressors. It is a monument to obedience that Catholics throughout the world supported the oppressors. In reality, of course, there were oppressors and oppressed on both sides, but that is not the way it was presented at the time.

The Spanish Civil War was one of the great mythical wars of modern times. People everywhere, and especially abroad, saw what they wanted to see. A vast ideologic mythology was created by both sides. Each was seen by its partisans as driven by pure intentions against a corrupt enemy. It was, of course, not true: few struggles are.[20] But historians have perpetuated the myth, emphasizing the fury or the scandal according to their sympathies.

The war was filled with ironies. The liberal and working-class anticlericals wanted to destroy the Catholic cultural ethic that, they believed, impeded Spain's progress. They fought the war, in part, for this cause. Traditionalist Catholics fought the war for religion as well, backing the Nationalists because they were committed to preserving and restoring that ethic. Yet within thirty years after the war ended, the ethic was changed, albeit not purposely, by the person the clergy backed, Francisco Franco. He industrialized Spain, and with industrialization came modernization and ultimately secularization. It can be argued that the Republicans would have industrialized and modernized earlier. Perhaps, but it would have been difficult, especially considering the turbulence of the 1930s and the world war in the 1940s.

---

tober 1944), pp. 81–85, called the war a turning point in the history of English Catholicism and claimed that it caused a decline in conversions. Lunn had been a publicist for the Nationalist cause during the war.

20. Former international brigadier Philip Toynbee notes: "The war was not fought between good men and evil men; it was certainly not fought between kind men and cruel men." *The Distant Drum*, p. 180.

As it was, the clerical triumphalists won the war, but their victory sounded the death knell of triumphalism.

The Spanish war was dominated by circumstance. It forced partisans of each side to support those they had no sympathy with. Frequently geography determined partisanship. This fact is most obvious in the case of the Catholic Basque autonomists, whose actions are difficult to understand otherwise. By the same token it is equally difficult to understand the attitude of those clergy and laypersons who contributed to the scandal of silence about the reprisals except to argue that the circumstances of war likewise dictated their response.

The history of the Spanish war also shows the degree to which people will fight for their religion. For the committed Catholic, religion is the marrow, the very essence of life. It offers a ritual connected with nature, the seasons, and life that answers an elemental need within his soul. It becomes the lifeblood of the person, to which all else is secondary: life without the Church is unthinkable. Birth, marriage, death, and the thousands of events in between are all celebrated in a transcendent ritual that clothes them in a garment of permanence.

People will fight for this kind of tradition—indeed, they will fight for it more tenaciously and more fiercely than they will fight for money or power. The liberal anticlericals confused this ritual and tradition with the cultural ethic they wanted to destroy. The two were not the same, but the liberal anticlericals were so blinded by the need for change that they failed to recognize the difference; nor were the clergy and Catholics any more perceptive in their defense and identification of ritual and tradition with ethic. The ideological proletarians were probably more aware of what they were doing. They were replacing one ritual and one mystery with another: the brotherhood of the working class for the mystical body of Christ, the red flag for the altar banner, the revolutionary pantheon for the communion of saints.

It would be tempting to generalize from the Spanish experience and argue that the clergy's role in Spanish history has proven the validity of the liberal criticism—that the clergy should stay out of politics and attend only to the spiritual welfare of the faithful. Unfortunately this view assumes a compartmentalization of life that does not exist in reality and in any event is certainly woefully inadequate to apply to a society so permeated with religion as Spain's was. A better moral would be to argue that the clergy have a responsibility to condemn injustice, wherever it may exist, but without attaching themselves to particular parties, groups, or partisan movements.

Perhaps the last words on the religious events of the war—and religion here should be taken to include all ideologies, political and social as well, for they also are based on transcendent faith, in the individual or society, if not in God—were spoken by two participants and writers. From his presidential palace in Barcelona the hapless Manuel Azaña in 1937 wrote an epitaph on the war, *La velada en Benicarló*. In this essay-dialogue his character Eliseo Morales, a writer like Azaña, speaks of Spaniards:

> Everyone is rehabilitating oppression and intolerance, and the surge does not catch us unprepared. This kind of thing lies at the roots of our being. Some shoot school-teachers; others shoot priests. Some burn churches; others burn Socialist clubs. Descendants of the inquisitors are burning temples. The purifying virtue of fire continues as a Spanish myth.
>
> Moreover, the Spaniard needs to believe in something. He doesn't realize his potential . . . until some faith possesses him. Catholic, Moslem, or revolutionary. Then our ardor for domination makes us try to impose our authority on our neighbor or to exterminate him, separate him from the national body. You spoke of unity, a dangerous inclination, cousin to intolerance. With us unity is not measured by physical frontiers but by lines of belief. Strictly speaking, our nation has a moral, not a territorial base. We warm no hearths; we don't love the duration of things. We have a nomadic soul that takes pleasure in lonely wastelands. The Spanish soul carries within itself its own desert, where it dominates.[21]

The French writer and aviator for the Republicans, André Malraux, in his novel *L'Espoir* says it more simply: "I suppose," his character Colonel Ximenes says while considering the Catholic cultural ethic and looking at a burnt-out church, "the nobler a cause is, the more scope it offers to hypocrisy and lies."[22]

---

21. See the English translation by Josephine and Paul Stewart, *Vigil in Benicarló* (Rutherford, New Jersey, 1982), pp. 122–23.

22. From the translation, André Malraux, *Man's Hope*, p. 175.

Chronology

	October–November: Debates on anticlerical constitution
	December 9: Anticlerical Constitution of 1931 promulgated
1932	January 1: Spanish bishops' collective pastoral condemns anticlerical provisions of the Constitution of 1931
	January 23: Society of Jesus dissolved by decree
1933	April 12: Isidro Gomá named archbishop of Toledo and primate of Spain
	May 23: Cortes passes anticlerical Law of Religious Denominations and Congregations
	May 25: Spanish bishops' collective pastoral condemns Law of Religious Denominations and Congregations
	June 4: Pius XI condemns anticlerical legislation in encyclical *Dilectissima Nobis*
	November 19: Center-Right Cortes with Catholic (CEDA) representation elected
1934–35	Execution of much of the anticlerical legislation suspended
1934	October 6: Anticlerical violence in uprising in Asturias
1935	November: Gomá and Tedeschini named cardinals
1936	February 16: Anticlerical Popular Front government elected
	February–July: Sporadic anticlerical violence
	April 10: Luis de Zulueta named Spanish ambassador to the Holy See
	June: Felipe Cortesi named papal nuncio to Spain; Tedeschini recalled
	July 18: Nationalist uprising; Civil War begins

Civil War

1936

July–December	Anticlerical fury (nearly 7,000 clerics killed)
July 25	Last public mass sanctioned by ecclesiastical authorities said in Republican Spain (except in Basque provinces)
July 27	Republicans decree nationalization of all church property
July	Silverio Sericano becomes chargé d'affaires at Madrid nunciature
July 29	Cardinal Vidal escapes into exile in Italy
August 8	Bishops of Vitoria and Pamplona issue pastoral instruction
August 15	Nationalist reprisals in Pamplona

September 4   Nationalists ban all textbooks other than those with a
                  Christian moral basis
                  Manuel de Irujo appointed minister without portfolio in
                  Republican government
September 8   Bishop of Vitoria's explanation of pastoral instruction
September 14   Pope Pius XI addresses Spanish pilgrims in Rome
September 30   Ambassador Zulueta leaves Rome; Nationalist Antonio
                  Magaz occupies Embassy to the Holy See
October 7   Basque Nationalist party takes political control of
                  Vizcaya
October–   Execution of 14 Basque clerics by Nationalists
November
October 14   Bishop Múgica of Vitoria exiled to Rome
November 4   Gomá writes pastoral arguing that the war is a conflict
                  between two concepts of civilization
December 19   Cardinal Gomá named "Confidential and Semiofficial
                  Representative to the Nationalist Government" by the
                  Holy See
December–   Public exchange of letters between Cardinal Gomá and
March 1937   Basque President José Antonio Aguirre

                                    1937

March   Nationalist invasion of Vizcaya
                  Pope issues three encyclicals: *Mit Brennender Sorge* (on
                  the problems in Germany); *Divini Redemptoris* (on
                  Communism); and *Firmissiman Constantiam* (on
                  Mexican problems)
May 10   Franco requests collective pastoral letter
May 17   Manuel de Irujo becomes minister of justice in
                  Republican government
June 4   Paul Claudel's poem "To the Spanish Martyrs" published
June 19   Bilbao falls to Nationalists
June   Salvador Rial named vicar-general of Tarragona
July 1   Bishops' collective letter issued (but not published until
                  late August)
                  Jacques Maritain's article "De la guerre sainte" published
July   Ildebrando Antoniutti sent on special mission by Holy
                  See to Nationalist Spain
August 7   Republicans authorize private religious services
September 7   Antoniutti named chargé d'affaires from Holy See to Na-
                  tionalists
September   Segura named archbishop of Seville
October 4   Open Letter of 150 American Protestants published
October 14   American Catholic response to Protestant Open Letter

1938

March 1	Republican decree authorizing conscripted priests to be placed in noncombat positions
March 2	Nationalists suspend divorce legislation
March 12	Nationalists abolish law allowing civil marriage
April	Georges Bernanos publishes *Les Grands cimitières sous la lune*
May 1	Republican premier Juan Negrin proposes peace plan including religious freedom
May 3	Nationalists allow re-establishment of Society of Jesus in Spain
May 16	Holy See grants diplomatic recognition to Nationalist Spain; Gaetano Cicognani named nuncio; José de Yanguas Messia named Nationalist ambassador to Holy See
September 25	Nationalists decree annulment of all civil marriages contracted in Republican Spain
October 23	Republicans establish military chaplaincy
December 10	Nationalists abolish law secularizing cemeteries

1939

February 7	Bishop of Teruel assassinated by Republicans
February 2	Nationalists abolish Law of Religious Denominations and Congregations
February 10	Pope Pius XI dies
March 2	Eugenio Pacelli elected Pope Pius XII
April 1	Civil War ends

Post-Civil War

1941	June 7: Accord signed between Holy See and Spain
1943	September 22: Cardinal Vidal dies, still in exile
1953	August 27: Concordat signed between Holy See and Spain
1971	September: Majority in Joint Assembly of Bishops and Priests begs forgiveness for clergy's actions during Civil War
1975	November 20: Francisco Franco dies
1978	December 29: New Spanish constitution disestablishes Church
1979	January: New Concordat signed between Holy See and Spain

Bibliography

Works cited in the notes, along with other helpful studies

Books, Articles, Pamphlets

Abad de Santillán, D. *Por que perdimos la guerra.* Madrid: G. del Toro, 1975.
Abella, Rafael. *La vida cotidiana durante la guerra civil: la España nacional.* Barcelona: Planeta, 1973.
———. *La vida cotidiana durante la guerra civil: la España republicana.* Barcelona: Planeta, 1975.
Aguirre Prado, Luis. *The Church and the Spanish War.* Madrid: Ed. del Servicio Informativo Español, 1965.
Albonico, Aldo. "Los católicos italianos y la guerra de España." *Hispania* 139 (1978), 373–99.
Aldecoa, Raymond. *Le Christ chez Franco.* Translated by Rolland-Simon. Paris: Les Editions Denoel, 1938.
Alonso Lobo, Arturo, OP. "¿Se puede escribir así la historia?" *La Ciencia Tomista* 88 (1961), 301–76.
Alpert, Michael. "Humanitarianism and Politics in the British Response to the Spanish Civil War, 1936–9." *European History Quarterly* 14 (1984), 423–40.
Altabella Gracia, Pedro. *El catolicismo de los nacionalistas vascos.* Madrid: Editora Nacional, 1939.
Analisis sociológico del catolicismo español. Barcelona: Ed. Nova Terra, 1967.
Antoniutti, Ildebrando. *Memorie Autobiografiche.* Udine: A. Friulare, 1975.
Arbeloa, Victor Manuel. "Anticlericalismo y guerra civil." *Lumen* 24 (1975), 162–81, 254–71.
———. *Socialismo y anticlericalismo.* Madrid: Taurus, 1973.
Arrarás Iribarren, Joaquín, ed. *Historia de la cruzada española.* 8 vols. Madrid: Ediciones Españolas, 1940–43.
Arteche, José de. *El abrazo de los muertos: diario de la guerra civil 1936–39.* Zarauz: Editorial Icharopena, 1970.
Atholl, Duchess of. *Searchlight on Spain.* Harmondsworth: Penguin, 1938.
Ayerra Redín, Marino. *No me avergoncé del evangelio.* 2d. ed. Buenos Aires: Editorial Periplo, 1959.
Azaña, Manuel. *Obras completas.* 4 vols. México: Ediciones Oasis, 1968.

213

————. *La velada en Benicarló*. Buenos Aires: Editorial Losada, 1939. (Translated by Josephine and Paul Stewart as *Vigil in Benicarló*. Rutherford, New Jersey: Fairleigh Dickenson University Press, 1982.)

Azpiazu, Iñaki de. *7 meses y 7 dias en la España de Franco*. Caracas: Ediciones Gudari, 1964.

Azpilikoeta, Dr. de. *The Basque Problem as Seen by Cardinal Gomá and President Aguirre*. New York: The Basque Archives, 1938.

Bahamonde y Sánchez de Castro, Antonio. *Un año con Quiepo*. Madrid: Ediciones Españolas, 1938. (Translated as *Memoirs of a Spanish Nationalist*. London: United Editorial Ltd., 1939.)

Ballesteros y Beretta, Antonio. *Historia de España y su influencia en la historia universal*. Vol. VIII. Barcelona: Salvat Editores, 1936.

Barea, Arturo. *The Forging of a Rebel*. Translated by Ilsa Barea. New York: Reynal and Hitchcock, 1946.

Barrett, Richard A. *Benabarre: The Modernization of a Spanish Village*. New York: Holt, Rinehart and Winston, 1974.

Bayle, Constantino, SJ. "La cárcel de mujeres en Madrid." *Razón y Fe* 113 (April 1938), 435–50.

————. "Los comuniones en la España roja." *Razón y Fe* 117 (May 1939), 72–85.

————. "El culto a la eucarística en la España roja." *Razón y Fe* 115 (December 1938), 378–85.

Bell, J. Bowyer. "French Reaction to the Spanish Civil War, July–September, 1936." In *Power, Public Opinion, and Diplomacy*. Edited by L. P. Wallace and W.C. Askew. Durham: Duke University Press, 1959. 267–96.

————. "Ireland and the Spanish Civil War, 1936–1939." *Studia Hibernica* 9 (1969), 137–63.

Ben-Ami, Shlomo. *Fascism From Above: The Dictatorship of Primo de Rivera in Spain, 1923–1930*. Oxford: Oxford University Press, 1983.

Benavides, Domingo, *El fracaso social del catolicismo español. Arboleya Martínez 1870–1951*. Barcelona: Editorial Nova Terra, 1973.

Benson, Frederick R. *Writers in Arms: The Literary Impact of the Spanish Civil War*. New York: New York University Press, 1967.

Bernanos, Georges. *Les Grands cimitières sous la lune*. Paris: Plon, 1938. (Translated by Pamela Morris as *A Diary of My Times*. London: Boriswood, 1938.)

Bertrand de Muñoz, Maryse. *La guerra civil española en la novela*. 2 vols. Madrid: Ediciones José Porrúa Turanzas, 1982.

————. *La guerre civile espagnole et la littérature française*. Ottawa: Didier, 1972.

Blinkhorn, Martin. *Carlism and Crisis in Spain 1931–1939*. Cambridge: Cambridge University Press, 1975.

Bolloten, Burnett. *The Spanish Revolution: The Left and the Struggle for Power during the Civil War*. Chapel Hill: University of North Carolina Press, 1979.

Borkenau, Franz. *The Spanish Cockpit: An Eyewitness Account of the Political and Social Conflicts of the Spanish Civil War.* London: Faber and Faber, 1937.

Bosworth, William. *Catholicism and Crisis in Modern France.* Princeton: Princeton University Press, 1962.

Brademas, John. *Anarcosindicalismo y revolución en España: 1930–1937.* Translated by J. Romero Maura. Barcelona: Ariel, 1974.

Bravo Morata, Federico. *Historia de Madrid.* Vol. III. Madrid: Fenicia, 1968.

Brenan, Gerald. *Personal Record 1920–1972.* New York: Knopf, 1975.

——. *The Spanish Labyrinth: An Account of the Social and Political Background of the Civil War.* 2d. ed. Cambridge: Cambridge University Press, 1950.

Brinton, Henry. *Christianity and Spain.* London: United Editorial Ltd., 1938.

Broué, Pierre, and Emile Témime. *The Revolution and the Civil War in Spain.* Translated by Tony White. Cambridge, Mass.: MIT Press, 1972.

Buckley, Henry. *Life and Death of the Spanish Republic.* London: Hamish Hamilton, 1940.

Burgo, Jaime del. *Conspiración y guerra civil.* Madrid: Alfaguara, 1970.

Callahan, William J. *Church, Politics, and Society in Spain, 1750–1874.* Cambridge, Mass.: Harvard University Press, 1984.

——. "The Origins of the Conservative Church in Spain, 1793–1823." *European Studies Review* 10 (1980), 199–223.

Calvo Serrer, Rafael. "La iglesia en la vida pública española desde 1936." *Arbor* 25 (1953), 289–324.

——. *La literatura universal sobre la guerra de España.* Madrid: Ateneo, 1962.

Cambio social y religión en España. Barcelona: Ed. Fontanella, 1975.

Campbell, Colin. "Analyzing the Rejection of Religion." *Social Compass* 24 (1977), 339–46.

Campbell, Roy. *Flowering Rifle.* London: Longmans, Green, 1939.

——. *Light on a Dark Horse. An Autobiography (1901–1935).* Chicago: Henry Regnery, 1952.

Canetti, Elias. *Crowds and Power.* Translated by Carol Stewart. New York: Viking, 1962.

Canterbury, Dean of, et al. *Report of a Religious Delegation to Spain, April 1937.* London: Victor Gollancz, 1937.

Cantril, Hadley, and Mildred Strunk, eds. *Public Opinion, 1935–1946.* Princeton: Princeton University Press, 1951.

Cárcel Ortí, Vicente. "La iglesia durante la II República y la guerra civil (1931–39)." In *Historia de la iglesia en España.* Vol. V: *La iglesia en la España contemporánea.* Edited by Vicente Cárcel Ortí. Madrid: BAC, 1979. 331–94.

Caro Baroja, Julio. *Introducción a una historia contemporánea de anticlericalismo español.* Madrid: Ediciones Istmo, 1980.

Carr, Raymond. *Spain, 1808–1939.* Oxford: Oxford University Press, 1966.

———. *The Spanish Tragedy: The Civil War in Perspective.* London: Weidenfeld and Nicolson, 1977.

———, and Juan Pablo Fusi. *Spain: Dictatorship to Democracy.* London: George Allen and Unwin, 1979.

Carreras, Luis. *The Glory of Martyred Spain.* London: Burns, Oates and Washbourne, 1939.

Casanova, Manuel. *Se prorroga el estado de alarma (memorias de un prisionero).* Toledo: Editorial Católica Toledana, 1941.

Castells, José Manuel. *Las asosiaciones religiosas en la España contemporánea (1767–1965): un estudio jurídico-administrativo.* Madrid: Taurus, 1973.

Castro Albarrán, Aniceto de. *El derecho al alzamiento.* Salamanca: Cervantes, 1941.

———. *El derecho a la rebeldía.* Madrid: Gráfica Universal, 1934.

———. *Este es el cortejo: héroes y mártires de la cruzada española.* Salamanca: Cervantes, 1938.

———. *La gran victima: la iglesia española mártir de la revolución roja.* Salamanca: Cervantes, 1940.

Castro Delgado, Enrique. *Hombres made in Moscú.* Barcelona: L. de Caralt, 1964.

Cattell, David. *Communism and the Spanish Civil War.* Berkeley: University of California Press, 1955.

Centro de Información Católica Internacional. *El clero y los católicos vascoseparatistas y el movimiento nacional.* Madrid: M. Minuesa, 1940.

Charles-Roux, François. *Huit ans au Vatican, 1932–40.* Paris: Flammarion, 1947.

Christ or Franco? London: The Friends of Spain, 1937.

Christian, William A., Jr. *Person and God in a Spanish Valley.* New York: Seminar Press, 1972.

Cierva, Ricardo de la. *Bibliografía general sobre la guerra de España (1936–1939) y sus antecedentes históricos.* Madrid: Ariel, 1968.

———. *Los documentos de la primavera trágica.* Madrid: Ministerio de Información y Turismo, 1967.

———. *Historia de la guerra civil española.* Vol. I: *(1898–1936).* Madrid: Editorial San Martín, 1969.

———. *Historia ilustrada de la guerra civil española.* Madrid: Editorial Danae, 1970.

———. *La historia se confiesa: España 1930–1976.* 10 vols. Barcelona: Planeta, 1976.

Clark, Robert P. *The Basques: The Franco Years and Beyond.* Reno: University of Nevada Press, 1979.

Claudel, Paul. "Aux Martyrs Espagnoles." *Sept* (Paris), June 4, 1937. (Translated by John O'Connor in *The Colosseum* 4 [September 1937], 108–17.)

Le Clerge Basque: Rapports présentés par des Pretes Basques aux Autorités Ecclésiastiques. Paris: H.G. Peyre, 1938.

Comas, Ramón. *Isidro Gomá—Francesc Vidal i Barraquer: Dos visiones antagónicas de la iglesia española de 1939*. Salamanca: Editorial Sígueme, 1977.

Cooper, Norman B. *Catholicism and the Franco Regime*. London: Sage Publications, 1975.

——. "The Church: From Crusade to Christianity." In *Spain in Crisis*. Edited by Paul Preston. Hassocks: Harvester Press, 1976. 48–81.

Corbin, Jay P. *G.K. Chesterton and Hilaire Belloc: The Battle Against Modernity*. Athens, Ohio: Ohio University Press, 1981.

Cortada, James W., ed. *Historical Dictionary of the Spanish Civil War, 1936–1939*. Westport, Conn.: Greenwood, 1982.

Coutrot, Aline. *Un courant de la pensée catholique. L'hebdomadaire "Sept" (Mars 1934–Aout 1937)*. Paris: Editions du Cerf, 1961.

Coverdale, John F. *Italian Intervention in the Spanish Civil War*. Princeton: Princeton University Press, 1975.

Crosby, Donald F. "Boston's Catholics and the Spanish Civil War: 1936–1939." *New England Quarterly* 44 (March 1971), 82–100.

Cuenca Toribio, José Manuel. "El catolicismo español en la restauración (1875–1931)." In *Historia de la iglesia en España*. Vol. V: *La iglesia en la España contemporánea*. Edited by V. Cárcel Ortí. Madrid: BAC, 1969. 277–329.

——. *Sociología de una élite de poder de España e Hispanoamérica contemporáneas: la jerarquía eclesiástica (1789–1965)*. Córdoba: Escudero, 1976.

Cunningham, Valentine, ed. *The Penguin Book of Spanish Civil War Verse*. Harmondsworth: Penguin, 1980.

Curtiss, John S. *The Russian Church and the Soviet State, 1917–1950*. Boston: Little, Brown, 1953.

Dansette, Adrien. *Religious History of Modern France*. Vol. II: *Under the Third Republic*. Translated by John Dingle. New York: Herder and Herder, 1961.

Dendle, Brian J. *The Spanish Novel of Religious Thesis 1876–1936*. Madrid: Editorial Castalia, 1968.

Deportista, Juan. *Los rojos*. Valladolid: Librería Santarém, 1938.

Díaz Mozaz, José María. *Apuntes para una sociología del anticlericalismo*. Barcelona: Ariel, 1976.

Díaz de Villegas, J. "Nuestra cruzada no fue jamás una guerra civil." *Guión* 266 (1964), 25–29.

Documents on German Foreign Policy, 1918–1945. Series D (1937–1945). Vol. III. *Germany and the Spanish Civil War (1936–1939)*. Washington, D.C.: U.S. Government Printing Office, 1950.

Doering, Bernard E. *Jacques Maritain and the French Catholic Intellectuals*. Notre Dame: University of Notre Dame Press, 1983.

Eby, Cecil. *The Siege of the Alcázar*. New York: Random House, 1965.

Edwards, Jill. *The British Government and the Spanish Civil War, 1936–1939*. London: Macmillan, 1979.

Enciclopedia Universal Ilustrada Europeo-Americano. Suplemento Anual, 1936–1939 (segunda parte). Bilbao: Espasa Calpe, 1944.

Eppstein, John. *The Catholic Tradition of the Law of Nations*. London: Burns, Oates and Washbourne, 1935.

Escobal, Patricio P. *Death Row: Spain 1936*. Translated by Tana de Gámez. Indianapolis: Bobbs-Merrill, 1968.

Espina, Concha. *Esclavitud y libertad: diario de una prisionera*. Valladolid: Ediciones Reconquista, 1938.

Estelrich, Juan. "La cuestión vasca y la guerra civil española." *La Ciencia Tomista* 56 (1937), 319–48.

———. *La persecución religiosa en España*. 2d. ed. Buenos Aires: Editorial Difusión, 1937.

Estivill, Jordi, and Gustau Barbat. "Anticlericalisme populaire en Catalogne au début du siècle." *Social Compass* 27 (1980), 215–30.

Falcoff, Mark, and Fredrick B. Pike, eds. *The Spanish Civil War, 1936–39: American Hemispheric Perspectives*. Lincoln, Nebraska: University of Nebraska Press, 1982.

Falconi, Carlo. *The Popes in the Twentieth Century*. Boston: Little, Brown, 1967.

Fernández Areal, M. *La política católica en España*. Barcelona: Dopesa, n.d.

Fernsworth, Lawrence. *Spain's Struggle for Freedom*. Boston: Beacon Press, 1957.

Flynn, George Q. *Roosevelt and Romanism: Catholics and American Diplomacy, 1937–1945*. Westport, Conn.: Greenwood, 1976.

Foss, William, and Cecil Gerahty. *The Spanish Arena*. London: Right Book Club, 1938.

Franco's Rule: A Survey. London: United Editorial, n.d.

Fraser, Ronald. *Blood of Spain: An Oral History of the Spanish Civil War*. New York: Pantheon, 1979.

Freeman, Susan Tax. "Faith and Fashion in Spanish Religion: Notes on the Observation of Observance." *Peasant Studies* 7 (1978), 101–23.

Fusi Aizpurúa, Juan Pablo. *El problema vasco en la II República*. Madrid: Ediciones Turner, 1979.

Galíndez, Jesús de. *Los vascos en el Madrid sitiado*. Buenos Aires: Vasca Ekin, 1945.

Gallego, Gregorio. *Madrid, corazón que se desangra*. Madrid: G. del Toro, 1976.

Gallegos Rocafull, José Manuel. *Crusade or Class War: The Spanish Military Revolt*. London, 1937.

Gallin, M.A. "Revolution." *New Catholic Encyclopedia*. Vol. XII. New York: McGraw-Hill, 1967. 450–51.

Gárate Córdoba, José María. *Mil dias de fuego: Memorias de la guerra del trienta y seis*. Barcelona: Luis de Carolt, 1975.

García, Ángel. *La iglesia española y el 18 de julio*. Barcelona: Acervo, 1977.

García Duran, Juan. *Bibliografía de la guerra civil española*. Montevideo: Editorial El Siglo Ilustrado, 1964.

García Escudero, José María. *Historia política de las dos Españas*. 4 vols. Madrid: Editora Nacional, 1975.

García-Nieto, María Carmen, and Javier María Donezar. *La guerra de España 1936–1939 (Bases documentales de la España contemporánea)*. Vol. X. Madrid: Guadiana de Publicaciones, 1974.

García Venero, Maximiano. *Historia del nacionalismo catalán (1793–1936)*. Madrid: Editora Nacional, 1944.

————. *Historia del nacionalismo vasco*. Madrid: Editora Nacional, 1969.

————. *Madrid julio 1936*. Madrid: Editorial Tebas, 1973.

Garosci, Aldo. *Gli intellettuale e la guerra di Spagna*. Turin: Giulio Einaudi, 1959.

Garriga, Ramón. *El Cardenal Segura y el nacional-catolicismo*. Barcelona: Planeta, 1977.

Gay, Francisque. *Dans les flammes et dans le sang*. Paris: Bloud et Gay, 1936.

Gibson, Ian. *The Death of Lorca*. Chicago: J. Philip O'Hara, 1973.

————. *Paracuellos: como fue*. Barcelona: Editorial Argos Vergara, 1983.

Gil Mugarza, Bernardo. *Espana en llamas 1936*. Barcelona: Acerbo, 1960.

Gilmore, David D. *People of the Plain: Class and Community in Lower Andalusía*. New York: Columbia University Press, 1980.

Gironella, José María. *Cien españoles y Dios*. Barcelona: Ediciones Nauta, 1969.

————. *The Cypresses Believe in God*. Translated by Harriet de Onís. New York: Knopf, 1955.

————. *One Million Dead*. Translated by Joan MacLean. Garden City, New York: Doubleday, 1963.

Gomá y Tomás, Isidro. *Por Dios y por España*. Barcelona: Rafael Casulleras, 1940.

Gómez Casas, J. *Los anarquistas en el gobierno*. Barcelona: Bruguera, 1977.

Gomis, Juan. *Testigo de poca edad (1936–1943)*. Barcelona: Nova Terra, 1968.

González-Anleo, Juan. "Vida religiosa." *Informe sociológico sobre la situación social de España, 1970*. Madrid: Fundación FOESSA, 1970. 435–70.

González Oliveros, W. *Falange y Requeté organicamente solidarios*. Valladolid: Francisco G. Vicente, 1937.

Granados, Anastasio. *El Cardenal Gomá, Primado de España*. Madrid: Espasa Calpe, 1971.

Greaves, H.R.G., and David Thomson. *The Truth about Spain*. London: Gollancz, 1938.

Greene, Thomas R. "The English Catholic Press and the Second Spanish Republic, 1931–1936." *Church History* 45 (1976), 70–84.

Gurney, Jason. *Crusade in Spain*. London: Faber and Faber, 1974.

Guttmann, Allen. *The Wound in the Heart: America and the Spanish Civil War*. New York: Free Press of Glencoe, 1962.

Gwynne, H.A., and A. Ramos-Oliveira. *Controversy on Spain*. London: United Editorial, 1937.

Hamilton, Bernice. *Political Thought in Sixteenth-Century Spain: A Study in the Political Ideas of Vitoria, DeSoto, Suárez and Molina.* Oxford: Oxford University Press, 1963.

Hellman, John. *Emmanuel Mounier and the New Catholic Left, 1930–1950.* Toronto: University of Toronto Press, 1981.

Hennesey, James. *American Catholics: A History of the Roman Catholic Community in the United States.* New York: Oxford University Press, 1981.

Hermet, Guy. *Les Catholiques dans l' Espagne Franquiste.* Vol. I. Paris: Fondation Nationale des Sciences Politiques, 1980.

Hernando, Bernardino M. *Delirios de cruzada.* Madrid: Ediciones 99, 1977.

Herr, Richard. "El significado de la desamortización en España." *Moneda y Crédito* 131 (1974), 55–94.

Hoskins, Katherine Bail. *Today the Struggle: Literature and Politics in England During the Spanish Civil War.* Austin: University of Texas Press, 1969.

Hughes, H. Stuart. *The Obstructed Path: French Social Thought in the Years of Desperation, 1930–1960.* New York: Harper and Row, 1967.

Huidobro Pardo, Leopoldo. *Memorias de un finlandés.* Madrid: Ediciones Españolas, 1939.

Ibarruri, Dolores. *El único camino.* Habana: Imp. Nacional de Cuba, 1962. (Translated as *They Shall Not Pass.* New York: International Publishers, 1966.)

Irujo, Manuel de. *La guerra civil en Euzkadi antes del estatuto.* Madrid: Fuenlabroda, 1978.

———. *Memorias.* Vol. I: *Un vasco en el ministerio de justicia.* Buenos Aires: Vasca Ekin, 1976.

Iturralde, Juan de. *El catolicismo y la cruzada de Franco.* 3 vols. Vienne and Toulouse: Editorial Egui-Indarra, 1960, 1965.

Jackson, Gabriel. *A Concise History of the Spanish Civil War.* New York: John Day, 1974.

———. *Entre la reforma y la revolución 1931–1939.* Translated by Ramón Fernández Sol. Barcelona: Ed. Crítica, 1980.

———. *Historian's Quest.* New York: Knopf, 1969.

———. *The Spanish Republic and the Civil War, 1931–1939.* Princeton: Princeton University Press, 1965.

Jato Miranda, David. *Madrid, capital republicana.* Barcelona: Acervo, 1976.

Jellinek, Frank. *The Civil War in Spain.* London: Gollancz, 1938.

Jerrold, Douglas. *Georgian Adventure.* New York: Chas. Scribner's Sons, 1938.

Jiménez de Aberásturi, Luis María and Juan Carlos. *La guerra en Euskadi.* Barcelona: Plaza y Janes, 1978.

Jiménez Duque, Baldomero. "Espiritualidad y apostolado." *Historia de la iglesia en España.* Vol. V: *La iglesia en la España contemporánea.* Edited by V. Cárcel Ortí. Madrid: BAC, 1979. 395–474.

Joubert, H. *La guerre d'Espagne et le catholicisme.* Paris: SGIE, 1937.

Kamen, Henry. "Clerical Violence in a Catholic Society: The Hispanic World, 1450–1720." *The Church and War.* Edited by W.J. Sheils. London: Basil Blackwell, 1983. 201–16.

Kemp, Peter. *Mine Were of Trouble*. London: Cassell, 1957.

Kern, Robert W. *Red Years/Black Years: A Political History of Spanish Anarchism*. Philadelphia: Institute for the Study of Human Issues, 1978.

Knoblaugh, H. Edward. *Correspondent in Spain*. London: Sheed and Ward, 1939.

Koestler, Arthur. *Spanish Testament*. London: Gollancz, 1937.

Kurzman, Dan. *Miracle of November: Madrid's Epic Stand, 1936*. New York: G.P. Putnam's Sons, 1980.

Laird, Megan. "A Diary of Revolution." *The Atlantic Monthly* 158 (November 1938), 513–33.

Langdon-Davies, John. *Behind the Spanish Barricades*. New York: Robert M. McBride, 1936.

Lannon, Frances. "A Basque Challenge to the Pre-Civil War Spanish Church." *European Studies Review* 9 (1979), 29–48.

————. "Modern Spain: The Project of a National Catholicism." *Religion and National Identity*. Edited by Stuart Mews. Oxford: Basil Blackwell, 1982. 567–90.

————. "The Socio-Political Role of the Spanish Church—A Case Study." *Journal of Contemporary History* 14 (April 1979), 193–210.

Lasky, Melvin J. *Utopia and Revolution*. Chicago: University of Chicago Press, 1976.

Legarreta, Dorothy. *The Guernica Generation: Basque Refugee Children of the Spanish Civil War*. Reno: University of Nevada Press, 1984.

Lera, Ángel María de. *La masonería que vuelve*. Barcelona: Planeta, 1980.

Lewy, Guenter. *Religion and Revolution*. New York: Oxford University Press, 1974.

————. "The Uses of Insurrection: The Church and Franco's War." *Continuum* (Autumn 1965), 267–90.

Lincoln, Bruce. "Revolutionary Exhumations in Spain, July 1936." *Comparative Studies in Society and History* 27 (April 1985), 241–60.

Linz, Juan J. "Religion and Politics in Spain: From Conflict to Consensus above Cleavage." *Social Compass* 27 (1980), 255–77.

Lisón Tolosana, Carmelo. *Belmonte de los Caballeros: A Sociological Study of a Spanish Town*. Oxford: Oxford University Press, 1966.

Lizarra, A. de. *Los vascos y la república española: contribución a la historia de la guerra civil, 1936–1939*. Buenos Aires: Vasca Ekin, 1944.

Lizarza Iribarren, Antonio. *Memorias de la conspiración: cómo se preparó en Navarra la cruzada, 1931–1936*. Pamplona: Editorial Gómez, 1953.

Llordés Badia, José. *Al dejar el fusil: memorias de un soldado raso en la guerra de España*. Barcelona: Ariel, 1968.

Llorens, Josep M., and Joan Comas. *La iglesia contra la república española*. Vieux: Domaine de l'Espaliou, 1968.

Lobo, Leocadio. *Primate and Priest*. London: Spanish Embassy, 1937.

Loewenstein, Prince Hubertus Friedrich of. *A Catholic in Republican Spain*. London: Gollancz, 1937.

Luca de Tena, Juan Ignacio. *Mis Amigos Muertos*. Barcelona: Planeta, 1971.

Lunn, Arnold. "The Catholics of Great Britain." *The Atlantic Monthly* 174 (October 1944), 81–85.

———. *Spanish Rehearsal.* London: Hutchinson, n.d.

McCormick, R. A. "Morality of War." *New Catholic Encyclopedia.* Vol. IV. New York: McGraw-Hill, 1967. 802–7.

McCullagh, Francis. *In Franco's Spain.* London: Burns, Oates and Washbourne, 1937.

McLeod, Hugh. *Religion and the People of Western Europe 1789–1970.* Oxford: Oxford University Press, 1981.

Madariaga, Salvador de. *Spain: A Modern History.* New York: Praeger, 1958.

Malraux, Andre. *L'Espoir.* Paris: Gallimard, 1937. (Translated by Stuart Gilbert and Alastair Macdonald as *Man's Hope.* New York: Grove, 1979.)

Maragall, Joan. "La iglesia cremada." In *Obras completes d'en Joan Maragall (serie catalana): Escrits en prosa.* Vol. I. Barcelona: Gustau Gili, 1912. 221–30.

Maret, François. *Les Grands chantiers au soliel.* Paris: F. Sorlot, 1938.

Maritain, Jacques. "De la guerre sainte." *La Nouvelle Revue Francaise,* July 1, 1937, 21–37.

Marquina Barrio, Antonio. *La diplomacia Vaticana y la España de Franco (1936–1945).* Madrid: CSIC, 1983.

———. "El Vaticano contra la cruzada." *Historia 16* 22 (February 1978), 39–52.

Marrero Suárez, Vicente. *La guerra española y el trust de cerebros.* Madrid: Punta Europa, 1961.

Martín Artajo, Javier. *No me cuente Ud. su casa.* Madrid: Biosca, 1955 (Translated by Daniel Crabb as *The Embattled.* Westminster, Maryland: Newman Press, 1960.)

Martínez, Juan de la, SJ. *¿Cruzada o rebelión?* Zaragoza: Librería General, 1938.

Martínez-Alier, Juan. *Labourers and Landowners in Southern Spain.* London: George Allen and Unwin, 1971.

Massot i Muntaner, Josep. *L'Esglesia catalana al segle XX.* Barcelona: Curial, 1975.

Maura, Miguel. *Así cayó Alfonso XIII.* Barcelona: Ariel, 1966.

Mayeur, Françoise. *L'Aube. Etude d'un Journal d'Opinion. 1932–1940.* Paris: Armand Colin, 1966.

Menéndez-Reigada, Ignacio G., OP. "Acerca de la 'guerra santa,' contestación a M.J. Maritain." *La Ciencia Tomista* 58 (1937), 356–74.

———. "La guerra nacional española ante la moral y el derecho." *La Ciencia Tomista* 56, 57 (1937), 40–57, 177–95.

Mendizábal, Alfred. *The Martyrdom of Spain: Origins of a Civil War.* Translated by C.H. Lumley, with a preface by Jacques Maritain. New York: Chas. Scribner's Sons, 1938.

Mercader Riba, Juan. "Origenes del anticlericalismo español." *Hispania* 33 (1973), 101–23.

Mews, Stuart. "The Sword of the Spirit: A Catholic Cultural Crusade of 1940." In *The Church and War*. Edited by W.J. Sheils. Oxford: Basil Blackwell, 1948. 409–30.

Miguel, Florindo de. *Un cura en zona roja*. Barcelona: Casals, 1956.

Ministerio de Justicia. *Causa General: La dominación roja en España*. Madrid: Ministerio de Justicia, 1943.

Mintz, Jerome R. *The Anarchists of Casas Viejas*. Chicago: University of Chicago Press, 1982.

Miranda, Soledad. *Religión y clero en la gran novela española del siglo XIX*. Madrid: Ediciones Pegaso, 1982.

Mitchell, Peter Chalmers. *My Home in Málaga*. London: Faber and Faber, 1938.

Molnar, Thomas. *Bernanos: His Political Thought and Prophecy*. New York: Sheed and Ward, 1960.

Moloney, Thomas. *Westminster, Whitehall and the Vatican: The Role of Cardinal Hinsley, 1935–43*. Turnbridge Wells: Burns and Oates, 1985.

Montero, José R. *La CEDA: el catolicismo social y política en la II República*. 2 vols. Madrid: Ed. de la Revista del Trabajo, 1977.

Montero Moreno, Antonio. *Historia de la persecución religiosa en España, 1936–1939*. Madrid: BAC, 1961.

Montserrat, Victor. *Le Drame d'un Peuple Incompris: La Guerre au Pays Basque*. Preface by François Mauriac. Paris: H.G. Peyre, 1938.

Mora, Constancia de la. *In Place of Splendor: The Autobiography of a Spanish Woman*. New York: Harcourt, Brace, 1939.

Múgica, Mateo. *Imperativos de mi conciencia*. Buenos Aires: Liga de Amigos de los Vascos, 1945.

El mundo católico y la carta colectiva del episcopado español. Burgos: Centro de Información Católico Internacional, 1938.

Muntanyola, Ramón. *Vidal i Barraquer: el cardenal de la paz*. Translated by Victor Manuel Arbeloa. Barcelona: Estela, 1971.

Murall, José, SJ. "The Martyrdom of Six Spanish Jesuits." Translated by Leo P. Burns. *The Jesuit Bulletin* 16 (January 1938), 4–6.

Noel, Charles C. "Missionary Preachers in Spain: Teaching Social Virtue in the Eighteenth Century." *The American Historical Review* 90 (October 1985), 866–92.

Núñez Morgado, Aurelio. *Los sucesos de España vistos por un diplomático*. Buenos Aires: L.J. Rosso, 1941.

O'Donnell, Peadar. "An Irishman in Spain." *The Nineteenth Century* 120 (December 1936), 698–706.

O'Duffy, Eoin. *Crusade in Spain*. London: Robert Hale, 1938.

Onaindía, Alberto de. *Hombre de paz en la guerra*. Buenos Aires: Vasca Ekin, 1973.

One Year of War 1936–1937. New York: Paulist Press, 1937.

Ordóñez Márquez, Juan. *La apostasía de las masas y la persecusión religiosa en la provincia de Huelva, 1931–36*. Madrid: CSIC, 1968.

Ortega, Joaquín L. "La iglesia española desde 1939 hasta 1976." In *Historia de la iglesia en España*. Vol. V: *La iglesia en la España contemporánea*. Edited by V. Cárcel Ortí. Madrid: BAC, 1979. 665–714.

Ossorio y Gallardo, Ángel. *La guerra de España y los católicos*. Buenos Aires: Patronato Hispano-Argentino de Cultura, 1942.

Pala, Lucio. *I cattolici francesi e la guerra di Spagna*. Urbino: Argalia editore, 1974.

Palacio Atard, Vicente. *Cinco historias de la República y de la guerra*. Madrid: Editora Nacional, 1973.

———. "La guerra de España (1936–1939)." *Diccionario de historia eclesiástica de España*. Madrid: CSIC, 1972–75. II, 1184–88.

Palau, Gabriel, ed. *Diario íntimo de un cura español (1919–1931)*. Barcelona: Herederos de Juan Gili, 1932.

Paul, Elliot. *The Life and Death of a Spanish Town*. New York: Random House, 1937.

Payne, Stanley G. *Basque Nationalism*. Reno: University of Nevada Press, 1975.

———. *Spanish Catholicism: An Historical Overview*. Madison: University of Wisconsin Press, 1984.

Paz, Abel. *Durruti: The People Armed*. Translated by Nancy MacDonald, New York: Free Life Editions, 1977.

Peers, E. Allison. *Catalonia Infelix*. New York: Oxford University Press, 1938.

———. *Spain in Eclipse, 1937–1943*. London: Methuen, 1943.

———. *Spain, the Church and the Orders*. London: Burns, Oates, and Washbourne, 1945.

Peiró, Francisco. *El problema religioso-social de España*. Madrid: Razón y Fe, 1936.

Pérez López, Francisco. *A Guerilla Diary of the Spanish Civil War*. Translated by J.D. Harris. London: André Deutsch, 1972.

Pérez de Olaguer, Antonio. *El terror rojo en Cataluña*. Burgos: Ediciones Antisectarias, 1937.

Pérez de Urbel, Justo. *Los mártires de la iglesia*. Buenos Aires: AHR, 1956.

Pike, David Wingeate. *Conjecture, Propaganda and Deceit and the Spanish Civil War: The International Crisis over Spain, 1936–1939 as Seen in the French Press*. Stanford: CIIS, 1968.

———. *Les Français et la Guerre d'Espagne*. Paris: Presses Universitaires de France, 1975.

Pitcairn, Frank. *Reporter in Spain*. London: Lawrence and Wishart, 1936.

Pitt-Rivers, J.A. *The People of the Sierra*. Chicago: University of Chicago Press, 1961.

Pius XI. *The Church and the Reconstruction of the Modern World: The Social Encyclicals of Pius XI*. Edited by Terence P. McLaughlin. New York: Image, 1957.

———. "Discourse of Pope Pius XI to the Spanish Refugees, September 14, 1936 at Castel Gandolfo." *The Catholic Mind* 34 (October 8, 1936), 385–94.

A Preliminary Official Report on the Atrocities Committed in Southern Spain in July and August 1936 by the Communist Forces of the Madrid Government. 4th ed. London: Eyre and Spottiswoode, 1936.

Preston, Paul, ed. *Revolution and War in Spain 1931–1939.* New York: Methuen, 1984.

Raguer i Suñer, Hilari. "El cardenal Gomá y la guerra de España." *Arbor* 61 (April 1982), 43–81.

———. *La espada y la cruz (La iglesia 1936–1939).* Barcelona: Bruguera, 1977.

———. "Los obispos españoles y la guerra civil." *Arbor* 62 (July–August 1982), 7–32.

———. *La Unió Democràtica de Catalunya i el seu temps (1931–1939).* Montserrat: L'Abadia de Montserrat, 1976.

———. "El Vaticano y la guerra civil española (1936–1939)." *Cristianesimo nella Storia* 3 (April 1982), 137–209.

———. "Le vicaire du cardinal: Mgr Salvador Rial Lloberas, vicaire général de Tarragone pendant la guerre civile espagnole." *Revue d'Histoire Ecclesiastique* 79 (April–June 1984), 370–415.

Ramírez Jiménez, Manuel. *Los grupos de presión en la Segunda República Española.* Madrid: Tecnos, 1969.

Ramos-Oliveira, Antonio. *Politics, Economics and Men of Modern Spain, 1808–1946.* Translated by T. Hall. London: Gollancz, 1946.

Rémond, René. "Anticlericalism: Some Reflections by Way of an Introduction." *European Studies Review* 13 (1983), 121–26.

———. *Les Catholiques, le Communisme et les crises, 1929–1939.* Paris: Armand Colin, 1960.

Revuelta González, Manuel. "La iglesia española ante la crisis del Antiguo Regimen (1808–33)." In *Historia de la iglesia en España.* Vol. V: *La iglesia en la España contemporánea.* Edited by V. Cárcel Ortí. Madrid: BAC, 1979. 3–113.

Rey, Juan, SJ. *¿Por qué lucho un millón de muertos?* 2d ed. Santander: Sal Terrae, 1962.

Rhodes, Anthony. *The Vatican in the Age of the Dictators 1922–1945.* New York: Holt, Rinehart and Winston, 1973.

Ricart Torrens, José. *Un obispo antes del concilio: Biografía del Exmo. y Rdno. doctor don Manuel Irurita Almandoz, obispo de Barcelona.* Madrid: Religión y Patria, 1973.

Robinson, Richard A.H. *The Origins of Franco's Spain: The Right, the Republic and Revolution, 1931–1936.* Pittsburgh: The University of Pittsburgh Press, 1970.

Rodríguez Aisa, María Luisa. *El Cardenal Gomá y la guerra de España: Aspectos de la gestión pública del Primado, 1936–1939.* Madrid: CSIC, 1981.

Rogers, F. Theo. *Spain: A Tragic Journey.* New York: Macaulay, 1937.

Roja, Carlos. *La guerra civil vista por los exiliados.* Barcelona: Planeta, 1975.

Romero, Luis. *Tres dias de julio (18, 19 y 20 de 1936).* Barcelona: Ariel, 1967.

Romero Maura, Joaquín. *La Rosa de Fuego.* Barcelona: Grijalbo, 1975.

Roy, Ralph Lord. *Communism and the Churches*. New York: Harcourt Brace, 1960.

Rudd, Margaret Thomas. *The Lone Heretic: A Biography of Miguel de Unamuno y Jugo*. Austin: University of Texas Press, 1963.

Ruíz Rico, Juan. *El papel político de la iglesia católica en la España de Franco (1936–1971)*. Madrid: Tecnos, 1977.

Ruíz Vilaplana, Antonio. *Burgos Justice*. Translated by W.H. Carter. New York: Knopf, 1938.

Rumi, Giorgio. "Mondo Cattolico y Guerra Civile Spagnola: L'Opinione Ambrosiana." *Rivista de Storia della Chiesa in Italia* 36 (January–June 1982), 35–48.

Salas Larrazábal, Ramón. *Pérdidas de la guerra*. Barcelona: Planeta, 1977.

Salter, Cedric. *Try-out in Spain*. New York: Harper, 1943.

Sanabre Sanromá, José. *Martirologio de la iglesia en la diócesis de Barcelona durante la persecución religiosa*. Barcelona: Editorial Librería Religiosa, 1943.

Sánchez, José M. *Anticlericalism: A Brief History*. Notre Dame: University of Notre Dame Press, 1972.

————. *Reform and Reaction: The Politico-Religious Background of the Spanish Civil War*. Chapel Hill: University of North Carolina Press, 1964.

————. "The Second Spanish Republic and the Holy See: 1931–1936." *The Catholic Historical Review* 49 (April 1963), 47–68.

Sánchez del Arco, Manuel. *El sur de España en la reconquista de Madrid*. Seville: Editorial Sevillana, 1937.

Sarolea, Charles. *Daylight on Spain: The Answer to the Duchess of Atholl*. London: Hutchinson, n.d.

Sanz de Diego, Rafael M., S.J. "Actitud del P. Huidobro, S.J., ante la ejecución de prisioneros en la guerra civil. Nuevos datos." *Estudios Eclesiásticos* 60 (Oct.–Nov., 1985), 443–84.

Sebastián y Bandarán, José, and Antonio Tineo Lara. *La persecución religiosa en la Archidiócesis de Sevilla*. Seville: El Correo de Andalusia, 1938.

Seco Serrano, Carlos. *Historia de España*. Vol. IV: *Epoca contemporánea*. 3d. ed. Barcelona: Instituto Gallach, 1971.

Sencourt, Robert. *Spain's Ordeal: A Documented History of the Civil War*. London: Longmans, Green, 1938.

Sender, Ramón. *Counter-attack in Spain*. Translated by Peter Chalmers Mitchell. Boston: Houghton, Mifflin, 1937.

Serrahima, Maurici. *Memories de la guerra i de l'exili, 1936–1940*. Vol. I: *1936–1937*. Barcelona: Ediciones 62, 1978.

Soria, Georges. *Guerre et revolution en Espagne, 1936–1939*. 5 vols. Milan: Editoriale Ambrosiane, 1975.

Southworth, Herbert Rutledge. *Guernica! Guernica! A Study of Journalism, Diplomacy, Propaganda and History*. Berkeley: University of California Press, 1977.

————. *El mito de la cruzada de Franco.* Paris: Ruedo Ibérico, 1963.

Sperber, Murray A., ed. *And I Remember Spain: A Spanish Civil War Anthology.* London: Hart-Davis, MacGibbons, 1974.

Steer, G.L. *The Tree of Gernika: A Field Study of Modern War.* London: Hodder and Stoughton, 1938.

Stein, Louis. *Beyond Death and Exile: The Spanish Republicans in France, 1939–1955.* Cambridge, Mass.: Harvard University Press, 1979.

Sturzo, Luigi. *Church and State.* Translated by Barbara B. Carter. Notre Dame: University of Notre Dame Press, 1962.

————. *Politics and Morality.* Translated by Barbara B. Carter. London: Burns, Oates, and Washbourne, 1938.

Tangye, Nigel. *Red, White and Spain.* London: Rich and Cowan, 1937.

Taylor, F. Jay. *The United States and the Spanish Civil War.* New York: Bookman Associates, 1956.

Thomas, Hugh. *The Spanish Civil War.* Revised and enlarged ed. New York: Harper and Row, 1977.

Toni Ruíz, Teodoro, SJ. *Iconoclastas y mártires (por Avila y Toledo).* Bilbao: Santa Casa de Misericordia, 1937.

Torrent García, Martín. *¿Qué me dice usted de los presos?* Alcalá: Talleres Penitenciarias, 1942.

Toynbee, Arnold J. *Survey of International Affairs, 1937.* Vol. II: *The International Repercussions of the War in Spain (1936–1937).* Oxford: Oxford University Press, 1938.

Toynbee, Philip, ed. *The Distant Drum: Reflections on the Spanish Civil War.* London: Sidgwick and Jackson, 1976.

Traina, Richard P. *American Diplomacy and the Spanish Civil War.* Bloomington: Indiana University Press, 1968.

Tuñon de Lara, Manuel. *El hecho religioso en España.* Paris: Librarie du Globe, 1968.

Tusell Gómez, Juan. *Historia de la democracia cristiana en España.* 2 vols. Madrid: Cuadernos para el Diálogo, 1974.

Ullman, Joan Connelly. *The Tragic Week: A Study of Anticlericalism in Spain, 1875–1912.* Cambridge, Mass.: Harvard University Press, 1968. (Translated into Spanish as *La semana trágica* by Gonzalo Pontón. Barcelona: Ariel, 1972.)

————. "The Warp and Woof of Parliamentary Politics in Spain, 1808–1939: Anticlericalism versus 'Neo-Catholicism.'" *European Studies Review* 13 (1983), 145–76.

Urra Lusarreta, Juan. *En las trincheras del frente de Madrid (Memorias de un capellán de requetés, herido de guerra).* Madrid: Fermín Uriarte, 1967.

Valaik, J. David. "American Catholic Dissenters and the Spanish Civil War." *Catholic Historical Review* 53 (January 1968), 537–55.

————. "American Catholics and the Second Spanish Republic, 1931–1936." *Journal of Church and State* 10 (1968), 13–28.

————. "Catholics, Neutrality and the Spanish Embargo, 1937–1939." *The Journal of American History* 54 (1967–68), 73–85.

Van Allen, Rodger. *The Commonweal and American Catholicism.* Philadelphia: Fortress Press, 1974.

Vicuña, Carlos, OSA. *Mártires Agustinos del El Escorial.* 2d. ed. El Escorial: Monasterio de El Escorial, 1945.

Vidal i Barraquer, Francesc. Arxiu Vidal i Barraquer. *Esglesia i Estat durant la Segonya República Espanyola, 1931–1936.* 4 vols. Edited by M. Battlori and V.M. Arbeloa. Montserrat: Monestir de Montserrat, 1971, 1976.

Vignaux, Paul. "Cattolici francisci di fronte ai fascismi e alla guerra de Spagna." *Cristianesimo nella Storia* 3 (October 1982), 343–408.

View From the Right: Support for the Nationalists (Seeds of Conflict. Series 3 The Spanish Civil War 1936–1939). Nerdeln: Kraus, 1975.

Villa-San Juan, José Luis. *¿Así fue? Enigmas de la guerra civil española.* Barcelona: Nauta, 1971.

[Vilar Costa, Joan] JVC. *Montserrat: glosas a la carta colectiva de los obispos españoles.* Barcelona: Instituto Católico de Estudios Religiosos, 1938.

The Voice of the Church in Spain. London: Burns, Oates and Washbourne, 1937.

Watkins, Keith W. *Britain Divided: The Effect of the Spanish Civil War on British Political Opinion.* London: Thomas Nelson and Sons, 1963.

Weber, Eugen. *Action Française: Royalism and Reaction in Twentieth-Century France.* Stanford: Stanford University Press, 1962.

Weintraub, Stanley. *The Last Great Cause: The Intellectuals and The Spanish Civil War.* New York: Weybright and Talley, 1968.

Weisser, Michael R. *The Peasants of the Montes: The Roots of Rural Rebellion in Spain.* Chicago: University of Chicago Press, 1976.

Winston, Colin M. *Workers and the Right in Spain, 1900–1936.* Princeton: Princeton University Press, 1985.

Ynduráin, Francisco. "Resentimiento español. Arturo Barea." *Arbor* 24 (January 1953), 73–79.

Zeldin, Theodore. *France, 1848–1945.* Oxford: Oxford University Press, 1977.

Zumeta, Ángel de. *Un cardenal español y los católicos vascos.* Bilbao: Minerva, 1937.

Newspapers and Periodicals

L'Action Française (Paris)
America (New York)
L'Aube (Paris)
The Catholic Digest (New York)
The Catholic Mind (New York)
The Catholic News (New York)
The Catholic Worker (New York)

The Catholic World (New York)
The Church Times (London)
La Ciencia Tomista (Salamanca)
The Colosseum (London)
The Commonweal (New York)
La Croix (Paris)
Cruz y Raya (Madrid)
The Daily Mail (London)
Esprit (Paris)
Etudes (Paris)
Le Figaro (Paris)
G.K.'s Weekly (London)
The Manchester Guardian
The Month (London)
The Nation (New York)
New Blackfriars (London)
The New Republic (New York)
The New York Times
La Nouvelle Revue Française (Paris)
L'Osservatore Romano (Vatican City)
Razón y Fe (Burgos and Madrid)
The Saint Louis Post-Dispatch
Sept (Paris)
Studies (Dublin)
The Tablet (London)
Temps Présent (Paris)
The Times (London)
La Vie Intellectuelle (Paris)

Index

Abella, Rafael, 110
Acción Católica Nacional de Propagandistas (ACN de P), 34
L'Action Française (Paris), 161, 162, 164, 166
Adoratrices nuns, 26, 31
Aguirre, José Antonio de, president of the Basque autonomous government, 85; polemic with Gomá, 85–86, 92; and Vatican attempt to mediate war, 128
Ajuriguerra, Juan, 78
Álava, 71, 74
Alfonso XIII, 1, 35, 82, 105, 120, 153
Almansa (Albacete), n56
Almería, bishop of, 10, 18
Alsasua (Navarre), 113
Altuna Mendi, 75
Álvarez del Vayo, Julio, 133, 142
America (American Jesuit weekly), 186, 196, 198; on anticlerical fury, 188–89; views of Franco, 188–89, 191; support of Nationalists, 188–90; on uprising, 189; on communism, 190; on Basque refugee children, 197
American Catholic bishops, 184–85, 195
American Catholics, 184–98; reaction to anticlerical fury, 187–90, 195; views of Franco, 188–89; open letter (1937), 194–95
American congressmen and greetings to Spanish Cortes (1938), 196
American Protestants, and war, 184–85, 191–96, 198; clergy, 193–95; reaction to anticlerical fury, 194; open letter (1937), 194–95; bishops' open letter

American Protestants (*cont.*)
(1938), 195–96; letter to Pius XII, 198
American secular agnostics, 185, 187, 191–93
Americans and anticlerical fury, 187–90
anarchists, n11, 16, n21, 37–38, 50–51; press, 38
Anderson de Cienfuegos, Jane, 187
Anglican Church—*see* Church of England
Añoveros, Antonio, 113
anticlerical fury (1936), 8–59, 81; in Basque Provinces, 74–76; Catholic reaction, 106; Republican reaction, 132; effect on French, 162–63, 168; British reaction to, 174–77; American reaction to, 187–90, 195; as climax, 204
anticlerical legislation, 7; abolished, 106, 131, n133
anticlerical violence, pre-1931, 4–5; 1931–36, 7–8, 37, 48; pre-1936, 47–49. *See also* anticlerical fury
anticlericalism, pre-1931, 2–7, 21, 33–34; 1931–36, 7–8, 22–23, 33–39; incendiary, 47–55. *See also* anticlerical fury
Antoniutti, Ildebrando, Vatican *chargé* to Nationalist government, 128–30; and Basque refugee children, 180
Arboleya Martínez, Maximiliano, 67
Argentine clergy in Spain, 56–57
Asturias uprising (1934), 8, 48
Atholl, Duchess of, n175
L'Aube (Paris), 162, 163, 164
Auden, W.H., 182

231

ABOUT THE AUTHOR

José M. Sánchez is professor of history at Saint Louis University, St. Louis, Missouri. He has been studying Spanish religious history for over thirty years. His earlier works include *Reform and Reaction: The Politico-Religious Background of the Spanish Civil War* (University of North Carolina Press, 1964), an examination of the political and religious events that led to the Spanish Civil War, and *Anticlericalism: A Brief History* (University of Notre Dame Press, 1972), a study of the development and varieties of that phenomenon.